A Walk in Ireland

A WALK IN
IRELAND

AN ANTHOLOGY
OF WALKING LITERATURE

COLLECTED AND ARRANGED BY
MICHAEL FEWER

First published in 2001 by
Atrium
Cork
Ireland

A Walk in Ireland © Michael Fewer 2001

Atrium is an imprint of Attic Press Ltd,
Crawford Business Park, Crosses Green, Cork

British Library Cataloguing in Publication Data
A CIP catalogue record for this book is available from the British Library

ISBN 0 953535 32 0 HB

Library of Congress Cataloging-in-Publication Data
A Walk in Ireland: an anthology of walking literature / Michael Fewer.
    p. cm.
    ISBN 0-9535353-2-0 (alk. paper)
    1. Ireland–Description and travel.   2. Walking–Ireland.   I. Fewer, Michael.

    DA969.W35 2001
914.1504–dc21   2001045135

Typeset by Mark Heslington, Scarborough, North Yorkshire
Printed by MPG Books Ltd, Cornwall

Contents

Acknowledgements

This anthology could not have been completed without the encouragement, advice and scholarly assistance of many, including Jonathan Williams, Peter Healy, Ciaran MacAnally, Paddy and Gloria Smith, Aidan Heavey, Joss Lynam, Brendan Grimes, Dr Christopher Woods, and Fred Collins of Greene's Bookshop. I was particularly grateful for the kindness and encouragement of the authors whose permissions I sought and received, including Colm Tóibín for an extract from *Walking along the Border*, Peter Somerville-Large for an extract from *From Bantry Bay to Leitrim*, Cameron McNeish for an extract from *The Great Outdoors ...*, Mike Harding for an extract from *Footloose in the West of Ireland*, and David Boyd for an extract from his forthcoming book on his walk around Ireland. I want to thank Peter Healy for permission to use photos and extracts from John Healy's diaries, Mary, Aidan and Bridget Wall for permission to use photos and extracts from Claude Wall's journals. Unfortunately, some who helped on this project have passed on, including the late Peg Malone, who gave permission to use extracts from J. B. Malone's journals, and the late Peter Tynan O'Mahony, who gave permission to use an essay by Nora Tynan O'Mahony. I am particularly grateful to Jim O'Malley for his translation of Ó Dúinnín, and to my old friend Dick Cronin for his translation of Ó Liathain. For all their suggestions and advice I thank the Literature and Publishing MA students at the National University of Ireland, Galway: Carlin, Neasa, Eddie, Paula, Trisha, Ciara, Shane, Deirdre McHugh and Deirdre Nolan, David, Anthony, Mary, Bernadette, Lesley, Levi, Jen, Aoileann, Karen, Paul and Suzanne.

Thanks to HarperCollins for an extract from *Round Ireland in Low Gear* by Eric Newby, and to Hamish Hamilton for an extract from *The Kingdom by the Sea* by Paul Theroux.

Although every effort was made to identify and contact copyright-holders both in Ireland and abroad, in some cases I was not successful.

The publishers wish to thank the National Library for permission to reproduce a print of the Killarney Lakes from the Devils Punch Bowl on Mangerton.

Introduction

Introduction

I took up hill walking about thirty years ago when the gentle, rounded, blue-grey forms of the Dublin mountains drew me to them at weekends, in search of wildlife, clear air and the calming balm of solitude. As I climbed each of the summits, more and more layers of mountain became visible to the south, and I was drawn farther and higher into their spell. I gradually extended the scope of my walking to include seacoasts and riverbanks, always seeking the quiet, out-of-the-way places, wildernesses where man was an infrequent visitor and threatened flora and fauna found asylum. Some of the paths I followed had clearly been routes for thousands of years, and in these places also vestiges of man's past were often well preserved, allowing my imagination to people the landscape with ghosts of previous ages. I was delighted to find friends who shared my interests, and to agree with Balzac's sentiments when he wrote, 'We must acknowledge that solitude is a fine thing; but it is a pleasure to have someone to whom we can say that solitude is a fine thing'.

When asked why I got so much delight from walking and climbing, I found it difficult to offer a simple explanation. What was the source of the pleasure, often quite sublime, from which springs the happy glow I have observed on the faces of companions at the end of a long and often uncomfortably wet day on the hills, a glow that does not simply emanate from the relief that it is all over, or that a pint in front of a pub fire is an imminent prospect? Fred Hoyle, the astronomer, had a sensible answer: 'Mountaineers are always being asked why they climb mountains and I am always surprised when they allow themselves to be trapped into offering reasons. The truth of the matter is surely this. Any purpose that can be precisely explained is always temporary . . . It is a curious paradox of human existence that purposes which can be clearly defined and explained have a limited life-span. And conversely, the things in life that last indefinitely cannot be explained and defined.' Seeking further opinions, I gradually unearthed many accounts of walking that reached back through the centuries and confirmed my personal experiences. For instance, Conrad Gesner, the eminent zoologist and botanist, wrote in 1541: 'I have made up my mind . . . that henceforth, as long as it please God to let me live, I shall every year climb a few mountains, or at any rate one, at the time when the flowers are at their best, so that I can examine them and combine a grand exercise of the body with enjoyment of the mind. Is that not true bliss? What rapture must fill the mind of him who looks in wonder at the vastness of these great mountain ranges and lifts his head, as it were, into the bosom of the clouds!' My satisfaction was complete when I discovered

I

long-forgotten descriptions of treks over familiar ground in Ireland, where the writers had experienced the same wonder as me.

It seemed clear that the descriptions of walking travellers provided a special view of the world, and sometimes contributed valuable historical insights into the state of things at the time they walked. After all, walking travellers, because of their very mode of travel, have closer, more intimate contact with the places they pass through and the people they meet along the way than those who travel by any other means.

Walking travel is as old as mankind, but the literature of walking is relatively new. It probably had its beginnings two and a half centuries ago in that area of Europe where France, Germany and Switzerland come together. After many years during which wars raged back and forth across the continent, the second half of the 1700s brought an era of peace. The economic and social development brought about by the beginnings of the Industrial Revolution gave birth to a golden age of science and scholarship, and improvements in governance, laws, and communications all assisted in allowing people to travel more widely; tourism became a new industry. Allied with this new ease of travel, interest in the natural world, from the scenic as well as the scientific point of view, grew rapidly. As early as 1730, Albrecht von Haller's poetic work on the Alps, *Die Alpen*,[1] had achieved worldwide readership, and had begun to nurture a fascination for the region that has continued to this day. In 1761, Jean-Jacques Rousseau published the novel *La nouvelle Heloïse*, which encouraged people to take a new look at the countryside and nature; it was the forerunner of European Romantic literature. The villages of Vevey and Clarens on the shores of Lake Geneva, where the novel was set, attracted curious tourists for decades after it was published. In 1770 Oliver Goldsmith's *The Deserted Village*, based on the countryside around Lissoy in County Westmeath where he spent his childhood, drew similar interest. Rousseau's *Reveries of a Lonely Wayfarer*, written on an island on the Lake of Bienne,[2] and later, Goethe's accounts of his tours in Switzerland engendered considerable interest in the idea of travelling on foot through countryside and wilderness areas, although Goethe referred to the idea of actually climbing mountains as 'profane and barbaric'. In spite of this, the myriad peaks and glaciers of the Alps attracted the more robust pedestrian explorers, and when in 1786 Dr Michel-Gabriel Pacard, a physician from Chamonix, made the first ascent of Mont Blanc, mountain climbing, the most energetic form of walking, began to become popular.

[1] Von Haller (1708–1777) was a celebrated Swiss physician who was also considered one of the greatest poets in the German language in the eighteenth century.
[2] A Swiss lake situated at the foot of the Jura mountains: Rousseau lived on the islet of St Pierre on the lake for two months to avoid imagined persecutors.

William Coxe's[3] *Sketches of the Natural, Civil and Political State of Switzerland* of 1779 excited interest in Alpine landscape amongst those living in the British Isles, and in particular, impressed and inspired the young William Wordsworth. Coxe, although not exclusively a pedestrian traveller, much preferred to travel on foot, and constantly enthused about the freedom that walking offered. Coxe's writings inspired many adventurous travellers to embark on their own pedestrian tours, including Wordsworth, who set off in autumn 1790 on his own walking tour of Europe. He walked through France and Switzerland with Robert Jones, a fellow student, to whom he subsequently dedicated one of his early poems, which described the Alpine scenes they visited.[4] He went on to become the premier poet of pedestrianism in the English language.

By the early nineteenth century walking had become a widely used and acceptable mode of leisure travel for the well-off and for members of the emerging educated middle class. A popular 'walking craze' swept England at the time, broadening the focus of pedestrianism from scholarly exploration to manly prowess and physical stamina. Attempts to achieve great feats of speed and distance became common, and countryfolk would gather at crossroads to catch sight of famous pedestrians such as John Stokes, who had begun to walk to combat 'excessive corpulancy', and who became well known for his speed-walking. In one trek in 1815, he walked 1,000 miles at the rate of 50 miles in 12 hours each day.[5]

Mainstream pedestrians, however, concerned themselves with exploring and discovering the countryside, glorying in the exertion involved, and places like the Lake District in England, already a centre for picturesque travel, now began to attract large numbers of walking tourists. By the 1820s, popular travel guides had begun to include sections on pedestrian travel.

The central driving force for the pedestrian traveller then was, as it is today, the thrill of self-sufficient exploration, something that is afforded completely only by walking. In 1821 travel writer Robert Newell summed up the advantages of walking thus:

> The best way of seeing a country is on foot. It is the safest, and most suited to every variety of road; it will often enable you to take a shorter track, and visit scenes (the finest perhaps) not otherwise accessible; it is healthy, and, with a little practice, easy; it is economical: a

---

[3] William Coxe (1741–1828) was a historian, biographer and traveller. His descriptive accounts of his travels were so successful that they were translated into French, German, Spanish and Italian and widely published.

[4] *Descriptive sketches, taken during a pedestrian tour among the Alps*, 1790.

[5] *Romantic Writing and Pedestrian Travel*, Robin Jarvis, 1997.

pedestrian is content with almost any accommodation; he, of all travellers, wants but little, 'Nor wants that little long'. And last, though not least, it is perfectly independent.[6]

It was this independence and freedom of movement that walking allows which appealed to the adventurous traveller; whether to follow a track, scramble up a hill, or cross a stream, all possibilities were open. In addition, walking provided the maximum opportunity for pause and delay to allow one to observe; stopping to sniff the fragrance of a flower or to watch a grazing butterfly is so much simpler when travelling on foot.

The first significant accounts of pedestrian travel in Ireland began to appear towards the end of the eighteenth century when Ireland was relatively peaceful and enjoying a brief golden age. In 1783 the English parliament renounced its claim to legislate for Ireland, and until the turn of the century it existed as an independent kingdom and had its own parliament. This newborn, energetic but short-lived Ireland attracted the curiosity of outsiders and encouraged tourists, including pedestrians, to explore the western-most outpost of Europe, the more remote reaches of which held a seductive mystique for those from the 'mainland' or from the Pale, that civilized colony of England centred on Dublin. With the exception of recent motorways, the road network that exists in Ireland today was well in place 200 years ago, and all parts of the country, other than remote parts of Cork, Kerry and Mayo, were easily accessible to travellers.

Initially, pedestrian travellers were regarded with some suspicion in Ireland. In 1802 the song-collector Patrick Lynch had to flee from a mob in Belmullet, because he was an educated man travelling on foot, and, just a few years after the horror of the aftermath of the French invasion at Killala, he had been observed asking questions and taking notes in shebeens. The aptly named pedestrian traveller John Trotter commented that in 1814, pedestrians 'are not well received at inns in Ireland. The Irish are too much given to respect external splendour, and the pedestrian is liable at their inns to be considered a very suspicious character. He may be deemed a Tax Collector, or a play-actor, or a runaway – for they are fond of stigmatizing a stranger in this way'. He also commented that pedestrians frustrate the curiosity of locals: 'we hurried on, disappointing the curious gaze of several in this country-town, who, as is too customary in Ireland, having little business to occupy them, are devoured with curiosity to know that of others. Pedestrians of a genteel appearance very much puzzle these characters; and as there are no servants to question, no equipages to examine, and no postillions to listen to, these persons are left

[6] From *Letters on North Wales*, 1821, written and illustrated by Robert Haswell Newell (1778-1852).

in suspense.' Eventually, however, pedestrians were not only accepted, but, unlike other travellers in carriages or on horseback, were able to enjoy full peasant hospitality, that amazing trait of the poorest of the poor the world over to share what they have with passing strangers.

The earliest walking travellers in Ireland mainly followed the roads, departing from them only to explore well-known places such as Croagh Patrick in Mayo, the Giant's Causeway in Antrim, or Mangerton in Killarney, long thought to be the highest peak in Ireland. As mentioned above, the road network was as extensive at the beginning of the nineteenth century as it is now, although the quality of surface left much to be desired. Two hundred years ago much of the national network, apart from the main routes, was in the form of green roads, which were comfortable to walk on; but as commercial traffic increased, many of these were surfaced with crushed stone, which made walking uncomfortable. This may have been one of the reasons why, subsequent to the 1880s, many walkers, inspired by such stalwarts as Henry Hart, began to eschew man-made routes and take to the moors, hills and mountains.

I have selected for this anthology passages from the writings of a wide variety of people who walked in Ireland between the years 1783 and 1995. Although I have tried to include a broad range of locations, owing to the proximity of Ireland's capital city to Wicklow, most of the extant written material relates to this area, and it is impossible not to be somewhat east-coast heavy. Other than the fact that they chose to travel on foot, the people whose work I have selected have little in common with each other. Together, however, their accounts of their walks, long or short, tell much about the progress and development of Ireland and its people over the years, and provide a chronological travelogue of a country in the process of change. The Ireland of today bears little resemblance to the land that the earlier walkers explored; a few aspects, however, clearly remain unchanged, including the high mountains (some of the old descriptions of these wilderness places will be very familiar to those who walk in Ireland today), and the state of Protestant/Catholic relations in the northern part of the island.

Some of these pedestrian travellers covered great distances, others wrote of short strolls. Some favoured level terrain, while others were attracted to and challenged by the mountains. Some set out to experience at first hand the social and political situation that existed in the country, others to seek flora and fauna, and still others enjoyed walking as a prelude to hearty drinking and singing. I have gathered them all to offer them to you, the reader, and all those who have been my companions on the mountains, as a celebration of walking in Ireland.

Anthology

Dr Samuel Johnson (1709–84)
County Kildare in c.1783

[Boswell comments in his *Life of Dr Johnson* that Johnson always showed an aversion to travelling to Ireland, and he is, of course, known for comments about the country; in response to Boswell's question, 'Is not the Giant's Causeway worth seeing?', he replied, 'Worth seeing? Yes; but not worth going to see.' He was, however, sympathetic to Ireland, and had friendships with Irishmen such as Goldsmith and Burke; indeed, his doctorate was awarded by Trinity College Dublin. Boswell reports him telling an Irish visitor, 'Do not make an union with us, Sir. We should unite with you, only to rob you. We should have robbed the Scotch, if they had any thing of which we could have robbed them.'

According to *Walker's Hibernian Magazine*, Johnson did pay a short visit to Ireland, possibly in 1783, the year before his death; his description of the visit was published in the *Hibernian Magazine* in November 1783. After a sojourn in Dublin he tired of society there and accepted an invitation to accompany two ladies, Mrs Greville and Mrs Jephson, on a short tour of County Kildare. There he visited Celbridge Abbey, the seat of Colonel Marlay, which earlier in the century had been the home of Esther Vanhomrigh, Swift's Stella. The house still stands today, overlooking the river Liffey and an island formed by taking a short canal off the river. Dr Johnson and his two companions visited the island and then went for a stroll along the banks of the Liffey; I include in my chosen excerpt his description of what happened on this short walk.]

Whether it was mentioned to me seriously by Dean Marlay, or was only the extemporaneous effusion of female pleasantry, I cannot now precisely determine, but I think I heard that Vanessa, then Mistress of Celbridge, had put down a laurel for every brilliant couplet of which Dr Swift or her vanity told her she was the subject and he the author. Had the subsequent possessors of Celbridge with counteractive industry deracinated a laurel for every distich published by his posthumous editors disgraceful to the memory of that singular genius, the island of Celbridge would be destitute of a laurel. We left the bower, the laurels and the island, and proceeded to an irregular bridge of I know not how many arches. From the central part of the bridge some miles of the river, and the gentle declivities of the ground appear to great advantage. Colonel Marlay possesses a considerable tract on either side of the river, a circumstance of distinguished advantage, as the view from either bank cannot be prejudiced by the malicious hostilities of an opposite neighbour, nor by a cause less reprehensible, though more to be apprehended, the vicious appetite for altering the landscapes of nature without genius to embellish them. As both shores call him master, he can sleep secure without the fear that his verdant banks will be tortured into terraces, the winding stream quadrated into fish ponds; that hares and greyhounds of lead may take their eternal place in the fields before him; or that a whitewashed Neptune will be forever recumbent in his sight upon an urn like a bagpipe, from which will issue neither moisture nor melody.

While I was admiring the fantastical ramifications of some umbelliferous plants that overhang the margins of the Liffey, the fallacious bank, imperceptably corroded by the moist tooth of the fluid, gave way beneath my feet, and I was sudden-submerged to some fathoms of profundity; presence of mind in some constitutions not naturally timid is generally in proportion to the imminence of peril; having never learnt to move through the water in horizontal progression, had I desponded, I had perished; but being for a moment raised above the element by my struggles, or by some felicitous casualty, I was sensible of the danger, and instantly embraced the means of extrication; a cow at the moment of my lapse had entered the stream within the distance of a protruded arm, and being in the act of transverse navigation to seek the pasture of the opposite bank, I laid hold on that part of the animal which is loosely pendant behind, and is formed of a continuation of the vertebrae; in this manner I was safely conveyed to a fordable passage, not without some delectation from the sense of progress without any effort on my part, and the exhilarating approximation of more than problematical deliverance. Though in some respects I resembled the pilot of *Gyas jam senior madidaque fluens in veste*,[1] yet my companions, unlike the barbarous Phrygian spectators, forebore to acerbitate the uncouthness of embarrassment by the insult of derision, shrieks of complorance testified sorrow for my submersion, and safety was made more pleasant by the felicitations of sympathy; as the danger was over, I took no umbrage at a little risibility excited by the feculency of my visage, upon which the cow had discharged her graminous digestion in very ludicrous abundance: about this time the bell summoned us to dinner, and as the cutaneous contact of irrigated garments is neither pleasant nor salubrious, I was easily persuaded by the ladies to divest myself of mine; Colonel Marlay obligingly provided me with a loose covering of camblet; I found it commodious and more agreeable than the many compressive ligatures of modern drapery; that there might be no

[1] Here Johnson refers to a passage describing a boat race in Virgil's *Aeneid*, where the fall of an elderly coxwain into the sea is greeted with derision by the spectators.

violation of decorum, I took care to have the loose robe fastened close before with small cylindrical wires, which the dainty fingers of the ladies easily removed from their own dress, and inserted into mine at such proper intervals to have no aperature that could awaken susceptibility of temperament, or provide the cachinations of levity.

Anonymous
*c.*1790

[Rambling songs were popular at the end of the eighteenth century, usually providing entertaining descriptions of the experiences of travelling rakes combined with a litany of place-names. The one I have chosen, translated from Irish, appeared in *Anthologia Hibernica* in 1793. It tells of the experiences of Fiachra McBrady during a ramble from his home in County Cavan around Ireland, via Dublin, Waterford, Cork, Killarney and Galway, before returning to his wife and family.]

The Peregrinations of Fiachra McBrady

If ye heard each disaster, of your poetaster,
And Irish scholmaster, since leaving Stradone;
Thro' thick and thin splashing, the rain on him dashing,
My friends in compassion, you'ld Brady bemoan.
The bri'rs my cloaths tatt'ring, my new nail'd brogues clatt'ring,
The mud my legs spatt'ring, I strove to grope home;
Whilst tir'd, wet and weary, I'd rather, I swear ye,
Be 'n the cabin with Mary, than bishop of Rome.
I got over mountains, thro' bogs, and by fountains,
Pierc'd woods without counting, to Croghan, alone;
Whence to Arran I scamper'd, with baggage not hamper'd,
To Sligo's sea rampart, Kinnard and Tyrone.
Continuing my hurry, I dash'd on to Newry,
Thence to Down like a fury, where they robb'd me *oghone*!
O'er Sliav Gullin I darted, from Drogheda parted,
Where against a ship carted, I broke my jaw bone.
I shouted out murder, to the ship's crew if further,
I got near the border, I'd fall in and drown;
Whilst the rascals kept funning, never fear, you're too cunning,
And the people came running, from all parts of the town.
For fear of no quarters, from this crew of sea tartars,

I swam o'er the waters, in stockings and shoes;
Thence to Garristown common, where I met an old woman,
Who told me my coming was announc'd in the news.
'Tis not to be wondered, that I found myself founder'd,
Like a horse that on ground hard, had plough'd by the tail;
But St Patrick's bells ringing, my heart set a springing,
And I reach'd Dublin singing *'Brave Grainne Weal'*.
The first thing I'll mention, that gain'd my attention,
And my eyes kept in tension an hour I swear;
'Twas King William of Britain, on an iron horse sitting,
As fierce as a kitten, the post office near.
Desirous of knowledge, I went to the college,
Where I am forc'd to acknowledge, but little I found;
So sooner than argue, I steer'd for Portlarga,
With of whiskey a cargo, my sorrows to drown.
I drank till quite mellow, then like a brave fellow,
Began for to bellow, and shouted for more;
But my host held his stick up, which soon cur'd my hiccup,
As no cash could I pick up, to pay off the score.
To prison he sent me, here I 'gan to repent me,
I knew I must Lent keep, until my release;
But the next day they stript me, and out of doors kick'd me,
So my choler to quit, see, I damn'd the police.
With wet and cold, shiv'ring, my broken jaw quiv'ring,
I thought oft the river in, my body to throw;
And it still is a mist'ry, when I con o'er' my hist'ry,
By what means I mist free, the waters below.
I visited Blarney, Birr, Cork, and Killarney,
McMahon of Farney, and Galway's rich shore;
From Croagh Patrick with hot head, to Dromole I trotted,
With an oak stick well knotted, and so to Balore.
Here a lodging I'd taken, but lothe to awaken,
For fear of my bacon, or man, wife, or babe;
Brush' d on in a passion, and thro' the ford dashing,
I reach'd the mud mansion of Brian McCabe.
The potatoes were boiling, but his brats kept such squalling,
With the itch their hands mawling, the road I set to;
And at home found Moll Brady, with Owen and Thady,
As they'd heard I was drowned, all crying *'Whillaloo'*.

I remember McBrady - no lady, or village queen
But wish'd on a May-day, or play-day, his choice to've been;
To a barrel of liquor, none quicker, to run was seen,

Nor at fairs had a stick or club thicker, or brogues more clean;
Like a halfpenny candle, he'd handle his sapling green
Now alas! in Dunsandle, a bramble his grave doth screen.

Le Chevalier de la Tocnaye
Killarney and Tralee in 1796

[Jacques Louis de Bougrenet, Chevalier de la Tocnaye, was a Breton Royalist, and he was in his twenties in 1791 when he was forced to leave France for England in the wake of the Revolution. He had armed himself with sufficient letters of introduction, and having travelled widely in England and Scotland for a few years, he wrote *Promenade dans le Grande Bretagne*, published in 1795. The success of this travelogue spurred him to come to Ireland with the same motive in mind. He arrived in Ireland in 1796, and took a year and a thousand miles to travel round the island on foot, after which he published a description of his journeys under the title *Promenade d'un français dans l'Irlande*.

His story of his travels is a wonderfully readable, witty and perceptive view of late eighteenth-century Ireland; he is very observant, and records for his readers not only the major events but all the little things that go towards painting a detailed and often humorous pictures of the countryside and people of the time. He was a well and broadly educated man, and clearly clever; his suggestions for improvements in the countryside, particularly in relation to the canalization of Ireland, were all eminently sensible and far-sighted. Some of his notions subsequently came to pass, and who is to say, considering his contacts with the gentry in each area he passed through, that he did not at least plant the seed of such developments? One of his ideas, however, while maybe not considered so outlandish in his day, would be regarded as somewhat crackpot now: he suggested that if the great lakes of the Shannon basin were drained, an additional 200,000 acres of farmland would be gained.

He must have cut an unusual figure as he walked, a typical, if down-at-heel, dandy of the period, his few belongings (including powder bag and powder puff!) wrapped in a handkerchief and slung over his shoulder on his sword-stick, onto which he attached an umbrella. He takes pride in listing his 'complete equipment' for walking, and states that 'although [his] baggage was inconsiderable, [he] wanted for nothing, and had the means of appearing in society as well dressed as others.' In addition to the clothes he wore, he carried a razor, a comb, a scissors, needles and thread, dress shoes, a pair of silk stockings and a pair of breeches, two shirts, three cravats and three handkerchiefs. This paucity of 'equipment' suggests that he was a hardy man, which is borne out by the 28 miles a day he covered, but it is clear that either he was fearless or very foolish in the manner in which he skipped around the country in his powdered wig and tights.

He had a healthy way of laughing at himself and his ideas, and he was a fearless optimist who rarely seemed to plan his route carefully or think about the time it would take him to walk from place to place, a neglect which often leads to difficulties. His weakness for women is clear in the way he describes his admiration of them, and it seems a wonder that he did not find himself in trouble in this regard.

In this extract, La Tocnaye describes his arrival and stay at Killarney, and then the continuation of his tour to Tralee. In addition to the beauties of the area, he describes a funeral and a fight, a wake and a holy well, and marvels at the power of the priests.]

The moment I quitted Kenmare I got into the mountains again; they were not, however, of so wild an appearance as the former.[1] When you become very tired of this wild country, on getting through a narrow passage at the foot of Mangerton, you are on a sudden charmed with the prospect of Killarney. The impression which its numerous islands and well-cultivated banks made on me, can be compared only to the sensation of a poor prisoner suddenly transported from his dungeon to the light of the sun. I continued my journey very slowly, not knowing which to admire most, the cloud-capt mountains covered with trees, the fine sheet of water at their feet, the islands, the peninsula which separates both lakes, or the charming country to the north.

I passed a week very agreeably at Lord Kenmare's, during which I was often on the lake. I shall venture to give a sketch of its beauties, which the soft frigid observer could not but admire.

People generally go two miles from Killarney to the island of Ross, the largest in the lake and separated from the country by a narrow stream, over which there is a bridge. In this island is to be seen the castle of Prince O'Donoghue, to whom this country belonged in ancient times, and who, according to its inhabitants, rides on the lake a certain day of the year.

Going eastwards the peninsula Mucruss[2] offers itself to the view. It is one of the finest places I have seen on account of the chequering of woods and plains, it meanders nearly about two miles.

The venerable ruins of the abbey inspire a sentiment of religious

---

[1] The Caha mountains, which he had crossed to reach Kenmare from Bantry.
[2] Muckross.

horror by no means unpleasing; the yew in the middle of it covers it entirely with its branches, and hardly admits the passage of a few rays of light which fall on the tombs and bones at the foot of it. The inhabitants believe that the rash mortal who would dare to cut it, or even pierce it would inevitably perish that year. They pay great devotion to the saint of the place and come to do pilgrimage and penance, which here, and in the rest of Ireland, consists of going round the building a certain number of times, all the while reciting prayers.

They also inter their dead here, and bring them from a prodigious distance; they bury them only on the south and east sides. The north is looked on as the devil's side, and the west is preserved for children that die without being baptized, and for soldiers and strangers. They look on it as a great piece of impiety to carry off the remains of the coffins; there are two large vaults in the abbey quite full of them. The bones are left scattered about, wherever they were thrown by the grave-diggers, but nobody would touch them for the world. In a corner outside there is a tremendous heap of them. Although at the Reformation the rich divided between them the plunder of the abbeys, they nowhere ventured to remove the graveyard. It is among the ruins of the old church the peasants wish everywhere to be buried, and it is impossible to dissuade them from it: it has often been tried here to make them bury their dead in another place, but without success. This would, however, be advisable, for, besides that on the rock, there is hardly sod enough to cover the dead, the churchyard is so full of corpses that it would not be prudent to dig there for some time. This gives them no uneasiness; those who were buried a year or two ago must make room for those who die later, and in this hideous-looking vault I saw more than one skull still covered with hair.

Some years ago an old well-looking man came to reside in one of the old chambers of this abbey. He made a bed for himself with some of the boards of the coffin and placed it in one of the windows, the only place sheltered. He soon got a reputation for sanctity, the peasants brought him provisions, and the gentry invited him sometimes to their table, where he behaved like a person accustomed to good company. When asked the reason of his penance, he answered that 'he could never do enough for his sins'. He was a handsome man, and once perceiving a lady looked attentively at him, 'Take care,' said he, 'those eyes have done much "harm"'. He lived about two years in this melancholy solitude, and at length disappeared. People have formed many conjectures, and invented several stories about him during his residence at Mucruss, but they are probably the suggestions of fancy.

The peninsula of Mucruss divides the lake into two; that which it forms is small and adds to the beauty of the prospect by variety. From thence you follow the current of the river which comes from the upper lake. In a certain part of the mountain called the Eagles Nest, because some eagles often fly over it, people amuse themselves with firing a cannon, the report of which is not re-echoed as is generally the case, but ceases for a time and then makes a noise like thunder. The banks of the river you sail up before you get to the upper lake, surrounded by wild towering mountains, presents a striking contrast with the lower, the banks of which are highly improved. When you come down the river into the lower lake, you are taken to see Sullivan's cascade in the middle of the wood, you go from thence to Innisfallen, a charming island, where there was formerly an abbey; it belongs to Lord Kenmare, and when a person is so lucky as to be at one of these parties on the lake, which he and Lady Kenmare often make up, after admiring the beauties of nature, he cannot avoid paying homage to their politeness and hospitality.

There are some stags in the woods, and sometimes they start one from the mountain, who then closely pursued gets into the lake, where the dogs and boats follow him and drive him out of the islands where he flies for shelter. A deal of company come here from every part of Ireland, but remain only to see the lake. They would remain longer if there were any public amusements or mineral waters; the latter especially would be highly advantageous, and I believe there are few places better adapted to repair a shattered constitution. There is an excellent mineral water in Lord Kenmare's park. Unfortunately no son of Esculapius[3] has hitherto taken it into his head to bring it into vogue, but this will happen sooner or later. The town is pretty enough, it appears new and is built in the form of a T.

Walking out one morning rather early, I heard dreadful groans and shrieks in a house. Attracted by curiosity I entered, and saw in a room about fifty women weeping over a poor old man, who [had] died a couple of days before. Four of them in particular made more noise than the rest, tore their hair and often embraced the deceased. I remarked that in about a quarter of an hour they were tired, went into another room and were replaced by four others, who continued their shrieks until the others were recovered; these after swallowing a large glass of whiskey, to enable them to make more noise, resumed their places and the others went to refresh themselves.

These assemblies are called wakes, and every peasant that dies is sure of having his friends and acquaintances in his room crying, weeping, drinking his health and singing his praises extempore in Irish verses, from the day of his death to that of his burial. It is rather an expensive custom, with which, however, the poorest person could not decently dispense; the

---

3 Aesculapius, the Greek god of healing.

expense was greater formerly, for it appears from the Brehon laws, that the quantity of meat and drink was regulated according to the rank of the deceased, to prevent excess and hinder families from being ruined by vying with each other. This explains the answer a poor widow, who was reproached with not sending for a physician, made: 'Oh!' said she, 'I thought it a deal for a poor woman like me to pay his funeral expenses.' I think the poor woman was right; the physician is a kind of moralist to the rich, he prevails on them to moderate their passions, and to repair the ravages of excess by temperance; but of what use could his advice be to the poor who never commit excess, to whom nourishing food would be the best remedy? If he recovered, the poor countryman must starve himself to pay the physician, and if he died his wife would be at double expense.

I was witness to an odd scene some days after. Hearing the church-bell ring I went to see the funeral pass; it was a poor old woman they were carrying to the grave. The coffin was as usual surrounded by a great number of women crying and singing the ululu in chorus; the men seemed to look on with indifference. When the funeral arrived at the cross road, an odd dispute arose between the husband and brother of the deceased; one of the roads led to the abbey Mucruss, the burying-place of the husband's family, and the other to Aghadoe, that of the brother's; the latter insisted she should be carried his way, the husband was equally clamorous for the interment of his dearly beloved in his family-place. The friends of the deceased were each pulling her to their own side, but finding they did not succeed, agreed to lay down the coffin and decide it by a fair battle. The cudgels were already brandished in the air, when Mr. Herbert, minister of the parish and Justice of the Peace, who was with me, leaped into the crowd, caught two of the principal combatants by the collar, and after inquiring into the fray, decided that the husband had a right to do what he pleased with his wife dead or alive; he then let him go, but kept her brother, and the funeral went towards Mucruss. I remarked that neither the battle, nor the discussion which followed it stopped the women who continued their ululu as if nothing had happened. When I saw the Justice of the Peace get into the crowd I was sure he would get an unmerciful flogging, and got on a wall to see the event; but I found I was mistaken: the peasants obeyed the magistrate and submitted immediately to his decision. This was certainly much better, but it appeared so curious to me that people should fight for a dead woman, that I was rather sorry the affair terminated so peaceably.

I went once to the top of Mangerton,[4] from whence a great tract of

[4] Mangerton (839 m) 10 km south of Killarney, was at the time thought to be Ireland's highest mountain.

country is seen, though it is not quite equal to the prospect of all the kingdoms of the globe. You see barren mountains covered with small lakes, that of Killarney appears a pretty sheet of water, in the midst of which the penisula of Mucruss juts out. There is a little lake on the summit of Mangerton called the devil's punch bowl, out of which I drank to the health of the saint of the place, and to that of his children, viz. the nine tenths of the human race, particularly the pretty girls.

As this town is much frequented in summer, beggars come here from every part of the country; they build wretched huts on the side of the road, and seize passengers. This might be prevented by a house of industry, where they should be obliged to work.

It would not be difficult to join the lake with the sea, either by a canal from it to the bay of Kenmare, or by rendering navigable the river which flows from the lake into the bay of Dingle. The first method would be better, for the bay of Kenmare is safer than that of Dingle, which has a sandy bottom; either way they would have only seven or eight miles to make a canal, which would undoubtedly be very beneficial to the town of Killarney and adjacent country.

On the road to Tralee I met a man who showed me three castles which formerly belonged to three brothers, who had been masters of the country, and were turned out by the English. I asked him why they were turned out. 'Because,' said he, 'they were not strong enough.' This is an argument *ad hominem.*

Tralee is a pretty town of some trade. The sea coast from this place to Limerick was formerly the chief residence of the Danes, who have left many of these round towers called Rath, or Liss, here. There are four of them at the distance of two hundred paces from each other at the mouth of the river in Tralee Bay. This town is frequented in summer by bathers and people who come to drink the mineral waters one or two miles off.

I went thence to Ardfert to Mr Dean Greaves's, where as usual I met with the delightful hospitality that soon makes me forget my fatigue. Ardfert was formerly a bishopric, but is now joined to that of Limerick. There were formerly many ecclesiastical establishments here; the ruins of the old cathedral are the greatest object of curiosity. The air of this place is said to be very wholesome, which had induced a surgeon to choose it for his burying place; he is alive yet, but his epitaph is engraved on his tomb as if he were dead.

In the church yard of the cathedral there was formerly a round tower, which though apparently very stable, fell down about fifteen years ago. What is remarkable is, that instead of falling towards one side, as a person would naturally expect, all the stones fell inside and formed a great heap on the place where the tower stood before.

I went to see the remains of the Franciscan abbey near Ardfert, where

I met two of the handsomest and most amiable women in Ireland, Lady Glandore and Mrs Woodcock, who had entered into the wicked resolution of retiring an entire year from the world. I know not if it was from good example, but I never felt so much inclined to be a hermit.

At some distance is one of these holy fountains where the inhabitants make their rounds; this is a very celebrated one, and people come to it from a great distance. They pretend it cures every complaint; their devotion consists in going round it barefooted seven or eight times praying, and kneeling each time before a black stone, which seems to have been a tombstone. They rub their hands very gravely to three death's heads on it; by dint of rubbing and kissing them, they are almost effaced. They then put the hand which they had rubbed to the stone on the part where they feel the pain, drink a large glass of water and wash their legs in the stream. They dip the children seven or eight times in the cold water. I often saw well-dressed people go through these ceremonies like the peasants. I saw even a very pretty girl kiss these ugly heads very devoutly; I could not help thinking I would have been a much better physician for her.

This fountain is very famous in the country, and even Protestants, of whom there are but few here, when they have tried other remedies in vain, make their rounds here and imitate the country people. The greater number of the peasants, however, seemed to come rather from a fondness for company than for devotion. I asked one of them what the water was good for? 'I do not know,' answered he. And when I asked him why he had made his rounds? 'To do like the rest,' said he, 'and to see the women.' At these fountains in fact many marriages are made up. In vain does the parish priest prohibit them from coming here; the people are so long accustomed to it that it would not be easy to prevail on them to lay it aside.

Nothing, indeed, can be more innocent than to walk about the well saying 'Oremuses', and then to take a glass of water; I am convinced that it might serve women by obliging them to take some exercise and to wash themselves. If they could be prevailed on not to confine the ablution to the legs it would be still better. But in order to produce this effect, there should be separate fountains for the men and women, in which case they would be soon neglected. The only thing the priest can do is to keep order at these meetings, and to prevent anything indecent from passing there; in this the parish priest of this place has succeeded. The good people come on Saturday morning, and conclude their penance at two o'clock; then the *cantien calle*, goes home with its *bonnie lassie*, *cracking* all the way.[5]

They are all Catholics here. They agree very well together; the people

<hr>

[5] An awkward translation: a later interpretation suggests: 'Then the young fellows make up to their girls and see them safe home to their mothers, chatting the while.

go to mass on Sundays, and the minister preaches to his family, without either of them caring of what religion they are the rest of the week, except on paying or receiving tithes. I went on Sunday to the Catholic chapel. The women there are always separated from the men, probably to prevent distractions. In the middle of the ceremony the priest made a long harangue in Irish in which he sent to all the devils in hell those who might be base enough not to pay him his dues.

These priests have great influence over the people; they are in a great measure judges, and decide all disputes with astonishing precision. It would be dangerous to displease them or to refuse to pay their scanty pittance. Government knew their power, and yet have made enemies of them by ill-treatment. The right method of gaining over the people would be to gain over the priests. I am convinced that a dozen fat benefices in favour of Catholic priests at the disposal of the Lord Lieutenant would soon make them as supple, as courteous, and as studious of pleasing as their dearly-beloved brethren, the bishops and ministers of the Protestant church.

The churches are built from east to west so that when the priest is at the altar, he faces the east. It is odd that this is universally the custom in Europe, even in the Lutheran churches, though few have remarked it. I recollect very well that all the old ones are built so in France, and that I never had remarked it; it is true the new ones are built either way, but , however, they mostly have the door towards the west, and the altar towards the east. This custom was universally introduced long before the establishment of Christianity, and appears to have been adopted by most nations. The reason assigned for it is that the Christian religion has originated to the east of Europe, and that it is a mark of respect due to the theatre of its miracles. In this case Christians in Persia should face the west. This seems to be equivalent to the reason Mahometans assign for turning also towards the east, on account of Mecca, the city of their prophet. Though I am not certain as to the real cause, I do not think it to be this; I am rather inclined to look on it as a universal homage paid to the rising sun.

The neighbourhood of the low sandy bay of Ballyheigh induces some company to come to Ardfert for the purpose of bathing in the sea. In the middle of the bay is a rock on which even moss does not grow, and which, however, an adventurer from this country settled as a dowry on a rich wife he got, and valued at two thousand a year. Walking along the coast through a country thinly inhabited, but where a person makes out his way by means of *go whil an slee a*,[6] I arrived at the mouth of the Shannon.

This is the largest river in Ireland. The inhabitants entertain a degree of veneration for it, of which it seems worthy; nobody is esteemed in this

[6] Probably '*ait go bhuil an sli*', or by following the way or track.

country who has not taken a dip in it, and as I wish to conform to the manners of the country I am in, this was my first operation. It is seven or eight miles broad at the mouth. On the banks are very high rocks, and deep caverns, into which the waves break with astonishing fury. At some distance on a rock separate from the others are ruins of the fortifications, and even of a little town; the streets and foundations of houses may be distinguished; the houses do not seem to have been larger than cabins, though the fortifications were extensive.

Continuing my journey along the coast, I passed the Cushin which falls into the Shannon; it rises at the foot of a hill, at the other side of which the Blackwater rises and falls into St George's channel at Youghal. No country in the world is better adapted for commerce than this, and nowhere could industry be more successfully employed in opening a communication by canals.

When the Royal Canal is finished, by which the Liffey will be joined to the Shannon, I believe it would be very advantageous to join the Black-water with the Cushin, and to render them navigable. They may easily join the Blackwater with the Suir, and even with the Lee. Ireland would then have an inland navigation of upwards of five hundred miles, which would establish a communication between the four principal cities of the south: Dublin, Limerick, Cork and Waterford; even Drogheda may be joined with them by this means, as the Boyne may be rendered navigable for boats as far as the Royal Canal.

Patrick Lynch
West Mayo in 1802

[Patrick Lynch was a Gaelic language scholar who was employed for a period in 1802 by the traditional music collector Edward Bunting, to collect music and songs in Connaught. He set out from Drogheda on foot in May of that year, and headed west on his quest. Over the next ten weeks he travelled widely over the wild north Mayo countryside between the towns of Castlebar, Ballina, Belmullet and Westport, and collected more than 200 pieces of music. By 1802 the vast bog landscape and wild coastline of north-west Mayo were still unmapped in detail. Taylor and Skinner's *Maps of the Roads of Ireland*, compiled twenty-five years previously, suggested that nothing significant existed west of Killala or north of Newport, and the westernmost reference in Sleator's *Topography* of 1806 is mention of a church at Crossmolina. While Lynch describes a desolate landscape scattered with mud cabins and shebeens, he finds, however, that the remote town of Belmullet is a bustling and seeming prosperous place, where tobacco and whiskey, the coinage of the song collector, are in good supply.

It was an area which only four years previously had witnessed the full violent might of the Crown when, in the wake of the failed French invasion at Killala, a bloody mopping-up operation was carried out involving many executions. This did not assist Lynch in his task; someone who spent long hours in public houses listening and taking notes must have attracted a lot of suspicion. One can imagine the difficulties and temptations he endured during the long series of late nights in whiskey houses, trying to coax obscure songs from shoemakers, farmers and mechanics; he reported to his employer: 'I stuck to the business both early and late, till I drained them of all the songs they had.' The following extracts from Lynch's letters to John McCracken of Belfast, who was acting for Bunting while the latter was in London, describe some of his experiences and treks in search of music and song.]

I left Drogheda on Monday 26th April. The rain came on. I stopped in Slane for two hours. Came to Navan, fourteen miles. I slept there, having suffered greatly by the rain. On Monday, waited awhile in Navan in order to see Dr Plunkett, Bishop of Meath, as I was advised in Drogheda. I did not get speaking to him; he was about some business. On Tuesday, from Navan, by Kells to Virginia, eighteen miles; on Wednesday, by Cavan to Belturbet, twenty-one miles; on Thursday, through part of Cavan and Fermanagh to the Black Lion, twenty miles; on Friday, to Manorhamilton, eighty-two miles from Drogheda;[1] and six miles more that evening, to a place called Killargy, near where Mr Bartley lives. I had a letter to him from Mr Pat Connor. I stayed there, at a public house, till Monday evening. I got but six songs from Mr Bartley; indeed, they are some of the best of Carolan's.[2] I got about sixteen more at the public house. I came three miles to Dromahare on Monday evening; took breakfast at Collooney, eight miles off, on Tuesday; came to a place called Skreen, in the Barony of Tyreragh, County Sligo, where I got five good songs from James Dowd, a farmer; that night I treated him and his family to some whiskey, where I got the five songs, some good potatoes and eggs, and a bed in the barn. I came to a public house on Wednesday night,

[1] These must be Irish miles; the distance from Drogheda to Manorhamilton is actually in excess of 105 miles.
[2] Turlough O'Carolan was a prominent Irish harpist and composer of the eighteenth century.

within eight miles of Ballina. Yesterday, 6th May, I came to this town. I found Dr Bellew very civil; I dined with him and his clergy. I wait here today to get a few songs from a Mrs Burke. I am advised to proceed directly to Irris, across the country; and to the Mullet, in the most westerly part of the County Mayo. I do not know how long this may take, but I am resolved to be always either writing or travelling, and to make the best I can for my employer. I am sure I shall be in want of money by the time I am at Castlebar. On my return from the mountains of Mayo, I know that every week will cost me a guinea, whether I travel or stop. Mr Bunting allowed me to keep account of every expense I should be at on account of the songs; but I find this cannot be well done, because my own travelling expense is so connected with the expense of procuring songs that I could not well keep a separate account. You will please to let Mr Bunting know that I expect he will allow me a guinea-and-a-half per week for altogether, and let me bear the expense for songs which may be to little purpose; at other times I will get a parcel of songs at less cost, and I would not wish to have any complaint at my return for extravagance. I am now convinced that the best way is to go to the shebeen-houses, and find out some little blasting schoolmaster, and warm his mouth with whiskey and he will find out the singers for me. For my own part, you may depend on it, I shall drink no whiskey nor spirits until I return to Belfast. I shall live as the case requires in this wild country. I hope I shall be able to show twenty-one songs for every week that I am on this tour, and more if I can. I have no place as yet that you could write to me; I suppose that I shall appoint Castlebar for my address . . .

I left Ballina on Friday, May 7th; went about five miles to Priest Conway of Ardagh. He was hospitable, directed me to a schoolmaster, Anthony Carrin, near Killala; I picked up two songs on the way – cost a little whiskey, and tobacco. On Saturday evening treated the schoolmaster in a shebeen-house, stayed there till night, got but little rest, came to the schoolmaster's house on Sunday morning early; took down two songs from him, went to Mass, from thence to another shebeen-house, where I got four good songs from the man and the woman of the house; the schoolmaster left me there; presently some people came in who began to whisper to the man and woman of the house, that I was come on some other device than looking for songs, and that I had written down their names, and would have them ruined for selling without license; the man of the house told me that he did not believe that I intended him any harm, but I found his wife growing very shy, and also a neighbour of theirs, who was to meet me and give me songs. I had to set off. I did not know where I should lodge that night; by good fortune I met the priest, who brought me to his own house where I stayed all night, and came to the schoolmaster on Monday morning.

I got but one song more from him – three in all, and four in the shebeen-house, and two on the way on Saturday before – nine since I left Ballina. Having travelled many miles through the Barony of Tirawlay, I set off in every direction to Crossmoligna, where I bought paper and tobacco, and set on Monday evening towards Erris, a dreary, bleak mountainous country. I came to a place called Duliag,[3] where there was but one house; I stayed there all night, and gave the people some tobacco for their hospitality. I got up early and made a journey of upwards of four miles that day. I had to cross a great moor,[4] such as I had never seen before, which fatigued me very much, until I crossed a great river, called Avonmore,[5] where abundance of salmon are caught. When I found myself growing very feeble, on the side of a mountain, I espied a sorry looking cabin, where I rested near an hour, got one song, gave them tobacco, they gave me potatoes and milk, and I found myself quite refreshed. I had now divided my tobacco. I enquired and found a place where they sold some, at three and threepence a pound; I bought half a pound of it, and came late in the evening to Daniel Kelly's near the entrance to the Mullet,[6] where I was entertained with potatoes, and eggs, and fresh oysters, with plenty of milk and butter. But they make no use of bread in this country. I came into the Mullet on Wednesday to Mr Richard Barrett's of Corn; I stopped at a shebeen-house hard by. I had been advised by Dr Bellew, Mr Conway, and others at Ballina, to go to Mr Barrett, he being a man of good information and of a happy retentive memory, a good singer, a born poet – in short, that he was equal to any of the bards if not superior.

Mr Barrett is certainly a very agreeable companion, and I found him exceedingly civil; yet I found myself greatly disappointed with respect to what I chiefly wanted. I got, after waiting some days, six songs from him, pretty good ones. He was short of tin. He keeps a little academy, for the gentlemen's children of the island. There are a great many genteel people, men of landed property in the Mullet. I suppose the young men of them had most of their education from Mr Barrett; they pay him great respect, and are very fond to see him in the evening in the whiskey house. I must tell you, Sir, that one evening, as Mr Barrett and I had been in company with three or four of these young bucks, a Mr O'Donnell called him aside, and after returning says, 'I think Mr Barrett has no right to give away his

---

[3] Dooleeg is a hamlet about 6.5 miles or 11 km from Crossmolina.
[4] The Sheskin area which Lynch crossed remains the largest area of blanket bog, and the largest but most sparsely populated townland, in Ireland.
[5] Called the Owenmore today. .
[6] The Mullet, or Belmullet, is a 25 km long landmass connected to the mainland by a narrow neck of land, for long one of the most remote places in Ireland.

own compositions, the fruit of his own brain, too cheap. If he is willing to give me the copy and copyright of all his own songs I shall be willing to give him five guineas for them.' 'Sir,' said I, 'I think Mr Barrett has a right to the profit of his own works, and I doubt not but they are worth more; meanwhile I have no orders to take the works of any poet now living.' 'How so, why so,' cries all the company, 'what have you come here for? Was there ever any poet in Connaught, ancient or modern, superior to Mr Barrett?' 'Gentlemen,' said I , 'I make no doubt of the excellence of Mr Barrett's compositions, but my orders are to collect the songs of the old bards, and I was told that Mr Barrett could give more old songs than any man in Connaught.' Thus it ended.

Whilst I stayed on the island I made three or four excursions, to different little villages, for their cabins are all in clusters on the sides of the hills, and they seem to live very comfortably. There are a good many neat slated houses interspersed through this peninsula where the owners have some free lands, having income, some £200, some £300, and some £500 a year, they live cheaply here and seem to be very happy. I was not invited to any of these gentlemen's houses, though I had seen and conversed with some of them; but I understand it is not their custom to invite anyone below their own rank; but if they come of their own accord they are welcome and treat them very hospitably. I had to call for whiskey wherever I applied for songs, and they sold whiskey everywhere. I left the Mullet on Thursday and came to Daniel Kelly's outside the peninsula where I got four songs; cost me 2s 8½d[7] for whiskey. Friday came to Avonmore; the flood was so high I stayed all night in Patrick Deane's by the riverside; he sent his horse with me over the river. Saturday morning I crossed the Craggy Mountain,[8] and the roughest road that ever was travelled; saw no house for sixteen miles, but one cabin at a distance, having waded to the knees through or across seven rivers, till I came to Strathfern[9] where I thought to stay, but the few huts dispersed about the place were hard to come at. I crossed a watery marsh to come at one of them, where I found one old woman, and a dozen of kids, and two young calves. I asked a drink, I got good milk, I returned tobacco, but I could see nothing like a bed in the house. I asked how far to Newport, they said four miles. I set off and crawled along very tired, came to Newport about ten at night.

[7] About 14p.
[8] Probably the Nephin Beg range.
[9] This place-name is now disused.

25

John Bernard Trotter (1775–1818)
Wicklow and Wexford in 1812

[John Bernard Trotter was born in County Down and he graduated from Trinity College in 1795 with a degree in Law. He did not enter the legal profession, however, and instead turned to writing and politics. His many anti-Union pamphlets and his family connections brought him to the attention of Charles James Fox, leader of a Whig splinter group and opponent of Pitt's Irish policy. At Fox's house in Arlington Street in London, Trotter met many of the Irish cognoscenti of the day, including Richard Brinsley Sheridan and Fox's cousin Lord Edward Fitzgerald. Trotter became a loyal devotee of Fox, and in 1806 went to work for him as private secretary, a task he took on with enthusiasm, although Fox died only months later – it is said, in Trotter's arms.

Trotter had a great interest in the revival of the Irish harp and was a founder member of the Dublin Harp Society. He was not a Gaelic revivalist, however, but was of that other grouping of Irish of the time which, while seeking a measure of parliamentary independence for Ireland, aspired to the culture and traditions of the English. He led a chequered life, sometimes seemingly well-off and other times enduring the debtors' prison, often profuse in his hospitality while at the same time being hounded by creditors. He was a prolific pamphlet writer and walking traveller, and we are fortunate to have his accounts of his travels, in the form of his collected letters to an Englishman he addresses as 'L'. In these he describes his walking journeys through Ireland in 1812, 1814 and 1817, advising on the state of the country, and admonishing 'L' on the mistakes England has made in the governance of Ireland.

It seems clear from the general style, the misspelling of place-names, which must have taken place when the letters were being transcribed, and typical passages where afterthoughts have been inserted into the flow of the letter, that Trotter did not live to edit his letters before publication. They were published under the title of *Walks through Ireland in 1812, 1814 and 1817 in a Series of Letters* in 1819, a year after his unfortunate and somewhat mysterious death, in extreme poverty, in the city of Cork.

With regard to the recent rebellion of 1798, although it seems clear that he is on the government side, he shows some sympathy with the rebel cause. He refers to Bagenal Harvey and John Colclough as 'amiable and spirited young men ... carried away by warm feelings and mistaken views', and regrets their executions.[1] Even what he regards as the upstanding yeomanry

---

[1] Harvey and Colclough were Wexford Protestants of liberal views and republican sympathies. They took a prominent part in the 1798 Rebellion, after which they

of the barony of Forth in Wexford, which he praises for their similarity to their English rural counterparts 'did not escape the fatal mania of 1798; and, as I have mentioned, formed a most formidable body of marksmen at Ross, but were soon sensible of their folly, and returned home. It is to be feared, that their tranquility had been unwisely disturbed, and some gross provocations had aroused them to this otherwise inconsistent conduct.'

The Anglo–French wars of the late eighteenth and early nineteenth centuries had created considerable wealth for Irish landowners as the price of livestock and food rose to feed the ever-hungry war machine. By 1812 the value of agricultural produce had reached a level which left the labouring classes, whose earnings had not kept pace with rising prices, finding it very difficult to feed themselves properly, while the landlords continued to get richer. Since much of the good quality food such as vegetables and meat was being exported, the peasantry were left to rely almost solely on the trusty potato, and the resultant lack in variety in their nutrition led to a deterioration in their general state of health. It is a chilling thought that many of the surviving children born to these peasants in the ensuing decade, enjoying poor health in their early years, were the undernourished adults who died in great numbers thirty years later when the potato crop failed repeatedly and the Great Famine occurred. Trotter's doubts about the long-term value of the potato diet of the countryfolk represents radical thinking for the time; he was concerned particularly about the spread of the potato as the main staple of the peasantry:

> I doubt ... whether this boasted and prolific vegetable has been really advantageous to Ireland. Before Sir Walter Raleigh introduced it, they had better food. From their cattle they were supplied with milk and butter. Their flesh gave plentiful repast. Corn supplied bread. Honey formed a species of wine. Fish, fruit and various vegetables completed their supplies. The population was less, because there was a smaller quantity of food, which is in fact its barometer. But they were better fed, less crowded, and, therefore, happier as to local advantages. This vegetable has spread with astonishing and rapid diffusion. The climate and soil suit it. Planted about 200 years ago in Ireland, it has at least quintupled the population. But the best food of men – meat, corn, butter etc. is almost all exported now, or only used by the better classes; the immense mass of the people has but miserable food; for daily meals of potatoes morning and evening, often without milk, are sorry repasts; the increase in numbers, as Ireland is

escaped to the Saltee Islands, but were subsequently captured and hanged on Wexford Bridge.

now situated, is really increase in wretchedness! I think, however, as neither potatoes nor men can be easily extirpated, that it is the duty of the government to manage the great family of the Irish nation as well as it can, under these circumstances.

It is clear that Trotter was not afraid of walking long distances. For instance, the sixteen- or seventeen-mile trek he takes on the very rough roads of the time, between Crusheen and Galway city, is more like 25 or 26 statute miles, because he uses the 'Irish mile' in his descriptions.[2] His accounts only rarely refer, however, to any physical tiredness or difficulty he experienced. In between travelling, he and his companions seem to take it easy for days at a time, hospitably entertained by the gentry.

In these extracts from Trotter's letters to 'L', he describes walking from Glendalough to the Vale of Avoca, and through south-east County Wexford.]

On leaving Glendaloch, we entered a fine valley, with a pleasant river meandering through it;[3] we also passed some woods, where the cheerful noise and movements of numerous woodcutters attracted our attention. The picture was gay, and relieved our minds of too serious thoughts. Happy privilege of the pedestrian; gradually changing, the scene is always new to him, and the fresh pages of the book of nature charm away melancholy, if it possess him.

Wishing to breakfast, we discovered a humble inn at the riverside, and there we heartily enjoyed our meal. The river and its banks were charming, and a fine wood spread to our left. It gave me a pain to see here, for the first time, a miserable and dilapidated little chapel. Every edifice erected to God ought to be respectable and respected. Want of money was the cause of its ruined state. Having breakfasted, we walked through a long and cheerful vale to Rathdrum. There is a good deal of the flannel manufactory in this part of the county of Wicklow, and a handsome flannel hall, built by Earl Fitzwilliam, at Rathdrum. But the people and their houses are wretched; their cattle small and bad. We learned that the gentry in this county have become great farmers, and that the people are reducing more and more to the situation of cotters, rather serfs, or

[2] An Irish mile equals 2,240 yards.
[3] The Avonmore.

villeins! The war has caused great prices for the produce of the land, and has generated high rents for gigantic farmers, with 1,500 or 2,000 acres in their hands. But labour is not raised in value, though the cottager lose all his land. He becomes annexed to an estate by the miserable tenure of necessity, and the rent of his roadside hovel is deducted from his yearly toil. His daily hire is 10d; perhaps less. This is £12 per annum; deduct £1 10s or £2 for house rent, £10 10s remain to procure potatoes, milk, clothes, medicine in case of illness – to pay the priest – send children to school – etc. etc. etc! £10 which the gambler or man of fashion casts away in a moment, in the circles of London, is the sum on which the existence of this family entirely depends!

Yet the poor Irishman endures with fortitude and humility, even with a degree of content. His common expressions are, however, very melancholy on enquiry into his circumstances. 'The poor, sir, have always suffered.' 'It is God's will it should be so.' 'The poor are little thought of in this country.' He will then sigh, and go to his daily toil. This system, my dear L, is a sad one! The degradation of the population of Ireland has endured from time immemorial, and they are themselves somewhat to blame for it. They want an independence of mind, which produces independence of station, and, with too indolent and obsequious a caress, they hug their poverty to their bosoms. The cottager and small farmer might make his house decent and comfortable in some degree, which it seldom is, and he might make his garden neat and useful with some good vegetables, as well as adorn it with a few humble flowers and shrubs. No! He prefers sitting at the fire, or in the sun, or a lazy walk to the alehouse in times of leisure, and leaves his little home as uncultivated and unadorned as his mind too frequently is. The system is erroneous, and too severely pursued by many, of exacting the utmost value of land by high rents or otherwise; but the most liberal of the gentry have a great deal to contend with, in the inveterate habits of these people. If a good lease of a large portion of ground be granted, they let and re-let; they divide and subdivide; and they do not think to improve, so much as to sell the commodity of land at a high rate. The causes of all this, I fear, lie so deep that few English ministries will be fond of analysing them.

The country people of Wicklow dress pretty well, are in general handsome, well-made, and very sagacious. Their communication with Dublin does not, however, improve them in any respect. Passing Rathdrum, a considerable and respectable country town, we arrived at Avondale, Mr Parnell's seat. It was made and greatly adorned by the late Colonel Hayes, who possessed true rural taste. This sweet place is charmingly situated, among grounds and woods undulating in the most beautiful manner. The romantic mountains of Wicklow everywhere around it, give variety and grandeur to the scene. The house is sufficiently good. You pass through the demesne to see the cottage built by the late Mr Hayes.[4] The walk to it is quite charming, a fine river rolling on your left, and the scenery I have described everywhere in full view; nor does the cottage disappoint expectation. It is large, and made in a perfectly rural manner, thatched and ornamented with rustic woodwork. The river flows immediately past it, and the impending opposite bank is bold and romantic; embowered in trees, and sheltered from every breeze, it seems truly the ritual of domestic peace and of the Muses! With reluctance we left this sweet abode, so far removed from the world's noise, and all its wearisome pomp. The melodious sound of the waters murmuring along, the pleasant song of birds, and the fragrant verdure of every shrub and tree made it most delightful. Mr Parnell was not at home, but we were received with great civility. This gentleman has distinguished himself by some writings in favour of Ireland, and bears a most amiable character. He has, we heard, set up a woollen manufactory near Rathdrum – but these things seldom do well in the hands of gentlemen unused to trade.

Leaving the fairy scenes of Mr Parnell's demesne, we regained the road, and, descending to the bridge and rivers called, 'The Meeting of the Three Waters,'[5] found fresh beauty calling on us for admiration. The descent by the road was rapid, and the picturesque assemblage of mountains, rivers, and woody vales of unrivalled beauty. Of this spot, Mr Moore says, or rather sings:

There is not in the wide world a valley so sweet,
As that vale in whose bosom the wide waters meet . . .[6]

Accompanied by such a murmuring and lovely stream, we continued, from this 'Meeting of the Waters', our walk through a most enchanting vale. . . .

This morning we viewed Wexford. Its market is plentifully supplied with fowl, flesh, fish, vegetables, etc. etc. This town is extremely populous, and far exceeds many towns on the continent of the same size, in its appearance of wealth and population. Calling at a shop to purchase a newspaper, we fortunately met with a lady both polite and intelligent, from whom we

[4] A rustic folly, which it was the fashion of the time to have constructed in demesnes for the amusement of visitors; in some places peasants, the older and more grizzled the better, were paid to pretend to live in the 'cottage', to make it appear more authentic.
[5] Still a beauty spot today, at Avoca.
[6] Extract from the poem 'The Meeting of the Waters', one of Thomas Moore's *Irish Meoldies*.

received considerable information as to Forth, and the road we should take.[7] She seemed fully to enter into all our ideas, and with a degree of promptness and grace which very much distinguish Irish ladies, even conducted us through her house and back garden, to a door opening on the street and road directly leading to the long-wished-for Forth. After taking leave of our hospitable and kind directress, whose mind and manners seemed equally pleasing, we set forward with great alacrity. We reflected that we were going to the first colony planted by the English above six hundred years ago, the estates and territory of Harvey de Monte Marisco, uncle to the Earl of Chepstow, a nobleman of high rank, one of the first who had come to Ireland, and a man of consummate prudence.

This new settlement enjoyed the protection of FitzStephen himself, who became seated in Wexford, and who manifested humanity and conciliating wisdom in his whole career in Ireland; and who aided, in all respects, as the prudent ally and sincere friend of the King of Leinster – never as the master or invader![8]

For some miles after leaving Wexford, nothing remarkable struck us. We at length reached the hamlet called Clinhin.[9] Here an immediate change was visible. The houses are large and commodious, much after the English manner; good gardens, orchards, and pleasant fields surround them. We pressed on with great satisfaction, and, walking briskly, soon found ourselves advanced in the barony of Forth. A new scene, to those accustomed to behold the wretchedness of Ireland, arose before us. Comfortable and well-sized farms with good houses, and agriculture quite superior to that of Ireland in general, joined to a peculiarity of manners, forcibly reminded us of an important alteration and improvement in this part of Ireland, effected by men long departed, but well entitled to her gratitude! Having walked about six miles into Forth, we rested to refresh ourselves at a decent public house. They furnished us with ale different

[7] The Barony of Forth, preserving with that of Bargy the boundaries of two ancient Gaelic *tuatha*, is situated at the extreme south-east corner of Ireland, somewhat isolated owing to its semi-peninsular nature, bounded on two sides by the Irish Sea. It is an area that was settled by foreigners in every era of Irish history, the settlement of the Normans having the greatest influence. Under their rule from late in the twefth century, Welsh, English and Flemish settlers were planted there and mixed easily with the incumbent Norse and native Irish, eventually evolving their own dialect called Yola, an amalgam of Old English, Norman French and Flemish.

[8] Robert FitzStephen, together with Hervey de Montmorency and Maurice de Prendergast, commanded the 600 adventurers who carried out the Norman invasion of Ireland in May 1169.

[9] Probably Killinick, a village with a population of about 500 people in Trotter's time, 8 km south of Wexford town.

from any we had ever seen or tasted in Ireland. It was clear, strong, and had a particularly perfumed taste, which I, for one, liked very much. It resembled the best ale in Wales, such as persons travelling from Ireland to England for the first time are so much pleased with tasting. Our landlord told us their harvest would be abundant, and that rents were moderate, but seemed to fear some change in this latter respect.

We pursued our delighted way through this Flanders of Ireland. The general cultivation was of wheat, oats, barley and beans, good patches of hemp, flax and very good potatoes. Every house had its garden of vegetables – was roomy, clean, and tolerably furnished.

As we were told of an interesting ruin, called the Church of the Island,[10] we resolved to see it. We continued our excursion, and found everywhere scenes that gratified us. Property appeared well divided. No great demesnes and parks, with haughty castle or mansion, overlooked the cottages of a starving and oppressed peasantry; but we found ourselves among a substantial yeomanry, each of them lord of his rural territory, and giving a faint idea of glorious England! Their continguity to the sea permits them to have abundance of manure, consisting of marine plants, sea-sand, etc. etc. All their farming is done in somewhat of an English manner. Their cattle are good, and well taken care of, and, in short, there is here a happy picture of rural life and independence, gratifying beyond measure to the beholder, after the painful contrast the rest of Ireland affords. We observed a large breed of large black Newfoundland dog generally spread through Forth.

Our walk carried us at length to the Church of the Island. This is an old ruin, not very large but romantic and wild in appearance. It was placed on a peninsula of great beauty, the sea spreading around it, and washing the sandy shore we had reached. The church stands in this lovely, but solitary scene. An exceedingly good and roomy farmhouse is the only one on the peninsula, which does not contain many acres. The church is a very much frequented and celebrated burying-place, and funerals are numerously attended here. We saw many rustic tombstones, and several of the simple garlands of white cut paper, curiously adorning a number of sticks bent as hoops, so often placed on the grave as a last mark of respect and affection, and so common in Ireland. For it is observable that the Irish and English customs and manners are happily blended in Forth. Neither are conquered, but both harmoniously assimilated. There is all the valuable independence of character which has made England a great nation; and there is a great deal of the sweetness and pleasantness of the Irish mind

[10] At Lady's Island, the ruins of an Augustinian priory dedicated to Our Lady still make a picturesque scene. The modern church here (1864) is by Ashlin & Pugin.

and manner united to it. We entered the farmhouse, near this great burying-place in Forth, where

> . . . each in his narrow cell, for ever laid,
> The rude fore-fathers of the hamlet – sleep,[11]

and found a civil reception from the good woman of the house. She gave us excellent milk, and we carried our own bread. Their accent is very peculiar, but we heard nothing of their ancient and celebrated dialect. It appeared to us very like the retired mountaineers of Wales speaking English. The tone and pronunciation was nearly the same.

The Catholic religion prevails universally in Forth. These descendants of the English, who have never changed their ancient faith, retain their honest simplicity, and manly characters. They are an excellent people in Forth – are not addicted to drinking – and few or no crimes are heard of amongst them. They preserve their own manner of speaking English, and have never adopted the Irish language. I forgot to say that the man of the house entered as we rested near the Church of the Island. He was curiosity personified. Not one, but a hundred questions assailed and oppressed us. Had we been Arabian or Chinese, we could not have met more inquisitorial research. His small piercing eyes seemed to dive into our every thought, as he sifted us and required to know our occupation, our thoughts, and pursuits. Nor was he easily satiated by reasonable answers to his enquiries, or repulsed by any reserve. Again and again he renewed his attack, till, sufficiently rested after our long walk, we were happy to bid himself and his family farewell.

[11] From *Elegy Written in a Country Churchyard*, the poet Thomas Gray's most popular work, published in 1751.

John Keats (1795–1821)
County Down in July 1818

[John Keats was born in London, studied medicine at Guy's Hospital, and although he worked hard at his medical studies, his chief interest was poetry. His first book, *Poems by John Keats*, was published in 1817. After the publication of *Endymion: A Poetic Romance* in May 1818, he set out with Charles Brown on a walking tour of Scotland. In July, in the course of his Scottish tour, he paid a brief visit to Ireland, during which he and his companion set out to walk from Donaghadee to the Giant's Causeway, a distance they were informed was 48 miles. On the way, they discovered that the 48 miles were 'Irish miles' – about 70 of the English variety. After 15 miles they reached Belfast, then in the worst throes of the early Industrial Revolution, and demoralised by what they found and the unexpected additional distance, they turned back to Donaghadee, from where they sailed to Scotland. Keats subsequently had to abandon his walking tour because of ill health. During the course of the following three years, in spite of declining health, he produced his best work, but he died early in 1821 at the age of twenty-six.

The following are excerpts from his letters of July 1818, to his sister Fanny and his brother Tom, describing his brief experience of Ireland, from *Letters of John Keats*, edited by Robert Gittings.]

To Fanny, from Dumfries, July 2nd 1818
My dear Fanny

I am ashamed of writing you such stuff, nor would I if it were not for being tired after my days walking, and ready to tumble int[o bed] so fatigued that when I am asleep you might sew my nose to my great toe and trundle me round the town like a Hoop without waking me – Then I get so hungry – a Ham goes but a very little way and fowls are like Larks to me – A Batch of Bread I make no more ado with than a sheet of parliament;[1] and I can eat a Bull's head as easily as I used to do Bull's eyes – I take a whole string of Pork Sausages down as easily as a Pen'orth of Lady's fingers[2] – Oh dear I must soon be contented with an acre or two of oaten cake a hogshead of Milk and a Cloaths basket of Eggs morning noon and night when I get among the Highlanders – Before we see them we shall pass into Ireland and have a chat with the Paddies, and look at the

---

[1] A thin, crisp gingerbread cake.
[2] Sweetbreads.

Giant's Cause-way which you must have heard of – I have not time to tell you particularly for I have to send a Journal to Tom of whom you shall hear all particulars or from me when I return – Since I began this we have walked sixty miles to newton stewart at which place I put in this Letter – tonight we sleep at Glenluce – tomorrow at Port Patrick and the next day we shall cross in the passage boat to Ireland . . .

My Dear Tom . . .

. . . Yesterday Morning we set out from Glenluce going some distance round to see some Ruins – they were scarcely worth the while – we went on towards Stranrawier in a burning sun and had gone about six Miles when the Mail overtook us – we got up – were at Portpatrick in a jiffy, and I am writing now in little Ireland – The dialect on the neighbouring shores of Scotland and Ireland is much the same – yet I can perceive a great difference in the nations from the Chambermaid at this nate Inn kept by Mr. Kelly – She is fair, kind and ready to laugh, because she is out of the horrible dominion of the Scotch kirk – a Scotch Girl stands in terrible awe of the Elders – poor little Susannas – They will scarcely laugh – they are greatly to be pitied and the kirk is greatly to be damn'd . . . It is not so far to the Giant's Cause way as we supposed – we thought it 70 and hear it is only 48 Miles – so we shall leave one of our knapsacks here at Donoghadee, take our immediate wants and be back in a week – when we shall proceed to the County of Ayr. In the Packet Yesterday we heard some Ballads from two old Men – one was a romance which seemed very poor – then there was the Battle of the Boyne – then Robin Huid as they call him – 'Before the king you shall go, go, go, before the king you shall go.' There were no Letters for me at Port Patrick so I am behind hand with you I dare say in news from George. . .

We stopped very little in Ireland and that you may not have leisure to marvel at our speedy return to Port Patrick I will tell you that is it as dear living in Ireland as at the Hummums[3] – thrice the expence of Scotland – it would have cost us £15 before our return – Moreover we found those 48 Miles to be irish ones which reach to 70 english – So having walked to Belfast one day and back to Donoghadee the next we left Ireland with a fair breeze – We slept last night at Port patrick where I was gratified by a letter from you.

On our walk in Ireland we had too much opportunity to see the worse than nakedness, the rags, the dirt and misery of the poor common Irish – A Scotch cottage, though in that some times the Smoke has no exit but at

[3] A Turkish bathhouse.

the door, is a pallace to an irish one – We could observe that impetiosity in Man [and b]oy and Woman – We had the pleasure of finding our way through a Peat-Bog – three miles long at least – dreary, black, dank, flat and spongy: here and there were poor dirty creatures and a few strong men cutting or carting peat. We heard on passing into Belfast through a most wretched suburb that most disgusting of all noises worse than the Bag pipe, the laugh of a Monkey, the chatter of women solus the scream of [a] Macaw – I mean the sound of the Shuttle – What a tremendous difficulty is the improvement of the condition of such people – I cannot conceive how a mind 'with Child' Of Philanthrophy could gra[s]p at possibility – with me it is absolute despair. At a miserable house of enter-tainment half way between Donaghadee and Bellfast were two Men Sitting at Whiskey one a Laborer and the other I took to be a drunken Weaver – The Laborer took me for a Frenchman and the other hinted at Bounty Money saying he was ready to take it – On calling for the Letters at Port patrick the man snapp'd out 'what Regiment'? On our return from Bellfast we met a Sadan[4] – the Duchess of Dunghill – It is no laughing matter tho – Imagine the worst dog kennel you ever saw placed upon two poles from a mouldy fencing – In such a wretched thing sat a squalid old Woman squat like an ape half starved from a scarcity of Biscuit in its passage from Madagascar to the cape, – with a pipe in her mouth and looking out with a round-eyed skinny lidded, inanity – with a sort of hori-zontal idiotic movement of her head – squab and lean she sat and puff'd out the smoke while two ragged tattered Girls carried her along – What a thing would be a history of her Life and sensations. I shall endeavour when I know more and have though[t] a little more, to give you my ideas of the difference between the scotch and irish – The two Irishmen I mentioned were speaking of their treatment in England when the Weaver said – 'Ah you were a civil Man but I was a drinker' Remember me to all – I intend writing to Haslam[5] – but dont tell him for fear I should delay – We left a notice at Portpatrick that our Letters should be thence forwarded to Glasgow – Our quick return from Ireland will occasion our passing Glasgow sooner than we thought – so till further notice you must direct to Inverness

Your most affectionate Brother John . . .

---

[4] A sedan chair.
[5] William Haslam, a close friend.

'G'
Wicklow in 1823

['G' was an anonymous traveller who described his perambulations with a female companion in the Wicklow Mountains in the summer of 1823, in letters to a 'friend in Edinburgh'. The letters were published in the short-lived *Belfast Magazine and Literary Journal* in 1825. Apart from the startling contrast between scenic beauty and extreme poverty that co-existed in the Wicklow of the day, the letters provide a clear insight into the class structure of the time. It seems quite acceptable for someone of the superior class – G's class – to walk unannounced and without invitation into a wayside cottage while the occupants are having breakfast, 'partly with a view to resting, and partly of becoming acquainted with the lower orders of people'.]

Dublin, July 1823

Well here I am in the heart of Ireland. It is not above ten days since I arrived in this country; yet what I have seen might fill a volume. Certainly no country in the world furnishes more materials for reflection – a single cabin might supply subject for a treatise on political economy, a single glen for an essay on the picturesque, and an unsophisticated Irishman, with all his bulls and blunders, ingenuity and kindness of heart, for a system of moral philosophy, or a treatise on phrenology. But I leave such general reflections, and my observations on the metropolis, of which you have read many accounts, to give you a few sketches of my rambles in a district less familiarly known, but one of the most beautiful in the country. I refer to Wicklow, in which romantic glens and mountains are blended with fertile and cultivated valleys, to a degree that I have nowhere else seen. The country is beautifully wooded, and everywhere presents a greenness and luxuriance of vegetation that is quite unrivalled. Even the ivy leaf is here a magnificent thing. In size it resembles some of the gigantic leaves of the tropical climates, and in the brilliance of its green far surpasses them. Yet when I tell you it is a land of glen and flood and mountain, you are not to expect the extensive glens, nor the majestic rivers, nor the vast and interminable mountains of the Scottish Highlands. You cannot, as you do there, travel weeks in a hill country. In a tour through Wicklow, you generally walk (if you are a pedestrian like me) in a level country, and only turn aside from the plains, to view what artists call 'a little bit of mountain scenery'. Its highest hills would not be above third rates in Scotland, and its largest rivers are not superior to Ettrick or Yarrow.

But before I proceed, I must inform you that you are not to expect from me a minute description of glens or mountains; I shall rather give you a portait of my own feelings, on the first view of a new country; and I shall endeavour to present you occasionally with some objects, which you may contrast with those with which you are already familiar. The tour of Wicklow properly begins at Bray, and here we commenced our walk. We had not proceeded far, when we were struck with a boy of extraordinary beauty, standing erect by a wall. I went up to him and asked him why he stood there; he bowed gracefully and held out his hand, into which I put a penny. He smiled intelligently and gratefully, but still said nothing. At first, I thought him dumb, but learned from some people who stood near that he knew no English, and that the only language he spoke or understood was Irish. This was the first specimen we had seen of a genuine Irishman ; he was almost naked; and though there were about him obvious marks of meagre living, yet his limbs were finely formed, and he had a face of the most perfect symmetry, lighted up with an animation, which neither hunger, nakedness, nor beggary, had been able to extinguish. What is this to Wicklow? I hear you say – Yes! my dear friend, I do think that the men and women I meet in Wicklow, form most important objects in the scene; and if you are of a different opinion, burn this letter, for they will often start up upon you.

We this morning entered an inviting looking wayside cottage, partly with a view to resting, and partly of becoming acquainted with the lower orders of people. The family were seated at a breakfast of tea, around a table on which was spread a clean tablecloth. This was a cottage of a superior order, though its walls were of mud, with an earthen floor. There were two wooden beds, on which were spread blankets, sheets and clean coverlids; the windows were of glass; and, as is usual in Scotland, the beds formed a partition between the apartment in which the family were sitting, and another behind it. The inhabitants of this neat little cottage were plainly but decently dressed. On entering into conversation with the master of the house, we discovered him to be a well-informed intelligent man; he was a Catholic, but spoke with great liberality of the Protestant gentry and clergy in his neighbourhood, [to] whom he gave credit for kindness and attention to the poor. He talked of Catholic claims with modesty, but with enthusiasm of the advocates of the cause in the House of Commons, adding that he trusted his friends would do nothing to forfeit their support. He said that the priests of this county had entered into a resolution not to administer the sacrament to any person who took any secret oath, or was in any wise connected with any secret society. As this man turned out to be a schoolmaster, we visited his school, which was in good order. When we entered, the children rose and bowed respectfully, and took their seats again with regularity, as a thing to which they had been accustomed. Some of the boys were engaged in the study of Latin, while in the cottage we observed a young woman reading a book, which we discovered to be the New Testament. 'I did not know you had been allowed to read the New Testament,' said my fellow traveller; 'Oh yes, Ma'am,' said the girl, with a mingled look of surprise and displeasure.

After leaving this interesting little mansion, in about an hour we reached the Glen of the Downs. On both sides the hills rise to above the height of 1,000 feet, beautifully wooded to the top; and so narrow is the glen, that there is merely room for the highway,[1] which winds along the banks of a bright little mountain stream. On the hill to your left, as you pass from Bray, are a cottage, banqueting hall and octagonal temple, erected by the taste of Mrs La Touche, which produces a pleasing effect, as they are seen peeping from the rich green woods with which this hill is clothed.[2] This glen is of no great length, but it opens on a scene not less interesting than itself – the magnificent demesne of Mrs La Touche, and the village of Delgany hanging like a bird's nest on the side of a romantic little hill. This beautiful village has grown up under the benevolent eye of Mrs La Touche. The cottages have a look of neatness and comfort that form a striking contrast to the wretchedness of other cabins; and I verily believe that the happiness of the inhabitants gives more pleasure to the mind of the admirable founder, than all the splendour of her own demesne. This village contains an excellent day-school for the children of the poor; to the honour of this good woman it is to be recorded that it was among the first of its kind in Ireland. And as we passed this noble demesne, we observed a number of decent-looking people, slowly moving along from different ways, and seating themselves near the gate, some of them apparently labouring under sickness and disease. We enquired the object of their pilgrimage, and were informed with looks of gratitude which lightened up their sad countenances, that the benevolent owner provided a dispensary, and a surgeon to attend twice a week, and they were going to receive the benefit of this blessed appointment.

The vicinity of Newton Mount Kennedy is celebrated for a number of beautiful demesnes, but as my taste has always led me to the study of nature at her rudest, rather than in her more cultivated appearances, we hurried into the Devil's Glen. This is a glen of the character of your

---

[1] At the time of writing, after a prolonged occupation of the woods here by 'Eco Warriors', Wicklow County Council is commencing work on the widening of the old road to a dual-carriageway.
[2] The 55-acre parkland of the La Touche demesne, with its 'Turkish Tent', octagonal temple, banqueting hall and a 254–foot-long conservatory filled with exotic plants, was laid out in association with Bellevue, a two-storey pedimented house built by Dublin banker David La Touche in 1754; it was demolished in the 1950s.

celebrated Roslyn.[3] The stream (the Vantrey) is larger than the Esk, and though, as in Roslyn, rude and precipitous rocks, that in some cases seem to be hanging in the air, are half hid by beautiful woods, yet certainly, in luxuriance of vegetation, and in freshness and brightness of green, the Irish glen has the advantage. One thing delighted me greatly – this was the first mountain stream deserving the name, that I had seen in Ireland, and the heart-stirring sound of the waters was music to my spirits. The north of Ireland, particularly, is deficient in rivers. The Lagan in Belfast is the least interesting river I have seen; a lazy laggard, crawling like a vile reptile over a bed of black slime. It has no pebbles, no rocks, no brightness, no music. But in this romantic glen, we have nature in her energies, triumphing over the tame efforts of art; vast jutting rocks, that seem self-supported; trees shooting their green heads into the air, when you see no earth to support their roots; and the river below foaming, and singing and dashing on its way, as in scorn of the rocks that would impede its progress. At the head of the glen there is a waterfall of about 100 feet high, which, as it shoots its whole length in one unbroken jet, produces a grand effect. But I must quit this interesting spot. The next place worthy of notice is Rosanna,[4] through which flows the Vantrey in peaceful brightness, as if reposing after the exertion and fatigue of forcing its way among the rocks of the Devil's Glen. The woods in this beautiful demesne are considered the finest in the country. But what gives this place its chief interest, is the memory of the late Mrs Tighe, the proprietor, and her daughter-in-law, Mrs Henry Tighe, the author of 'Psyche'.[5] The name of Mrs Tighe is synonymous with charity, and Mrs H. Tighe is nobly associated with the literature of Ireland. The amiable proprietor is said to have greatly encumbered a fine estate by acts of benevolence; and it was here that her ingenious daughter, under great bodily affliction, composed a work which will give Rosanna more celebrity than all its woods, and rich lawns, and noble mansions. The Irish are a grateful race. You never mention the name of La Touche, or Tighe, to those who have partaken of their boun-ties, or who had even heard of them, without drawing forth a torrent of blessings. 'What kind of woman was Mrs Tighe?' said Mr—to a man

[3] Rosslyn Glen, on the North Esk river south of Edinburgh, is a well-known Lothian beauty-spot, and was visited in the Romantic period by many seekers of the picturesque, including William and Dorothy Wordsworth, Burns, and Johnson and Boswell.

[4] Rossanagh is an early eighteenth-century house near Ashford built by the Tighe family. Although much altered, it is still extant. One of its finest features, however, an elaborately panelled dining room, was exported to the United States.

[5] In Greek mythology Psyche was the maiden with whom Cupid fell in love; Mrs Henry (Mary) Tighe's poem, written in 1805 when she was 32, was regarded by some critics as unreadable. She died in Woodstock in County Kilkenny, in 1810.

whom we met travelling through the demesne, 'An excellent lady!' was the answer; 'Was she charitable?' 'Oh yes – there was no such woman in Ireland, England or Scotland, nor in Europe.' This man, as he informed us, had been eighteen years in her service. His kind mistress was no more; there was nothing selfish in his praises – they were the genuine language of truth and good feeling. One thing is obvious in all I have seen in Ireland; where the gentry are resident and attentive to the poor the whole appearance of the country is improved, and the poor know no bounds to their gratitude. The Irish excel all nations in their manner of returning thanks for a favour; there is an eloquence in the language even of a beggar in the street or by the wayside, as he blesses you for an alms, no matter how small. We received more blessings for a few pence in Wicklow, than so many guineas should have bought in any other country in Europe.

After breakfast we walked two miles out of our way, to see a little summerhouse, to which Mrs Tighe was fond of carrying her guests. In this place there is nothing remarkable, except that the lawns open on a fine sea view. The lawn, which was kept in neat order in her lifetime, is going into disorder; the canal is full of weeds, the paths overgrown with grass; yet I felt a pleasure in seeing a place that had often formed a favourite retreat of this admirable woman and her ingenious daughter-in-law; but I have not mentioned the circumstance that induced me to mention this little deviation. While we were walking along the byway that leads to the cottage, I remarked an erection that attracted my notice and excited my curiosity. The front walls were of mud, about two feet high, the end walls might be about four feet; the roof resembled a conical top cut down the middle; it was built over the ditch, and the dyke formed the back wall; there was an opening in front at one end, by which a person, on his knees, might enter it. On looking in, I saw a woman sitting, who looked pale, emaciated and in dejection, and upon enquiry I found that she had been very ill of the typhus fever, and that this had been her only sick room. In this wretched place she had lived three weeks; but here nature triumphed over disease, and she was now in the progress of recovery. The people in this district have such a horror of the typhus fever, that the moment an unhappy being is discovered to be attacked by it, he is exiled from the habitations of men to those wayside huts; and the only attendance he receives, is from those whose fear is overcome by their humanity. This remark, however, will only apply to those who have no near relations, for so strong are the ties of nature, that those who have them are not so completely deserted. This poor woman was an unconnected individual, and one female, herself also without kindred, in the neighbourhood was the only person who had courage to perform for her the smallest of these offices that the sick require; and even these were performed at long intervals, and the patient was left the whole night, either to live or to die.

We passed through Rathdrum, a decaying village at the mouth of a romantic highland glen, and in the afternoon we reached the celebrated vale of Avoca. Here the genius of Moore[6] pervades everything, and flings a halo of light over a scene in itself of great beauty. The junction of the Avonmore and Avonbeg at the mouth of the glen, forms the meeting of the waters, which he has so sweetly and so faithfully described in his song of that name. It is singular, that while in your country, almost every glen and mountain call to mind some celebrated poet, and almost every stream borrows music from his song, in Ireland this is the first association of the kind we have experienced, yet its glens would give as well as receive glory. The poetry of Sir Walter Scott has opened the Highlands to thousands of strangers, who, but for it, would never have thought of them; but he has received as much as he has bestowed. The rocks of the Trossachs and Glen Ard will stand as an imperishable monument to his glory, and every time they are visited, his verses may be said to be re-read, as if they had been written on the beautiful tablets of nature. Oh! for a Sir Walter here; there are rich and ample materials for such a genius. But I must reserve my account of this lovely glen, and my subsequent wanderings, for another letter . . .

. . . The striking features of the celebrated vale of Avoca are its wood and waters. There is nothing in it magnificent, nor indeed very pictur-esque. The hills are low, but the greenness of the foliage and of the grass is truly Irish. The trees are nowhere of great size, but so thick are they, that the leaves resemble an immense parasol, which the rays of the sun never penetrate. After the conflux of the Avonmore and Avonbeg, the stream takes the name of the Avoca. It is nearly as large as the Ettrick at Tushelaw,[7] and remarkable for the purity and brightness of waters, as the grass is for its verdure. It is not a scene which a poet or a painter would visit if he wished to elevate his imagination by grand views of nature, or by images of terror; but if he desired to represent the calm repose of peace and love, he would choose this glen as their place of residence. At its mouth on the left side, overhanging the meeting of the waters, Castle Howerd is romantically situated, and farther down is Bally Arthur.[8] About four miles below the meeting of the Avonmore and Avonbeg, there is a second meeting formed by the junction of the Aughrin and Avoca at

[6] Thomas Moore was the first Irish Catholic writer to achieve international fame when his *Irish Melodies* was published in London in 1808; one of the songs in this collection, 'The Meeting of the Waters', refers to the Vale of Avoca.
[7] The Tushielaw Inn, located overlooking the river Ettrick south of Edinburgh, is still a well-known Scottish beauty-spot.
[8] Castle Howerd, designed by Sir Richard Morrison and completed in 1811, is still extant, as is Ballyarthur, a late seventeenth-century house at Woodenbridge.

the Wooden Bridge Inn. The birthplace of Homer was not more keenly contended for by the several cities of Asia, than the honour of the real meeting of the waters, by the inhabitants of the head and bottom of the valley. They are both well entitled to the honour, for both are very beautiful. A stone bridge is now built over the Aughrim, where there formerly was a wooden one. From the little hill above the inn there is a view of three finely wooded glens, the Avoca, the Aughrim and the Arklaw.

After enjoying this lovely prospect on a beautiful morning, we walked down to the bridge to amuse ourselves by examining it and the stream over which it is built – and even in this fairy valley, where wretchedness should never come, we discovered a scene of misery, more resembling what we would expect to find among the Pariahs of India, than the inhabitants of this fertile island. Looking over the parapet wall of the bridge, I observed smoke rising, and seeing a boy put out his head, I asked him if anyone lived there. As he made me no answer, we walked back to the inn to inquire into the cause of the phenomena, and were then informed that there was a family living in one of the arches of the bridge. We returned and examined this extraordinary habitation. The bridge was of three arches, and one of those we found inhabited by human beings. In summer when the stream is small, it flows within the middle arch and leaves this part completely dry. They had built a wall in the upper part of the arch so as to prevent the water from flowing in from above; this was no security in winter when the stream was swollen and flowed in from below on the wretched inhabitants, who were not unfrequently knee deep. This miserable family consisted of five, an old woman of nearly eighty, her daughter, a woman of nearly fifty, and three boys, her grandsons. The old woman, though racked to pieces by rheumatism in consequence of the damp dwelling, was still of a commanding figure. She was greatly above the common height, and a considerable bend forward rather added to, than took from, the dignity of her deportment. Her eye was unquenched by age, her voice was mellow and sonorous, and her conversation was by turns fiercely eloquent and thrillingly pathetic; she now awed the hearer, and now drew the tear into his eye; she seemed to feel that she was an outcast from society, but her mind was unsubdued by the cruelty of her fate. Her daughter sat knitting on a seat of sods, for there was nothing in the form of furniture in this wretched abode. While her mother gave us a history of the family she never lifted an eye, though she was a principal figure in the narrative. Her story was shortly this. Five or six years ago, the family had been in some degree of independence; the daughter's husband was then alive, and had by his exertions supported his own family, and the old woman. One winter day he fell from his car and received a mortal internal bruise; they were lodgers, and the fever into which he was thrown by this injury was mistaken by the landlady for the typhus, and nothing could induce her to keep them in her house another day. They were actually turned out; nor, from the same apprehension, would any other family receive them. In their despair, they carried him to the shelter of a wayside hedge, swept away the snow, and laid him down; there he lay three days in mortal agonies, and died! Soon after his death they had sought the shelter of the bridge, and had now been living in it for five years and upwards. I expressed my sympathy, and my wish that I had it in my power to provide them with a more comfortable dwelling, which drew from the woman a torrent of the most eloquent blessings I had ever heard. We could stand the scene no longer, but gave her a little money and escaped; while heart-chilling blessings followed us as we departed. At the inn we inquired into the truth of the narrative, and found it correct in all its parts.

I shall leave to the minerologist the description of the valuable mines with which the surrounding hills abound, being as rich within as they are beautiful on the surface. The next place that attracted our notice was Glendalough, or as it is more frequently called, the Seven Churches. This is a dark mountain lough overhung by naked precipices, and is certainly the only place we had seen in Wicklow to which the epithet 'sublime' could in the least apply. It is of no great extent, but the hills rise abruptly from it and fling over its waters their black shadows, in a manner that reminded me of some of our own Highland lochs. The most interesting objects here are the remains of the churches, seven in number; not that they are remarkable for the magnificence of their structure, or the beauty of their architecture, but because they formed one of the most ancient seats of Christian learning in Ireland. St Kevin, its founder and patron saint, was born in the year 498, and much of the learning and polish and piety of these early times must have been found here. No doubt in many cases, their great antiquity throws over such places a glory that did not originally belong to them. Like distance in landscape, it softens asperities, and so disposes the lights and the shadows as to hide deformities and to bring out beauties that vanish on narrower examination; yet there is an inspiration in the very soil and atmosphere of ancient celebrity, and the most unpatriotic and irreligious will feel a glow of pious or patriotic enthusiasm on the Isle of Patmos, or the field of Bannockburn.

From this to Luggalaw the country is flat and uninteresting, but this singular spot amply compensates the traveller for the dreary tract over which he has passed. In common cases, the sides of lofty mountains form the banks of lakes, but here the beds of two loughs, Dan and Tay, are mighty excavations, sinking as much beneath the level of the surrounding country as the mountains usually rise above it; the consequence of which is, that while travelling along a level upland region, all at once two lakes are seen in a valley far beneath you, the hills on one side beautifully wooded, on the other dark and rugged, and the brown side of the Douce[9] mountain crowning the whole. You then descend by a sloping path among overhanging woods till you reach the shores of Lough Tay, which, at the head of the lake, extend into a beautiful lawn, in which is the hunting seat of Mr La Touche.[10] I have never seen a spot that calls up in my mind, ideas of seclusion, solitude and peace, in a more eminent degree, than this interesting glen.

We reached Mr La Touche's cottage late in the evening, and in consideration of our benighted state, and because there was a lady in the party, we were accommodated there for the night. The evening was fine and there was a brightness over the scene never to be erased from my memory. Next morning we were advised by the housekeeper of this pleasant mansion, to ascend the Douce mountain and thus pass into the Powerscourt demesne, as this would both shorten the road and give us a magnificent view from the summit of Douce. We were also directed to call at the house of Mr La Touche's shepherd, who would show us the way over the mountain. We accordingly arose in high spirits and began to ascend the mountain, and reached the cabin of the shepherd, who to our disappointment was not at home. We entreated his wife to send someone with us as a guide, but she was inexorable, for she had no one, she said, to send. 'Cannot that boy go?' said my companion, pointing to a young person standing on the hearth. 'That boy!' said the woman, 'That boy, Madam, is my daughter!' On looking around the cabin, I saw a young woman sitting quietly in the corner, of a more promising aspect than the rest. 'Will you not walk up the hill with us,' said I, 'and put us on our way?' 'Oh, yes,' said she politely, in a voice that did not want sweetness. On the way, I soon found her to be superior to the good wife. In truth, she was the shepherd's governess; in both manners and knowledge she was far above her employers. This poor girl lived by teaching the children of several families of the neighbourhood to read, going three months to one, and three to another. She said that these poor people were kind to her, though they were Catholics and she was a Protestant, but that her salary was so small as not to be sufficient even to clothe her, as her apparel clearly showed – it was only one pound a quarter. She accompanied us nearly to the top of the mountain[11] and pointed out our way; but not long after she left us, there came on a mist so thick that we could not distinguish objects

[9] Now called Djouce Mountain, meaning uncertain.
[10] Built around 1790, it may have been designed by Francis Sands, who is said to have designed the 'Turkish Tent' at Bellevue. The house, much extended, is still extant, and in the ownership of Garech Browne of the Guinness family.
[11] The most likely route up Djouce from Luggalaw would be that which the Wicklow Way follows today.

a few yards distant. After wandering some time under this mist, I felt considerable uneasiness lest we should fall into some bog or over some precipice. We were indeed in a perilous state for nearly three hours, a time greatly more sufficient to reach the bottom of the hill, which I imagined we had crossed. Still there appeared no termination to our toils and dangers; now we met a swamp, which we were obliged to go around; then a torrent overhung by almost impassable rocks, which we were compelled to cross. The fortitude of my fellow traveller forsook at last, and after suffering above three hours of terror, she cried out in a voice of joy, 'There is a cottage chimney' – but it was the horn of a cow! We experienced many such delusions, and after wandering among the quagmires and precipices of this mountain, a sunbeam burst from a cloud, and showed us a little cabin glittering at no great distance. It was again almost instantaneously hid from our sight, yet I marked the place and we soon reached it; when to my astonishment, a hoarse laugh was raised, and a voice cried out in a tone of triumph, 'Did I not tell you, you could never cross the mountain?' This salutation I could not understand till looking around me for a moment, I observed that we were in the very shepherd's cabin we had left between three and four hours before. We had in truth never crossed the mountain. The family were seated around a table, on which lay a heap of potatoes and a jug of buttermilk, which seemed to travel round the party as they were desirous of partaking of its contents. In this group was the poor governess, but she seemed contented and even happy. I pressed the lady of the house to send one of her sons with us to guide us over the hill, for I did not like the idea of being foiled in the attempt, but she was more resolute in her denial than at first. I offered her a high bribe, but all to no purpose; he would be 'kilt' by his father, she said. This was quite decisive, and we were compelled to go round the bottom of the mountain, instead of over it, according to our morning plan.

After travelling several miles over an uninteresting tract, we reached the deer park at the head of the Powerscourt demesne. This is by far the most extensive and interesting demesne I have seen in Ireland. The road winds along the banks of a beautiful stream, and the gentle sloping hills are even richer in the garniture of groves than is usual in Ireland. The waterfall is much frequented, and I believe, much admired; but all these things depend on comparison. It is not remarkable either for its height, or the breadth of water that forms it, but the surrounding scene is beautiful. Towards the bottom of this lovely glen, Powerscourt House[12] stands on a

[12] Powerscourt was one of the finest of the great Georgian houses of Ireland, but was substantially destroyed by fire, with almost all its fine and irreplaceable furnishings, in 1974. It has since been partially rebuilt.

bank of considerable elevation, fronted by a lawn of considerable extent and beauty. The whole has an air of magnificence, suited to the noble family to whom it belongs. This ancient family boasts many eminent men; but no one is better entitled to the grateful recollections of posterity, than the late Lord Powerscourt, if magnificent donations devoted to the glorious cause of propagating genuine Christianity over the earth, deserve the gratitude of mankind. The Dargle was the last place we visited, and to describe it would be nearly to repeat what I have said respecting the Devil's Glen, to which it bears a strong likeness; yet it is softer in its character, and richer and brighter in its features. But I must now bid adieu to this land of crystal waters, and green leaves, and fair wild flowers.

Martha Blake
Connemara in 1823

[Henry and Martha Blake, a young London couple, emigrated in 1819 to the wilds of Connemara, and settled into Renvyle House, north of Ballynakill Harbour. Connemara was at the time a very remote, mountainous area, a stark landscape of bog, lake and rock, inhabited by peasants and fishermen who survived by doing some part-time smuggling. The nearest urban settlement at the time was the town of Westport, 36 miles away, and roads, where they existed, were very poor. The bustling town that is Clifden today had only one slated house in 1815.

During the years 1823 and 1824 Martha, her husband and her sister Anne, who lived with them, put together a book of their letters home to England, describing their pioneering life in the Irish wilderness. It was published in London in 1825 under the title *Letters from the Irish Highlands of Connemara*. The book was a considerable success, appealing as it did, with its scenic and botanical descriptions, to the new spirit of romanticism then taking hold in England. The extract below, from that publication, is Martha's description of an ascent of Lettery Mountain, today known as Benlettery or Bendouglas, the southernmost of the twelve Bens.

It was not till we had been absent from home a week that the weather was sufficiently settled to enable me to accomplish the great object of my wishes and ambition, by climbing the Lettery mountain. Although 800 feet lower than its proud rival in the county of Mayo, yet it is one of the highest mountains in Connemara. It rises on the north side of the Ballynahinch lake, and is reckoned among the Twelve Pins of Bennabola;

the middle peak of the three which crown the summit of the mountain, is 1,900 feet above the level of the sea.

We rode round the lake, and, leaving our horses at the foot of the hill, began to ascend by the side of a little rivulet, which throws itself into the sea under the arch of a stone bridge. The banks of the torrent are very picturesque; sometimes a young oak overhangs the stream; sometimes the bare rock stands boldly forward, overlooking the dark waters, and representing, in miniature, the spot from which the bard of Conway 'plunged into deep and endless night.'[1] At one time four falls were in view, the waters of each spreading out in a deep basin; but the finest and last was at a point where the torrent takes a direction round the rock, in a right angle with its former course, and breaks suddenly upon the eye. In winter, and after heavy rains, the water here falls in two parallel sheets, as nearly as I could guess, from thirty to forty feet high. On the opposite side, the rock is clothed with ivy, grasses, heaths and ferns; and the scathed trunk of an old yew tells what were once its leafy honours.

Upon leaving the waterfalls our ascent along the rocky shoulder of the mountain became more steep, though when we had really reached the summit, and looked back on our path, this part of it appeared scarcely more than level. Our march, however, was in very slow time, and as one of our party was a botanist, and a stranger, we had a good excuse for continual delay, in pointing out to him the many plants which were to be found on all sides, either rare or peculiar to a mountain district. At one time, a carpet was actually spread under our feet of the trailing arbutus (*a. uva urse*) with its red stalk and bright red berries, the club moss (*lycopodium selago*), and the blackberried heath (*empetrum nigrum*). We showed him too the Alpine lady's mantle (*alchemilla alpina*), and the London pride (*saxifraga umbrosa*).[2] This last forms a pretty border round your lowland gardens, but with us it is the natural ornament of the wildest spots, springing even from the crevices of the rocks, and throwing up its light and elegant blossoms with the utmost luxuriance, where it scarcely appears possible that the roots should find any soil to nourish them. None of these, however, excited his admiration half so much as the true Irish heath (*erica daboecia*),[3] which he had never before seen, even in a garden. Although this highland beauty shows herself in no other part of Ireland, yet with us she is to be met with on almost every mountain, and in almost every plain, and that too in no lowly guise; for instead of appearing, as she

[1] From the poem 'The Bard' by Thomas Gray.
[2] London Pride is called St Patrick's Cabbage in the Irish mountains.
[3] St Dabeoc's heath is widely distributed in parts of west Mayo and Galway, but is a distinctly different species from the Irish heath, which can also be found in the two counties.

does in your gardens, a poor puny dwarf, not above a few inches high, with us she holds her head so stately as almost to rank among the shrubs. Being one of the earliest heaths, the blossoms were already past their prime, but our companion soon found a luxuriant branch which he triumphantly placed in his hat.

The ardour with which we sought these mountain treasures was, however, often interrupted, and our eyes turned from the ground to the landscape which was opening around us. We began to distinguish the numerous bays with which the coast is indented, and to look for our own headlands stretching out one beyond another into the sea. To count the lakes that lay in the plain beneath would have been impossible. Most of them are so small, and so surrounded with boggy land, as to look very contemptible at a distance; though upon a nearer view, they have a borrowed beauty from the plants which they contain. Many of them are covered with the yellow and white water lilies; in others, along the shallow sandy margin, the delicate *lobelia dortmann* is seen with the *eriocaulon septangulore*,[4] like a West Indian beauty with her negro slave. How singular it is, that while the *lobelia* is to be found in most of the mountainous lakes of England, Scotland and Wales, the *eriocaulon*, which with us never appears to be separated from it, is with you so rare as to have been seen only in one spot!

The ascent of the conical point of the mountain was extremely rugged and precipitous. I was obliged to stop very often to regain my breath; meanwhile my companions amused themselves with rolling down immense stones, which, though of angular shape, were easily set in motion, and acquired amazing velocity in their progress. Some of them were several minutes ere they reached the bottom, and were carried a short distance up the opposite hill, breaking the rocks, and tearing up the turf as they bounded from one point to another.

No sooner we were seated on the highest point of rock, than some of our party, who certainly were unworthy of the honours of the expedition, called for the provision basket. The basket was produced, but it was little short of treason against the majesty of Nature, to fix those eyes on rolls of cold beef, which ought to have been directed to one of the noblest views in Cunnemarra.

Roundstone Bay and Biterbuy,[5] which would afford shelter to the whole navy of England, lay between the hills of Urrisbeg and Cashel. Beyond these might be seen the shores of the bay of Galway, and the numerous islands that lay off the coast. Had the atmosphere been perfectly clear, our sea view would have been very extensive. On the south

4 A plant of the pipewort family.
5 Bertraghboy Bay.

the land was rocky; a fine chain of lakes, varying in size and outline, opened by Ballynahinch river into the sea. The gradual improvement of the country was marked by the numerous roads, and by a few thickets, which, in some spots, under favour of the enclosures, had grown up sufficiently to make a little show. To the south east was the pass of Mam Main,[6] the most southern of the three passes that open into Cunnemarra. To the west lay the plain country, so low and so intersected by small lakes, which look like nothing more than bog holes, that it has the appearance of an extensive salt marsh, liable to be overflowed every spring tide. This low boggy ground extends from Urrisbeg to the bay of Ardbear; the hills then rise round Clifden, and the white spire of the little church can be distinguished on the side of the hill.

The bay of Ballynakill was clearly seen with the big hill of Renvyle,[7] as the country people call it, which, rising from the very edge of the water, never looked more bold or imposing. Beyond, was seen the large island of Boffin; then the graceful outline of Ennis Turc,[8] the sharp crags of Achill Head, and the line of Mayo mountains, with Clare Island defending the entrance of Clew Bay: names which, however harsh they may now appear, will, I am afraid, too soon become known to you as the scene of many a disaster to the unfortunate cruizers on this station. All this was seen in the interval between other majestic mountains in the foreground. The hill of Creig was the nearest, having the green marble quarry on the south-eastern side, and the white one to the north-west. The green valley before us lay in sunshine, and the winding course of the river was marked by the light yellow gravel in its bed. To the north-west several of the Pins, varying in height, in form and in colour, were arranged in the most picturesque groups; some green to the very tops, others brown with heath, and others again white with glistering quartz, from which every sod of turf had been either blown or washed away. It was indeed a more magnificent prospect than any which I have yet seen. The view from the summit of Mam Turc, as affording a greater variety of scenery, is more beautiful; but for the grouping of mountains, nothing on the same scale can, I think, exceed the north and north-east view from Lettery.

The clouds which, slowly rising from the sea, threatened to gather round the summits of the mountains, now warned us to depart; and I was not allowed time to search for the three little treasures (*Phleum alpinum*, *Agrostis minima* and *Juncus filiformis*), mentioned by Wade,[9] nor even to

[6] Mam Ean.
[7] Tully Mountain.
[8] Inishturk.
[9] William Wade (1770–1825), Professor of Botany of the Royal Dublin Society, and first curator of what was to become the National Botanic Gardens, carried out

find the purple saxifrage (*s. oppositifolia*) which we know to be an inhabitant of Lettery, as well as of other parts of Cunnemara. Our descent was no easy matter, for the south side of the mountain (we had ascended on the western side) was almost perpendicular, in some places wet and slippery, in others ragged with loose stones, yet supported on each side. I regained the valley without much fatigue, and in perfect safety. A mizzling rain now overtook us, and when we looked up to the summit of the mountain, we perceived that the seat we had just quitted was completely veiled in clouds. Leaving you this sketch to con over, as a lesson in geography, I shall bid you farewell.

John Barrow (1764–1848)
Fair Head, Country Antrim in 1836

[John Barrow was an Englishman who rose from humble origins to become a diplomat, second secretary to the Admiralty, founder of the Royal Geographical Society, and was created a baronet in 1835. He travelled Ireland in the same year, a decade before the Great Famine took hold, with the intention of publishing a description of his experiences. He had decided not to get involved in discussions of politics or religion, but of course that left little else, and he was inevitably drawn into these testy matters in order to have something to write about. He took a non-partisan stance, however, castigating the Catholic hierarchy about Lough Derg, ('the place confers no honour on the Catholic religion and, I believe, is not in accordance with Church ritual but mere tricks of the monkish priests to fatten on the credulity of the lowest, the most distressed, and most ignorant of the Catholic population ...') and Protestantism regarding Orange parades, which he calls 'ostentatious displays', and remarks that to 'triumph over and to insult five-sixths of an unoffending population[1] would appear to be as unmanly as it is indiscreet.'

Barrow travelled Ireland mainly by coach and on horseback, but I include an extract from his book *A Tour of Ireland*, describing a walk he took at Fair Head in County Antrim.]

---

pioneering work on the botany of Connemara. The first two plants are part of the grass family; the third is Thread Rush.

[1] The proportion of Catholics to Protestants in the all-Ireland context at the time.

On returning to the mountain road I fell in with that part of the new road, constructing by the Board of Works, which crosses Carey Mountain, and which was here finished, but not thrown open. The old road was rugged and steep enough, and with difficulty I kept my seat without being jolted off the car, till I reached Ballyvoy, a village of some fifty or sixty houses, little more than a mile and a half from Fairhead. The desire to see this celebrated spot was irresistible; I therefore left the car at Ballyvoy and walked to the point, among large enclosures that were walled in, and partly under cultivation with wheat, barley, oats and potatoes, but chiefly in pasture for sheep and cattle. I may observe that each parish has the land marked out and enclosed with ditches or walls, generally consisting of several hundred acres, which are called *townlands*; not that there is any town near them, that word signifying in Ireland, not a collection of houses, but enclosed ground. *Tuin* is the Dutch word for a garden, and I found the same word used in the same sense in Iceland: *toon*, a piece of enclosed ground near the house.

As I jogged along and alone on foot, the reflection crossed my mind, that there are certain spots in the globe, some nearer home than others, that every person, according to his respective fancy, must have felt a desire to visit, and a hope that, at some time or another, that desire might be gratified; at least it is so with me. I saw this bold headland the preceding year from the *Flower of Yarrow* yacht when driven by a storm to take shelter under Rachlin Island,[2] and there the thought came across me, that I should contrive some time or other to have a nearer view of Fairhead – indeed, I can trace this kind of feeling to a very early period of my life. Well do I remember when I was a boy, amusing myself with copying the engravings of the cathedral at Tronyem (Drontheim), and of the Kremlin at Moscow. I was wont to indulge in the hope of some day seeing both these places; that hope has already been realized – more than realized, for I have twice visited the most northern city of Europe.

But Fairhead took possession of a corner of my mind at a later period, and it was with feelings of no ordinary satisfaction that I was now approaching the brink of this noble headland, which, according to the measurement of Professor Playfair and Mr Jardin, rises to the height of six hundred and thirty-one feet above the level of the sea; of which height the columnar or, more properly, the prismatic shafts are not less than two hundred and seventy feet, without joint or articulation. Having procured a guide, my first object was to proceed to the highest summit, a small projecting part of the headland, where I took a nervous peep over the precipice while on my hands and knees.

[2] Rathlin Island.

From this point the prospect is very extensive. The island of Rachlin or, as it is usually called, Raghery, a short distance from the coast, lies stretched immediately under the eye, and the distant Mull of Cantyre [Kintyre], a fine bold headland, is seen to rise in the horizon. Here, too, the vast expanse of the northern sea lies open to the right and to the left – an object to me at all times the most impressive, as affording one of the noblest views in nature. The view alone was a source of satisfaction, but to examine more nearly the wonderful formation of the promontory was a subject of the deepest interest.

For this purpose I descended through an extraordinary cleft in the rock, which is termed the Greyman's Path, at the foot of which I was told would be obtained a full view of the huge prisms of basalt immediately overhead. In descending this gap, an opportunity is afforded of examining the formation of this gigantic prismatic structure. The irregular and jagged surfaces of the prisms, which protruded on either side of the narrow passage, seemed so exactly to fit and match each other, as if they had been torn asunder by some convulsion. This Greyman's Path is so called, as my guide informed me, from the circumstance of an old hermit having for many years lived in a small cave at the foot of the headland, who, either for pleasure or penance, was daily in the habit of ascending this path.

The descent was rugged and precipitous, and required some caution, on account of the numerous loose stones that roll from under the feet; but rough as it was, my guide prevented me from complaining, by assuring me that he had conducted many ladies down the path, and that they acquitted themselves quite as well as the gentlemen. Of this I doubt not, for I recollect hearing you say that you once took a lady (Lady Ann Barnard) up the gap in the mural precipice of the Table Mountain, which, I believe, is between three and four thousand feet high, she being the first female that had ever ascended that mountain; after which the Greyman's Path deserves not to be mentioned.

I cannot say that the view of the perpendicular precipice, as seen from below, fully answered the expectation I had formed of it; perhaps this is generally the case when the imagination has been strongly excited by exaggerated accounts of previous visitors. Be that as it may, I freely confess I was disappointed. I could not bring myself to think that 'the columnar range of Fairhead is by far the most magnificent basaltic facade yet discovered'; but I am most ready to admit that Fairhead, or, as it is usually called, Benmore, is a promontory that can never fail to arrest the attention and admiration of the spectator, though it can scarcely lay claim to the character of sublimity. It presents a bold and singularly marked face of rock of two hundred and seventy feet in height, supported, as it were, by a rugged buttress or sloping glacis of three hundred and thirty-one feet; but this very division into two unequal and dissimilar parts, a pyramidal facade rising out of a sloping mass of huge fragments, renders the unity defective, and ceases to impress on the mind a feeling of the sublime, which the vastness of an uninterrupted precipice could not fail to inspire. The facade, though not strictly columnar, consists of a succession of basaltic prisms, so clustered together as to give the appearance of that combination of columns which one often meets with in Gothic cathedrals. With these are intermixed large tabular masses, heaped on each other, and rising from the same sloping base to the summit. It would appear, however, from some of the enormous prismatic fragments that had been broken off, and fallen down from the rocky precipice, and which constitute a considerable part of the base sloping down to the sea, that there is a tendency in them to articulation, the fragments being generally broken into lengths, and the fractures conchoidal. Among them, too, are found pieces that have taken the forms of polygons.

Having satisfied my curiosity, so far as time and circumstances permitted, and tiring my legs not a little with the scramble, I returned to my car, passing by two small lakes at no great distance from the head, one called Lough na Cranagh, and the other Lough Doo. The distance to Ballycastle from Ballyvoy might be from two to three miles along the ridge of a glen through which the river Carey is seen to flow. The cottages along this line are neat and numerous. On the left stands the mountain of Knocklaide, 1,690 feet high, the loftiest and largest in this part of the country. On reaching the town I drove to the little inn which had the appearance of comfort and cleanliness; but on delivering my letter of introduction to Mr McNeill, he very kindly insisted on my taking up my abode with him, at least for the night.

Mrs Asenath Nicholson
County Tipperary in 1844

[Asenath Nicholson was a New Yorker who became fascinated by the cheerfulness and patience of the Irish emigrant poor in the city; she travelled to Ireland in 1844 and spent a year studying the people in their home environment, and reading to them from the Bible. She travelled extensively through Ireland, on foot and alone most of the time, often covering as much as twenty miles of rough road in a day, frequently suffering from blistered feet. She avoided the society of the well-off and delighted in spending most of her time in the countryside among the poor: '... we have had many

"Pencilling by the Way" and "Conciliation Halls" and "Killarney Lakes" from the top of coaches and from smoking dinner tables. But one day's walk on mountain or bog, one night's lodging where the pig, and the ass, and the horned oxen feed,

"like Aaron's serpent, swallows all the rest".[1]

After a brief return to New York, she came back to Ireland and stayed during the worst years of the Famine, buying and distributing food to the poor. She finally returned to the United States in 1852.

In this excerpt from her book describing her travels, *Ireland's Welcome to the Stranger*, she describes the hardship she endured walking towards Roscrea, County Tipperary in midwinter, and how a kind act on her previous visit there brought her good fortune.]

The morning was cloudy, and rain began soon to fall. I was five miles from Roscrea, and it being but about ten in the morning, thought best to go into a shelter till the rain might subside. A little cabin, with the tempting flowerpot standing in the window, saying, 'Here are order and content within,' induced me to call. It was built of rough stone, and was not whitewashed, but when I entered, the scene was changed. Such a room in cabin or cottage never had met my eyes. The room was small, and in the midst of it stood a centre table of the highest polish. On it were gilt-edged books, shells, flower baskets, specimens of Ireland's diamonds and gems; and under it were all the iron and tin utensils used for cooking, glistening like so many mirrors. There was no floor but the ground, but a nice straw mat was at the door, a hearth rug of no mean quality, a number of covered stools for the feet, a nice looking-glass and table, and a bed of the best appearance, with fringed curtains surrounding it. Two well-dressed ladies were sitting in the room, with a beautiful little lapdog on a soft mat at their feet. As I first entered, I thought of a room of fairies, and hesitated, to see whether the beautiful images made on my mind by Mary's neat cabin,[2] had not swelled to this fine picture. 'Walk in,' said one of the ladies, 'and take a seat from the rain.' They were sisters; one was married to a police officer, and told me she had not in her life been six miles from that cabin where she was sitting. How and where she acquired this taste, and where she had been taught such a finish of housekeeping, so distinct from all her neighbours, is difficult to understand.

[1] Exodus 8: 10–12.
[2] A tiny cottage in which she had previously lodged.

They sat till five o'clock without eating, though they gave me a biscuit, and they sat without working. The rain continued, but the young ladies told me that they had an engagement that evening to attend a christening and must be out. There was a lodging house near, and the unmarried sister offered to accompany me, adding, 'The woman is quite odd, and may tell you she can't lodge you, when she can.' We went. A positive denial was the result. I begged her to give me a shelter from the pitiless storm, giving her my usual password, 'American stranger', telling her that the Irish were so hospitable, and if she would visit my country I would do her all the good I could. All this cringing and coaxing was unavailing: 'I have told ye I wouldn't lodge ye, and that's enough'. There was an inviting bright fire upon the hearth. I begged her to let me lie down upon the chairs, and stop till the rain should cease, and I would go out at any hour. 'I shall not keep you, and that's enough.' I next went to an English family; they refused because they had just moved in. It was night and very dark, and the rain and storm increased. I set my face towards Roscrea, and was struggling with wind and rain when I saw the smoke of a cabin coming out at the door, which a woman had opened, with a pot of potatoes she was carrying in. I inquired the distance to Roscrea. 'You arn't a–goin' there tonight; turn into the house a bit; a smoky shelter is better than a stawrm. And why did ye not stop in the lodgin' house back?' Telling her I was refused: 'And did she think she never might be a wawkin', and want a lodgin' place? Ah, she's a blackguard; she stands there sellin' whiskey from mornin' to night, to the vagabonds about the place.'

This cabin had not one redeeming quality. Two pigs lay in one corner upon a pile of straw; three dirty children were on the hearth; a miserable bed, one chair, a stool or two, and an old tottering table, made the sum total of this domicile. And in addition to the smoke from the turf on the hearth, a copious volume was poured in from an adjoining room, from over a partition which extended midway up. What could I do here? Breathing was quite difficult, and, in or out, my case was no promising one. The poor man came in from his work and sat down by a little low table, and held his arms around the edge while the good woman poured the potatoes upon it. He picked out a large one, which he said weighed a pound, and, taking off the coat with his nails, presented it to me. I toasted it upon the coals, ate a part of it, and went to the door; and seeing that the rain had not abated, and that I must go, committed myself to him 'who rides upon the stormy sky', and went out. 'If I had a place, you should not go,' the poor man said as he saw me going.

My lot for the next two hours was not a pleasant one. The road was dreadfully clayey and hilly. I waded through darkness, mud and storm, sometimes on the road, sometimes in the ditch; and but once met a human being, whom I found to be an old man, who pitifully exclaimed, 'Ye'r lost!

Ye'r destroyed! And ye've two miles under yer fut to the town.' These two miles were replete with realities – no imagination here. I reached Roscrea about ten, and everything in town was still, but the loud pouring of the rain. I was bewildered, and knew not a single street, till I saw by a lamp a girl; and inquiring for the market, found the old stopping place of the kind woman who had invited me to stay, when passing through. And the first salutation when she saw me enter was, 'I have no place to put you here – I am obliged to sleep on the boards myself.'

My clothes were dripping with wet; it was past ten; and the rain was tremendous. 'I believe that I am not to have a lodging in Ireland to night,' was my answer. 'I will go with you to Mrs T.'s.' She went, I was refused, and the friend left me, and returned to her house. Mrs T. said she had taken two more than her usual number, and every bed was filled.

Now, kind friends, if you have followed me through rain and storm to Roscrea, remember the sixpence given to the poor woman when I passed through the town, and mark its progress. I stood, not knowing what to do. In a hotel I could not get a bed for want of money. A voice from a dark corner called out, 'Ain't ye the American lady that went through here a few weeks since?' I answered that I was. 'I've heard of you, and you shall have a bed if I sit up. You kept a cabin over a poor woman's head, and God won't let you stay all night in the stawrm.' The mistress was in bed; this woman went to her, told her who I was, and extolled my excellencies so vivid, that the mistress said, 'I have a bed in the garret where the servant sleeps, but there is nothing but a ladder that leads to it. I could give her clean sheets, and a chaff bed, but am ashamed to offer such a place.' I heard it, and said, 'A ladder is no objection; give me clean sheets, and all will be well.'

The mistress arose, made me a cup of coffee and brought bread and butter, and put me in a situation to dry my clothes. I ate some bread and took 'a sup' of milk, ascended the ladder, and never slept sweeter. 'Cast thy bread upon the waters, and after many days thou shalt find it.'[3] I had found my bread in the place where I left it, and at the very time I most needed it. But for that trifling sixpence, I should probably have stayed under some hedge that night, or been walking upon the street on my way to Urlingford.

At five in the morning I was down stairs, called for my bill, and was told it was threepence; nothing for the supper, and half price for climbing a ladder. I had now threepence, and but twenty-six miles before me. I went forth, the clouds were swept from the sky, the stars were looking out. It was December, and the day was just dawning; the grass was green, made young and fresh by the rain, and the morning bird had begun his song. I

[3] Ecclesiastes 11:1.

should be ungrateful to say that I was not happy. I was more than happy, I was joyful, and commenced singing. I was standing upon a green purse, looked at my threepence, and realised, if possible, my true condition. A stranger in a foreign land; a female, alone, walking with but threepence in my possession. I did so, and the sight of the pennies, rude and ungraceful as it might be, caused me to laugh. 'What lack I yet?' was my prompt reply, and then I was happy that I had been compelled to test my sincerity in visiting Ireland, and my firm unwavering belief in the promises and care of God. I had but just returned my purse to the bag, when I heard a carriage, and a call, 'Stop, and take a ride to the next town. Here is the American lady that stopped at my house.' This was the Quaker at whose place I stopped on my route to Galway. This ride carried me six miles from Roscrea to the place where I had stayed at the shopkeeper's, when on my way. I was met and welcomed at the car by a son of the family, with, 'We're glad to see you; Uncle has a letter for you at Urlingford, with money in it from America; but he found the seal broken at the office, and thought it might be unsafe to send it on to Galway.'

A breakfast was prepared. I passed the day in making repairs in garments sadly racked by storms and trials before unknown, and the next morning the boy and car were sent to carry me to Urlingford. My money was in waiting, my friends were as kind as when I left, and I sat down to rest and reflect.

John O'Hagan (1822–1890)
County Donegal in 1845

[John O'Hagan was born in County Down, educated in Dublin, and he graduated from Trinity College in 1842. He was an active member of the Young Irelanders, and at one time acted as legal counsel for his friend, Charles Gavan Duffy.[1] He became a Queen's Counsel in 1865, and later a judge, when he was appointed by William Gladstone, then Prime Minister, as the first Judicial Commissioner of the Irish Land Commission.

In 1844, at the age of 22, he travelled widely through the southern counties of Ireland in the company of Gavan Duffy, recording his experiences in

[1] Charles Gavan Duffy (1816–1903), a man of many parts, barrister, political activist, newspaper editor and author, he was also for a time Prime Minister of the State of Victoria in Australia.

a diary. In the summer of the following year he embarked on a walking tour of the North of Ireland with Duffy, John Martin and John Mitchell, who in spite of the extra 'l' that O'Hagan gives him, is most likely John Mitchel.[2] During the course of the tour Duffy received a message that his wife was ill, and had to return to Dublin. Although Mitchel and Martin appear to be seasoned walkers, it seems clear that O'Hagan is new to pedestrianism; he finds to his surprise that being out in the rain is not all that bad, and is thrilled to discover that he is capable of walking quite long distances. At Horn Head and Slieve League he is delighted to see eagles: 'they looked very majestic, sailing stately, without using a wing. One of them paused for some seconds with his claws spread out rigid as iron. I hoped he was going to take a stoop, but he sailed on'. His more experienced companions were pleased with O'Hagan's progress and he was euphoric about what he felt he had achieved during the tour, proudly claiming: 'Mitchell is to give me a certificate, "*Touristicas artes feliciter excolendi*".'[3]

This extract from his 1845 journal describes getting into difficulties on the wild east shore of Lough Veagh, twenty-five years before Glenveagh Castle was built and its gardens laid out along the eastern shore. In spite of their difficulties, he finds Lough Veagh very beautiful, and his musings on the future of the place have a curiously contemporary ring.]

Martin not being well and able to come out, Mitchell [*sic*] and I started from the hotel at 11 o'clock, with the resolution of crossing Durish Mountain,[4] seeing Lough Veagh, walking around it, and climbing Auge[5] on our way home. We found one of these objects quite enough for us, as will appear in the sequel. Our road lay by the side of Dunlewy Lake, or rather lakes, for there are two joined by a winding river. The upper lake appears from the hills above it something like the Upper Lake at Killarney in the first view we had of it from the hillside. The lake is in all about five miles long. We struck off the road about six miles from the hotel and began to climb Durish. There had been a great fall of rain during the night and the ground was very swampish. Moreover, a shower was just

[2] John Mitchel (1815–75) established the *United Irishman* newspaper in February 1848, was arrested, tried and convicted of treason-felony and transported to Australia in May 1848. He escaped in 1853 to the US, before returning to Ireland where he was elected MP for County Tipperary.
[3] Of successfully perfecting the 'touristic arts'.
[4] Today called the Derryveagh Mountains, the highest point of which is Dooish (652 m).
[5] Auge is probably the mountain known as Aghla Mor (584 m) today.

impending and the head of Durish was completely shrouded in mist. Kept never minding, however; took a sort of shelter during the first shower (we afterwards came to despise such a thing, and pushed on and plashed on). It was, as Mitchell said, a glorious day for the mountains, mist, wet and rainy; but for all that they did look very grand. Wet and rainy abovementioned are not tautological, the one referring to underfoot, the other to overhead. Got to the top. Still raining wickedly. No imaginable shelter except under a cow's belly, if they could be persuaded to stand. Directed our steps downward towards Lough Veagh, but made very slow progress due to the nature of the ground, which was a complete marsh with tufts rising from it at intervals, and I with my weak ankle could spring from one to the other but tardily. The day was wearing on and we began to feel hungry, so we took out our scrip, consisting of a few biscuits and some slices of meat. We were a little anxious to sit down, but there was no stone or rock, and every green substance was like a filled sponge. Lay down at length on the sand beside the stream, which, having drunk in the rain, was not so wet at the surface. Did not drink the water, being boggy. Still onward, hopping over tufts, though indeed, our feet by this time were soaked through. Came to a waterfall, not very large, looking very grand from its abrupt descent. Very peculiar effect of the spray when we looked at it from underneath. Got first sight of Lough Veagh below us. I do think – and Lord knows, I did not see it under the most favourable of circumstances – it is very little inferior to one of the Killarney lakes.

The hill is on one side bare, and on the other side a good deal of the remains of old forests. It was by the former side, which was the nearest to us, that Martin and Mitchell went when they were here before, but Mitchell said the path was dangerous, and we saw on the far side part of a road, which, there was every reason to believe, extended through the wood, all along the lake. Resolved to take it. Finished our descent of the mountain. The river at the head of the lake running between us and the other side. No ford. No matter, we could not well be worse than we were, so we coolly walked through it. There was a boat in the river which we coveted very much to bring us down to the far end of the lake; and heavens, it would have been a desirable consummation to have got it, but some workmen employed on the road told us it was private property, and not to be had. So we went on with, as we thought, a four-mile road around the lake, and a seven-mile road from there to the hotel, before us. But, behold you, after a few perches our road, which was only an inchoate one, terminated abruptly in a narrow path, which also soon ended; and there we were left to make our way, with no more assistance from art than one of Hugh Roe's mountaineers might have had. At one time we crept along the margin of the lake over the huge stones that bordered it, stepping perilously from one to the other. Again we would be driven to make our way through the wood, the ground being a complete quagmire, and the branches thick set. To add to our comfort, the night was falling, and set in before we made a mile. Fortunately we had moonlight, otherwise we might have made up our minds to pass the night there in our saturated clothes.

By moonlight we trudged on, sinking generally up to our ankles in slush, occasionally up to our knees. However, we never despaired; when things looked worst, Mitchell would propose to dance the Original Polka, so we laughed, took heart, and persevered. But it was a strange thing. Here was this beautiful lake, looking by moonlight as lovely a scene as one would wish to set eyes on, yet not a boat on it, not a house near it, no road on either side, but a dangerous path on one side and no path at all but primeval thickets on the other. I wonder if one returned here in twenty years, how it will be found; probably with a hotel at either end, and swarming with tourists. But to return to our transit. The greatest obstruction we met was a deep ravine with a river running through it. If the night had been dark, we might have met a very serious mischance. We let ourselves down by the branches of trees, but I was within an ace of sliding into a deep pool. We eventually, however, escaped all disasters but wet and fatigue, and arrived at the bridge at the foot of the lake.[6] We calculated it took us four hours to make our way along the lake. The length was scarcely so many miles. We were now, we thought, seven miles from our hotel, though in fact we were between ten and eleven.[7] I proposed to Mitchell to try and get stopping in some cottage for the night. But he represented that all the inmates of any cottage would be in bed (it was now about 11 o'clock), that we would not be able to get any bed, but would be obliged to sit all night in our damp clothes, and all we would get to eat would be a few bad potatoes, and on the whole we ought to strain every nerve to get to our dear Lord George.[8] If I had been less tired and hungry and wet, I should have enjoyed that moonlight walk excessively, for it was through a grand country of mountains and lakes. Noble Donegal! how ignorant I was, how ignorant are the mass of Irishmen, of what you are. We had Arrigal to our right, with his proud head still shrouded in mist. Mitchell had laid out in the morning that we should climb him on our way home and back to Guidore for tea!

But there was no use talking! We were both excessively tired, and our

[6] This bridge is where the Glenveagh Visitors Centre stands today.

[7] On current maps the distance between the bridge and Gweedore is nearer fourteen miles.

[8] The hotel in which they were staying had been established by Lord George Hill, an 'improving landlord' who spoke Irish and who owned 23,000 acres around the Gweedore area at the time.

feet so cold that our quickest walking could not warm them. Once we sat on the side of a bridge for about a minute, when Mitchell started up, exclaiming, 'I declare to God I was dreaming, and might have fallen over.' The hotel turned out to be three or four miles farther on than we thought, but at length we reached it at past two, famished and exhausted. We had our feet bathed, took a glass of brandy, cold meat and tea, and slept for some hours the sleep of the dead.

So ends 'Frank's day of adventures.' We had walked in all about five and twenty miles; and such walking! – equal to five and thirty on a common road. When I was in Dublin I was under the impression that I could not walk more than five or six miles; and as to such exertion as this, I would simply have pronounced it a physical impossibility. (Memo: There are fewer physical impossibilities in the world than we think.)

John Ashworth
West Mayo, *c*.1850

[John Ashworth was an Englishman who, owing to 'enactments, wise perhaps and expedient in themselves, but hastily carried out', got into finan- cial difficulties that forced him to think about emigration. He considered 'icy Canada', but dreaded the six months of snow and the possibility that Canada might be annexed by the United States; the 'burning Cape' of Good Hope, which he felt had too many 'hostile Boers and powerful and bloody Caffres'; and even Tasmania, 'a fine climate, the see of a bishop and free of aborigines'. A family friend, however, persuaded him to think about Ireland, where there was 'good land, a healthy climate, [and] estates to be had cheap.' He set out to investigate the western coast of the province of Connaught for suitability, and travelled extensively in western Galway and Mayo. He wrote of his experiences in a book called *The Saxon in Ireland, or Rambles of an Englishman in Search of Settlement in Ireland*, which was published in London in 1852. Research has not revealed whether or not he did subsequently bring his family to Ireland to settle, but he leaves no doubt in his writings that he is impressed by the people and the potential of the land. The following is an excerpt from his book describing a day's walking in the Nephin Beg Mountains in County Mayo.]

I am now resting at the inn at Newport, after one of the most fatiguing rambles I ever attempted. As I was sailing on the broad bosom of the Furnace Lough[1] I was so struck with the bold heights of the Nephin or Ballycroy mountains, rearing their craggy fronts to the westward, that I determined to ascend them, convinced that the views would amply repay the exertion. A guide was provided for me, and we commenced our walk from the House of Curreen, a solitary dwelling at the foot of the mountains, but inhabited by persons of consideration, if I may judge by the neat equipage, &c. which I met as I approached the dwelling. We soon struck off the mountain road, and faced the precipitous ridge which divides the two wild glens of Thaumaus and Glendahurk. I will not weary you with the details of my ascent, as these feats have been so often described by more practised pens than mine; and were I to attempt any delineation of the fine views that opened upon me as I rose higher and higher from the level plain to the very eyrie of the eagle, I could convey to you no idea of the reality. My guide was an active long-legged mountaineer, and an inhabitant of these wilds. I fancied he wished to tire out the Sassenach, and accordingly with becoming spirit I resolved to die game. We rested twice, and only then for a few seconds before we attained the summit of Cuscambecurragh,[2] and it was at his own suggestion that we stopped at all. The second time we seated ourselves was on a narrow ridge of rock which descends almost perpendicularly into Glen Thaumaus on one side, and into Glendahurk on the other. A curious fact here occurred perhaps worth mentioning, as showing the superstitious feeling prevalent in these regions. I took out my cigar case, and having only small wax lucifers, as soon as I lighted one it was extinguished by the driving sleet. I tried another, and a third, and was about to try a fourth, when my guide, one of the respectable sept hight[3] Macguire, laid his hand on my arm, and said somewhat sternly, 'No – I ask yer honour's pardon, but no more; if you do, I must leave you.'

It was a really sublime position we had attained. Thin vapours hurried over the summits of the mountains, sometimes veiling all below in obscurity; then again they rolled off, and the deep glens below, with their glittering streams, their verdant spots and craggy sides, browsed by the sheep, opened upon us with all the loveliness of a finished picture. I thought of Beattie's beautiful lines:

> And in mist the world below was lost;
> What dreadful pleasure! there to stand sublime,

[1] Three km north-west of Newport, County Mayo.
[2] Probably what is today called Ben Gorm.
[3] An Anglo-Saxon word meaning 'called' or 'named'.

Like shipwrecked mariner on desert coast,
And view the enormous waste of vapour, tost
In billows, lengthening to the horizon round,
Now scooped in gulfs, with mountains now embossed![4]

As we attained the peaked summit of Corranabinna,[5] nearly 2,500 feet from the level of Clew Bay, we found ourselves quite enveloped in thick clouds. A chill rushing wind met us, and we hurried on searching for the shelter of some overhanging rock. The vapours occasionally dissolved in rain, and my companion now disappointed all my previous expectations by assuring me that I had no chance, for that day at least, of enjoying the splendid view to the north and west of these heights. After we had wandered about on the top of the mountain for nearly half an hour, he at length told me it would be a work of no little danger to attempt a descent before the mist had in some measure cleared off, for the dangerous precipices overhanging the Corranabinna Lake could not be far from us. We had no alternative then but to shelter ourselves as best we could under the angle of a rock, a very indifferent protection against the driving sleet; but I had this especial comfort, it was yet early in the day, and I had already had enough experience of such situations to know that the changes from storm to sunshine were no less rapid and to be looked for, than those from fair weather to mists and darkness. The event fully justi-fied my spirit of resignation: a brisk rain descends, and the clouds seem lighter; now they sweep past us up the hill – they darken again, and are more thick than ever; now a break is distinguishable for a moment – some-thing like a ray of the sun seems to linger for an instant on a distant rock below us; now the sun breaks through – and never can I forget my sensa-tions as the scene opened upon us. We now found – for hitherto we could hardly see a foot before us – that we had been sitting all this time upon the very brink of that fearful precipice which overhangs the wild and solitary Lough of Corranabinna (or more properly, Carreg-a-Binniogh). Had we attempted during the mist to move our position, we must have been dashed to atoms. 'By dad, master *alanna*,' said my guide, looking in my face with a half-fearful expression, 'it was well you did not try the fourth match!'

It seemed here as if a gorge ran from the far-off plain into the interior of the mountains, dividing the heights of Meilroc and Corranabinna. At the extremity of this was a dark lake, hemmed in on three sides, partly by inaccessible cliffs, partly by green and heathery slopes. On the highest of these precipices we now stood a thousand feet above the lake; and so

[4] From *The Poet in Youth* by James Beattie (1735–1803), Scottish poet.
[5] Not named on current 1:50,000 maps, but noted at 716 m from sea level.

suddenly was the sense of our position forced upon us, that it was not till we had thrown ourselves on the ground and crawled along some distance from the fearful verge, that we dared to stand upright and gaze upon the glorious scene below. Plains, hills, lakes, rivers like threads of silver, distant ranges of mountains, bays, promontories, and far-off ocean rocks or islands, these all were beneath us, or stretching far away to the horizon. I could have stood and gazed for hours. The words of Goldsmith were at my heart though not upon my lips:

Creation's heir – the world – the world is mine.[6]

It was Nature's own map, and I soon, from my geographical knowledge of the district, made my eye familiar with my position. 'We are now,' said my companion, 'in Shrahduggane; and that lake to the left, as well as the dark one below us, are the sources of the Owenduff river, which empties itself yonder into Turlogh Bay.' 'Yes,' said I, 'close by Croy Lodge, where is the celebrated salmon fishery. That black and gloomy range to the left, in the far distance is, I suppose, Currawn Achill; and beyond are Slievemore and Croaghan, with Saddle Head to the north.' 'Right, Sir,' interrupted Macguire, 'and look off to sea as far as your eye can reach – that rock is called Deevelaun, famous for "agles and say birds"; and yonder is the country round Belmullet; and there Tyrawly lies, till it reaches Killala Bay and Crossmolina.' 'And,' continued I, 'yonder far bay, on which the sun is just now shining, is Blacksod Harbour, and beyond is the Mullet, and this lovely creek, that penetrates so beautifully inland, is Tulloghan Bay, and that inland lough is Fahy, on which the Castle of Doona is situated. What a glorious map is this.' 'You seem to know all about it,' said Macguire, looking surprised. 'I once came upon this mountain with a "foreigner", who asked me if we could see Snowdon in Wales. "And is it Wales you're talking about?" says I. "Faith, and he must have a keen eye that can see Snowdon, I'm thinking, even if he were on the top of Nephin," says I.

'Well, but Macguire,' I resumed, 'tell me the name of that round hill that stands, as it were, by itself on the plain below like a sentinel to the receding circular range around it.' 'That is Gloreslieve, about 1,000 feet high; and the mountain to the right is Scardaun, which forms the western side of Nephin Beg. And do you see a black speck just where the river seems to turn round a green knoll? That is the shooting lodge of Mr Vernon; and beyond, not far, is the house of Mr Lees, which he has built as a fishing station. The rivers of Ballycroy are famous among anglers all over Ireland, and some of those loughs you see there sparkling in the waste, have trout in them of seven and fourteen pounds weight!'

[6] From *The Traveller*, the first work published by Goldsmith under his own name.

'Did you ever try the Ballycroy river, Macguire, which empties itself near Croy Lodge into Tulloghan Bay ?' 'O yes, often. Last week I hooked a salmon which weighed twenty-two pounds, and we had a pretty severe "tussle" of nearly two hours before he was landed. He was as fat as a pig, pretty nearly the same thickness from his shoulder to his tail.' 'What river is that which joins the estuary there to the left with several branches ramifying over the flat plain till they meet in one stream above yonder bridge?' 'It is the old bridge of Bellaveeny; and that is the Bellaveeny river, or more properly the Owen-a-vrea. It rises in the lake on yonder mountainside, but the country through which it runs is anything but flat, though it seems to us so. It would be a first-rate stream for fish if preserved, and providing there was more water. It has large trout and might have a few salmon too, but for the night fishing. That might easily be prevented, for the poachers cannot conceal their light; it may be seen from a long distance. The way they do it is this: when the salmon come up to spawn, the poachers go by night, and, with a torch, perceive where the fish wallow to leave their spawn, and they take them out by means of a gaff.' 'It is an abominable practice,' said I, 'useless to the thief, and very injurious to the country; for fish so taken are not wholesome food.'

With such conversation, Macguire and I whiled away an hour on the mountain as we sat and overlooked the splendid scene below. At length it was time to commence our descent, for a cloud already rested on the summit of Nephin Beg, and the day still seemed uncertain. '*Facilis descensus Averni*':[7] not so into the plains of Ballycroy. Many a fall had we – many a time did we pause to select the safest slope, where, indeed, all were precipitous; and in several places Macguire stopped to make me listen where the underground torrents were rushing beneath the very earth on which we stood. This made careful walking necessary, for it would not have been very pleasant to sink below the surface into the depths of one of these subterranean pools. We at length attained the level of the two lakes which we had observed so far beneath us when on the summit of the mountain.[8] Two such valleys as those in which they lie are not often seen. The first we traversed was covered by immense blocks of rock scattered everywhere in strange confusion, and in every picturesque form. In one place, one had so rolled upon another as to form a natural cave, affording excellent shelter; others were half sunk in the ground, while some seemed almost to tremble in the air, merely resting on an angular point or leaning against some other neighbouring mass. Frequently crystal springs emerged from beneath these giant boulders,

[7] 'Easy is the descent to Avernus.' *Aeneid*, vi. 126.
[8] On current maps the two lakes bear the one name of Corryloughaphuill.

and marked their sinuous course into the plain beneath by a waving line of the freshest verdure. As we climbed a gentle knoll which separates these two wild glens, I looked back upon the scene we were leaving with a feeling of awe. The clouds already obscuring the summits of the precipice, the jutting cliffs above, the huge rocks below and the calm surface of the lake, formed a whole truly and strikingly sublime. It was close to this spot that the author of *The Wild Sports of the West*[9] met with the red deer, and here it was that the noble stag was killed. The other lake we have already described. Its waters were still and very dark, and the precipice rose around it on three sides, almost a thousand feet. This portion of the mountain range of Ballycroy was ever the favourite haunt of the wild deer, and here, I was informed, they still linger, though very few in number.[10] To have caught sight even of one would have completed the interest of the scene.

Leaving these romantic glens, we at length gained the fine slopes which everywhere distinguish the bases of these mountains; and I often paused to observe the rare capabilities of improvement which on every side presented themselves. A few judicious catch-water drains, if opened at the commencement of these slopes, would at once act beneficially upon many thousand acres on the plains below. It is from the innumerable springs that issue from the heights, that the plain is so saturated with moisture – once cut these off, and with the assistance of a few mains to convey them to the beds of the rivers, the ordinary quality of surface drains, of about two feet deep or less, would totally alter the whole aspect of the country. I never saw any tract of land where extensive and highly remunerative operations could be so easily and economically carried out. Draining, irrigation, and subsoiling, are all easy of performance, and in many parts the vegetable matter does not exceed two or three feet in depth. The plain which appeared so flat as viewed from the mountain, we found, on traversing it, sufficiently uneven, having many eminences in the midst of the moor, which appeared to contain abundance of clay and sand. Some of the sand I tested with muriatic acid,[11] and it effervesced briskly, of course exhibiting the presence of lime. Our walk to Macguire's cabin was nearly five Irish miles across the waste, though he protested it was 'just a step or so, and quite convanient.' But the genius of speculation was so alive within me, and I was so engaged as we strode along, that I did not grudge the distance. Every inch of land we traversed seemed reclaimable,

---

9 William Hamilton Maxwell (1792–1850), novelist and historian; *The Wild Sports of the West* (1832) is a hunting and fishing travelogue full of melodramatic anecdotes of the west.
10 There are no longer any deer in this area.
11 Hydrochloric acid.

possessing a fine sunny aspect, excellent slopes for draining, and rivers running far into the land, capable of bringing up lime and sea manure from the neighbouring islands and deeply indented shores. 'It is a shame,' exclaimed I to my companion, as we paused for a moment on a round knoll in the centre of the vast plain, 'it is a shame and a disgrace to every Celt and Milesian in the land, that such a fine tract as this should lie a mere useless waste, while in other parts every shallow deposit among the rocks, and even the very sands on the seashore, are eagerly sought after and dearly rented, in hopes of obtaining a scanty produce. I cannot understand it.' 'And faith I don't wonder,' replied Macguire archly, 'your honour does not know, perhaps, that all things are done in Ould Ireland by the rule of contrary. There is land here that will fat out sheep and bullocks, and I'm the man that know it, sure, for I've seen it myself.' I smiled at this remark, and set it down as one of the many instances I had met with of poetic exaggeration among this imaginative and lively people; but I afterwards was informed by a respectable proprietor of the district, that my companion was correct in his statement. In fact, as we walked along the banks of the Ballyveeny river, I remarked many extensive patches of deep alluvial soil, which only required enclosing with fences and ditches to render them, with a little dressing of lime, first-rate meadowland. I noticed also that as we approached the coast, every portion which had been worked by the cottar's spade exhibited crops of the heaviest and most promising description; and I felt satisfied that, so long as such land remained in Ireland neglected and almost unappropriated, it was sheer wickedness to ship off luckless emigrants to the barren plains of Australia, or the ferny wastes of New Zealand. After such a morning's walking, climbing, and bog-trotting as I had gone through, the rude, yet hearty hospitality of my friend Macguire's cabin was not to be despised. Her unvarying kindness to the stranger, her open-hearted profuse hospitality, her noble and generous contempt of 'remuneration', will ever endear Ireland to my memory. 'Sure, and it wasn't the money ye offered the woman!' said my guide vehemently to me as he entered the cabin and caught his wife's indignant look as she flung my offering to the winds – 'Would you eat the bread and then take away the blessing?' I was ashamed of myself and looked with reverence upon these poor people, and could only mutter my apology that I was an Englishman, and that in England no man ever refused what was offered him, &c. &c. The Irish have many faults, I grant you; but for courtesy, good humour, willingness to oblige, and kindness of heart to a suffering fellow creature, they have no equals. I have seen it, and experienced it too in a hundred instances. After a pleasant walk with Macguire along the banks of the Owen-a-vrea, I found a car waiting for me at the bridge of Ballyveeny, and was soon comfortably seated in mine own inn in the pleasant town of Newport, Mayo.

Achilles Daunt
Bray, Co. Wicklow in 1854

[Achilles Daunt was born in County Cork in 1832, and entered Trinity College at the age of sixteen, where he studied the classics and English literature. Although through his family connections (his grandfather was an influential member of parliament) he could have had a lucrative career at the Bar, he went instead into the church. After a busy and varied career working in parishes as far apart as Rincurran, west Cork and Dusseldorf in Germany, his final station was in Cork City, as the Dean of the Diocese.

   The excerpts included here are extracts from Daunt's diaries, written in 1854 when he was still a Trinity student, about sojourns he took in nearby County Wicklow. It is interesting to see that excursions out of the city by way of the then twenty-year-old coastal railway (the line to Bray opened only in 1854) had already become established as a popular and healthy activity for the general populace.]

Easter Monday is always enjoyed as a holiday by those whose business renders it difficult for them to emerge from the smoky streets of the city, save only on a few stated occasions. Hence the various means of exit from the good city of Dublin were very generally put into requisition by crowds of pleasure and healthseeking defectors from the shop, the office, the school and the college; amongst the representatives of which latter place, A. Daunt, junior, might be seen seated in a second-class carriage appertaining to the train that emerged from Westland Row Station at 9 o'clock, a.m., 'bound for' Kingstown[1] (fare, fourpence).

   Thence, ie. from Kingstown, this illustrious personage (who, be it remarked, was equipped with a cap, a decidedly second-rate coat, a pair of gloves that gave free access to the air and light of heaven, and a no-ways fashionable stick) – thence, I say, our traveller proceeded per 'atmospheric railway' to Dalkey,[2] and having crossed Killiney hills, descended into the valley beyond, and on to Bray *à pied*. The birds singing merrily, the sun shining gloriously, the sea and sky vying with each other in blueness and brightness – all looked beautiful, though spring seems yet to tarry.

   The good people of Bray seem much impressed with religious sentiments, albeit motley and discordant. Here are two chapels (RC), two

[1] Dun Laoghaire.
[2] At the time Dun Laoghaire and Dalkey were connected by a novel, hydraulically operated tramline.

Episcopal churches, one Scots' ditto, and one Methodist meeting house. From hence to Kilmacanoge, at the foot of the Great Sugarloaf, which is a very fine mountain and exceedingly imposing, its very peaked form and precipitous sides causing it to appear more elevated than it really is. Ascended for a few hundred feet to see the view, which was very splendid. Many of the interior peaks had the snow still shining on the summits and sides.

The descent proved the most difficult part of the enterprise, owing to the vast quantities of loose pieces of granite which lie about the great precipitancy of the hills. (All 'downhill movement' not quite so easy as I generally supposed it to be.) A few tosses ensued. Thence on to Enniskerry through the beautiful glen called the Dargle, one of the most delightful places I ever beheld. The fine trees – oaks, pines, etc. – are often wrapped in the most luxuriant ivy, which makes them look like innumerable old, ruined, ivy-mantled castles. The great charm of the spot to me was the perfect stillness, and the total seclusion here afforded. The broken nature of the ground, and the fine trees, with the gloomy mass of the Sugarloaf in the background, together constitute a scene that will amply repay a visit.

Proceeding onwards arrived at Enniskerry, an improving little village, lying snugly in the bosom of a sunny valley. Powerscourt demesne lies a mile or two beyond Enniskerry. Refreshed the inner man here at a very neat hotel, called (I think) Miller's; had a substantial luncheon of mutton chop, bread and butter *ad libitum*, porter, and vegetables, for which I was charged ninepence![3] Set off again, after a short rest, on foot for the city. Passed through the Scalp, a remarkable fissure between two high hills, nearly perpendicular, and strewn with huge blocks of granite and quartz. Progressing, arrived at Dundrum, where I 'took car' to Dublin, where I arrived at 5.30 p.m., having accomplished a journey of thirty-two miles – twelve by vehicle, twenty on foot – at a cost of two shillings, including refreshments. Altogether a pleasant day.

Was awakened by the shrill vocal melody of a vigorous band of the feathered tribe, who, taking up a position close to the lattice, gave vent to their warbling propensities in good earnest, headed by a noble thrush. After having studied with effect for two or three hours, I walked up to Bray Head through Mr Putland's demesne. The view from the hilltop was eximious, embracing the sea on the one hand, and the splendid valley of the Dargle, with its 'circumamplexive' wall of splendid mountains on the other. Hares and rabbits appear to be abundant here. I also saw a couple of

[3] Under 4p.

grouse. Lord Meath's demesne,[4] between Bray Head and the lesser Sugarloaf, is handsome, and the plantations, particularly, are very picturesque. The air here is bracing and salubrious. Much improved in health already . . .

Having been emboldened by the expedition of yesterday afternoon, to essay 'greater things', I set off to ascend the Great Sugarloaf, 1,700 or 1,800 feet high, one of the most remarkable mountains for its size I have ever seen, standing as it does alone, like a huge giant interposing his awful bulk between two valleys. There is a hamlet of neat houses, with a pretty little RC chapel, called Kilmacanoge, at the foot of the mountain.

I heard that the ascent was more practicable at the opposite side towards Enniskerry, but I resolved to go 'straight ahead', and accordingly scrambled up a ravine to the lower shoulder of the Loaf, and after three quarters of an hour's hard work among quartz rocks, bogs, and loose stones, got to the top, where a grand panorama rewarded my exertions. Roundwood was visible; the mountains round Glendalough, and the top of Lugnaquilla (the monarch of the Leinster Mountains, 3,050 feet high) rose over the Douce range majestically. All the coast as far as Arklow Head was discernible, and the Welsh mountains were also in sight. Powerscourt waterfall, Glencree valley, and other points of interest were all visible.

After luxuriating, 1,800 feet above the sea, on the food for the eyes and mind thus provided by kind nature, and on food for the body, in the shape of bread and cheese provided by myself (secondarily), I applied myself to the most difficult part of my task – descending. After many slides and scrambles 'on all fours' over loose rolling stones and yielding bog turf, down nearly perpendicular declivities, I got safely to Kilmacanoge, and reached Rock Cottage at 5 p.m. much delighted with the enterprise of the day . . .

Made a complete circuit of Bray Head, and was surprised to find it a perfect mine of curiosities, owing chiefly to the railway works,[5] which are being vigorously proceeded with on the sea side of this immense mass of bluff, and almost precipitous rocks which overhang the Irish Sea, much in the same manner that Penmanmawr does on the Welsh side. The footpath

---

4 Kilruddery House, an extensive Elizabethan Revival house designed by Sir Richard Morrison for the 10th Earl of Meath, stands in formal gardens on a grand scale, decorated with much statuary.
5 The extension of the Dun Laoghaire to Bray line; railway historians suggest that the local landowner, Lord Meath, did not want noisy, smelly trains passing through his demesne, and put Bray Head between him and the railway by donating the rocky and not too useful foreshore, free of charge.

is frequently hewn out of the face of the cliff, and the aspect of the place is very grand. There are two or three tunnels on the line of the railway, through different brows of the head. The works are very interesting. Some of the rock which they had to cut through is of an exceedingly hard description, like old red sandstone and quartz interfused. The cliffs are perpendicular in some places to a height of two hundred and fifty or three hundred feet. The long grass renders it dangerous to walk too freely on the upper ledges. A Mr Pennefather, I was told, fell over in this way, and lost his life.

An tAthair Peadar Ó Laoghaire (1839–1920)
Mangerton, County Kerry, *c*.1860

[Peadar Ó Laoghaire was born in Clondrohid, a Irish-speaking part of County Cork, and studied for the priesthood at Maynooth, where he became interested in Irish as a literary language. He served as a curate in many County Cork parishes before becoming the parish priest of Castlelyons in 1891. Soon after this he began to write in Gaelic, concentrating primarily on fiction which depicted Irish rural life at the time, but also producing contemporary versions of old tales and translations of Greek epics. His autobiography, *Mo Scéal Féin*, or 'My Own Story', appeared in 1915. I have selected an excerpt from this work in which he describes climbing, as a young man, Mangerton Mountain in County Kerry, which he had first attempted, alone, at the age of ten. The sights he saw must have greatly impressed him, since he clearly retained a detailed memory of the day well into his old age.]

Long after that I climbed to the summit of Mangerton, but I went up on the north side, from Killarney. I was older and stronger then than I was the day I went west to the 'letter that isn't read'.[1] I was alone and the day was very fine. I left Knockanerubill as soon as I had eaten my breakfast, and took every cut south-west until I was at the foot of the hill. Then I looked for the path that was, as I had been told, from the bottom of the

---

[1] Lettercannon, 6 km east of Kilgarran, from where as a young boy he had attempted to climb Mangerton.

hill up to the top, the path that had been made by the feet of the strangers who came to see Killarney and the grand scenery surrounding it. As soon as I found the path I began to climb. Whenever I started to pant I stopped and looked round at countryside that lay behind me. The view widened and became finer as I mounted. When I was a long way up, the prospect was so beautiful, so great and so wide, that I caught my breath when I gazed round at it. At last I reached the top. I stood there a long time looking all round me. It was a wonderful sight. The day was clear as crystal. There were small white clouds in the sky, but they were far up and there was not a speck of mist in the air beneath them, so that I could clearly see the land and the fields, the woods, some of the rivers, some of the churches and some of the dwelling houses which were not too far away. Killarney was there below me, seeming so close that I felt I could throw a pebble into the little town.

I was then on the brow of the hill. The fall was outside me sloping so steeply that I thought if I were to loose a stone it would not stop until it reached the bottom of the hill. Behind me was the flat top of the hill, wide and level, so that it seemed, when you moved in on it, that you were not on a hilltop, but on a wide broad plain. I moved in on it. I had no idea, until I paced hither and thither on it in this way, that the summit was so wonderfully long and wide. The other great hills, with little hills among them, were west, south and east of me. They seemed only like small beehives compared with the great beast under my feet. Only Carrantohill, yonder to the west, appeared to have any bulk or size. The Paps and Mullaghanish were east from me, looking very insignificant. I looked south to see if I could get a glimpse of the 'letter that isn't read'. I failed to see anything like it among the other mountains. The whole place was nothing but a collection of midget mountains. On the south I could see the inlets from the sea between the hills, so that you would think the hills were being submerged and that the sea would soon cover them; or maybe that the hills were rising from the water, and that soon the sea would have receded from the glens between the hills. Looking at them I noticed at once the exact resemblance between the hills and water I saw there and what you see when you look at the south-west corner of the map of Ireland on a school wall. I could not help staying a long while looking at that map that is still there, and how long ago it was put there I nor no one else can tell.

After spending a long time looking at it and thinking about it, I turned east through the fine broad plain on the summit. I had not gone very far when I was badly frightened. Right in front of me was a great wide hole, deep in the hill. It was just the kind of hole that would be left if one of the Paps was plucked from the middle of Mangerton and thrown over to where it now is, beside the other Pap, with the part that was in the hill on the ground, and the narrow end, that was in the hill, turned upward. You would think that if it were lifted from the ground again and put into the hole, with the narrow end of it downward, it would fill the hole, and the summit of Mangerton would be a flat plain, evenly level from side to side, as it was before the other hill was plucked from it.

If I spent a long while looking at the mountains and the inlets of western Ireland, from Berehaven to the Kenmare estuary and Tralee Bay and Dingle Bay, I spent still longer looking into the depths of that hole from which I thought the nearer of Dana's two Paps[2] had been taken long ago. I could not go too near the hole. The fall from the edge was too sudden and if I went too close to the brink the sod might go from under my feet and loose me down the slope. However, I came near enough to see the loch of water that was at the bottom. That loch looks remote and repulsive, dark and desolate.

It seemed to me that the loch was casting some spell on my sight, so long did I stay looking down at it. Whenever I looked about me, east to the two Paps or south to the inlets, before long my eyes would return to that ugly dark loch. Sometimes I glanced across at the eastern side of the hole and saw a beautiful sight; on that far side the sun was shining, and across it the shadows of the little clouds slowly drifted, just as the little clouds themselves were drifting over me in the sky. When I then looked at the loch, and moved a little back or forth, I thought the loch, away down at the bottom of the hole, moved, and swayed back and forth, as the top of the hill itself had done when I was looking north at it from the 'letter that isn't read'.

Whenever I grew tired of looking down at the repulsive, gloomy loch and across to the other side of the hole, and of swaying back and forth to see the swaying below, I looked at the beautiful countryside that lay to the north. By that time it was variegated like the far side of the hole, because the little clouds had spread themselves over all the sky, and the little shadows dotted the whole landscape. I never saw, before or since, a view so grand as the view that was spread before me when I looked west, north and east at that countryside, speckled all over with light and shade. The sky overhead was chequered in the same way, but with this difference: what was shade below was light above, and what was light below was shade above. The little clouds in the sky were white, lighter than the sky about them. The sunlight fell through the cloudless part of the sky, and it was the small white cloud that cast a shadow on the earth below it.

[2] *Dá Chích Anann*; the name is a reminder of the association of the goddess Ana with the province of Munster, to which, in her beneficent aspect, she gives prosperity.

I spent so much time looking at those fine sights, on the mountains and the inlets south of me, at the countryside – no, at the great spreading countrysides – north of me, at the awesome hole there at my feet, at the gloomy enchanted loch below, swaying and swinging at the bottom of the hole, and at the light and shade that was on them all, that evening was coming before I thought at all that Knockanerubill was a good distance to the north-east and that I had to go there for the night. Even then it was very hard for me to leave the view. It was growing still more beautiful as the sun sank and the light changed and the shadows darkened, and the loch below became, it seemed, still more gloomy and enchanted. I tried to leave. I stood still a little longer. I tried to go again and stood a little longer to look just once more at them all. In the end I ran from the place.

Going down the hill was much easier and swifter than going up. All the same I was a long time descending, because, while that wide prospect lasted, I had to stop and feast my eyes on it again and again. By the time I was at the foot of the hill it was night, so that I had scarcely enough light to cross the Flesk. I crossed it, however, without wetting my feet, and continued north until I set my foot on the Killarney road. By this time it was black night; but it was fine and calm, and before long the moon rose. When the moon was up and I had light it did not matter to me whether it was day or night. I followed on to the east, and came to a spot where a big high stone wall ran north of the road on my left, and on the other side of the wall an old castle. A few days before I had been told that the old castle and that part of the road had a bad name, that a pooka or a ghost or something unnatural of that kind was seen there. It was nearly midnight when I reached the spot. I was thinking of the pooka, but not because I was afraid of him. I was saying to myself that it was very foolish of people to think that pookas would be there at night any more than in the middle of the day. Just then, down the road towards me from the east comes some terrible animal at a fast gallop. There were trees on both sides of the road so that I had no chance of making out what kind of animal it was. I had a little stick in my hand. I raised it, small and trifling as it was. The animal ran towards me until it was in front of me. Just as it was going back past me it was levelled on the road. Half of it got up and continued west at a gallop and the other half stayed on the road. I was examining that half but I could not make out what kind of thing it was. Whereupon it rose from the road and made towards me.

'Stay out from me, whatever you are!' said I, with my little stick lifted. It spoke.

'Oh, wisha! That the divil may break your legs for a donkey,' said he, looking back the road after the thing that had galloped west. 'I beg your pardon!' said he to me. "Tis how I threw myself down off of that villain of a donkey. I levelled him in order to get down. East to Millstreet I'm going. I left Killarney this morning to go over to Millstreet. I was as far east as Barraduv when I met that donkey on the road. I caught him and jumped up on him to take him with me and have a ride a bit of the way. As soon as I was settled on his back and he found he couldn't throw me off, what did he do but turn back the road! I couldn't wheel him round without a reins or a winkers. He'd have me carried back to Killarney again only that I levelled him there on the road. I took a grip of his ear to turn him east, that's how I levelled him, the rogue of a villain!'

Then he told me who he was and why he was going east to Millstreet. He was from the poorhouse in Killarney and he was going on to the poorhouse in Millstreet. He was a boy of fourteen or fifteen. He planned to wrong the donkey, and the donkey gave him twist for twist.

We then continued east together, and were company for each other until we reached the boreen north to the house at Knockanerubill where my relations were living, and where I was going for the night. We parted from one another at that spot and I never saw him again alive or dead.

It was shortly before dawn when I arrived home. The people of the house were asleep, naturally enough. Food and drink were left for me by the fire. I ate and drank, said my prayers and went to bed. No fear but I slept soundly.

William Whittaker Barry (???–1875)
Enniskillen to Ballyshannon, and Killarney to Kenmare in 1865

[William Barry, who describes himself as 'an intelligent and well-informed Englishman', walked nearly a thousand miles through Ireland, visiting twenty counties over a period of ten weeks in 1865. Before travelling across the Irish Sea, he had read many travel books and guides to Ireland, but was anxious that his readers know that he took no notes or extracts from these sources, but rather let them 'pass through' the mind, so that he could write a strictly original, and impartial, description of the country. His account of his travels was published in 1867 under the title *Walking Tour around Ireland in 1865 by an Englishman*.

Barry delights in being a pedestrian traveller, and believes travel on foot is the best way to 'see a country thoroughly and to acquire correct impressions of the manners, habits and customs of the inhabitants, and to know something of their inner life and the way in which they treat strangers.' He is constantly subjected to the queries of fellow travellers he meets at inns about what it is like to travel on foot. They generally assume that he experiences and sees more then they do, and therefore must be more knowlegable about the country.

Barry, like Trotter fifty years before, notes the general denudation of the country by a peasantry seeking fuel, and comments when he is passing through a well-treed demesne, what a joy it is to hear birdsong again, something that, owing to the absence of hedges and trees in Ireland, is rare. He died in 1875 while on a walking tour in the Austrian Tyrol.

I include two extracts from his Irish tour. The first deals with part of his walk between Enniskillen and Ballyshannon, during which his experience of Irish inns leaves a lot to be desired, and he is forced to spend a night in the open. In the second, Barry sets out for Kenmare from Killarney; on the way he climbs Mangerton Mountain with a few companions, and relates an encounter with the mountain dew[1] girls, a curious feature of Killarney tourism of the time. Even through his polite Victorian language one can sense the sexual undertones of the encounter; the prettiness of the girls, the pairing off with the tourists, with each tourist having at least 'one belle to accompany up the mountain', and the lively conversation, in which his fellow travellers indulged in the 'highly reprehensible' practice of using 'double entendres'.]

ENNISKILLEN TO BALLYSHANNON

Having regained the high road, I walked along for many miles until dusk, along the shores of the lake, now and then obtaining good views.[2] The popular route from Enniskillen to Ballyshannon, whither I was bound, is to go by steamer as far as Beleek, and from the results of my own experiences, to be presently detailed, I should certainly advise the reader to follow that usual course. The road along the shore is evidently little traversed. A peasant remarked to me, 'We do not often see so nice a gentleman as you travelling along the road; I suppose you have been disappointed of a car.' I said, 'No, I am walking.' It was now getting dark, I fell into the company of a labouring man, who said I could be well accommodated at a roadside inn called Hazard's, two or three miles further on, and as it was becoming too dark to see much, he volunteered to show me the house. Having arrived there, I asked for a bedroom, and was shown a small room or kind of recess containing two beds, one of which was placed at my disposal. This accommodation I declined. I saw nobody about the place except the host and hostess, and I presumed therefore they would occupy the other bed. But the accommodation here was civilisation itself

[1] A mixture of goat's milk and poteen, the 'Baileys' of the day!
[2] Upper Lough Erne.

compared to my experiences further on. I had at an earlier part of this day's journey been recommended to Duffy's Inn, along this road, so on seeing a light I walked into a house and asked a young woman there, 'Is this Duffy's Inn?' 'Yes', she replied. 'Can I have a bed here?' I asked. 'Part of one,' was the answer. I don't know who my bedfellow or bedfellows was or were to be, whether man, woman, or child, or men, women, or children. I was too disgusted to pursue my enquiries any further, and so I left the house and pursued my journey.

It had now become quite dark, and I had to grope rather than walk along. Presently a private car passed me slowly. The occupants evidently observed the traveller, for they eyed me curiously, but made no observation. Though at this time a crust of bread and a cup of cold water would have been welcome fare, and a doormat a welcome couch, which I would have gladly accepted, I did not like to force myself on the attention of these strangers as a benighted traveller, so I said nothing. After walking a short distance a large black and white dog, which I had not observed, made a sudden lunge at my shoulder, but I managed to keep him off with my umbrella. The labouring man, in reply to some questions of mine, [had] said I might walk all night without being interfered with by man or dog. I thought this incident a practical commentary on such information. There was no moon this night, and the stars, which had furnished a flickering light, presently were enveloped by clouds, and the darkness was literally Egyptian, that which might be felt. At length much fatigued, and seeing no hope of meeting with an inn during the night, I turned into a hayfield, and making a pillow of my knapsack, laid down to rest under a haystack. However, though dreadfully tired, I scarcely slept. The geese cackled, reminding me perhaps that I deserved to be one of them for being there at all, the dogs barked and howled, and moreover, sundry insects kept creeping over my face. I felt thankful to St Patrick for having destroyed all the snakes in Ireland, and I laid me down to rest in the most perfect confidence that in this respect he had fully performed his mission. The novelty of sleeping or rather attempting to sleep in the open air, on the bare ground, was singular enough. I am accustomed to sleep with my window open during the summer months, and on awaking on this night from a slight doze it seemed as if more than one window was open; but of course on coming to consciousness I perceived that the windows of heaven were open, windows which no human hand could shut. One thing I observed during this sleepness night. How comes it that two or three insects which find their way into our beds are of a kind so fatal to repose, whereas here, on the dewy ground in an open field, the insects which play over my countenance neither bite, sting nor hurt, but seem only as it were to come and bid me welcome to their habitations? One thing more also occurred to me. This night though dark and dewy, was very fine; but on many wet nights, on the soaking ground, our brave soldiers have lain previously to a day of death or wounds to many, of extreme exertion to all.

The actual distance from Enniskillen to the hayfield where I sought my night's rest was only about nineteen miles, which was very provoking, as with a little forethought and by leaving early I might have reached Beleek ere night. As it was I did not start on my day's journey until 12 o'clock, then two or three hours were spent in the diversion towards Devenish Island, and another hour or so in the visit to Ely Lodge, and thus the day became much abridged. However, 'all's well that ends well'. I did not catch cold, and perhaps it is good to have one night's experience of a bed on the open field. But though in former walking tours I frequently was nearly benighted, yet I always managed to obtain a bed some time about midnight. And I shall be happy if this night's experience be the first and last of its kind.

KILLARNEY TO KENMARE

I left the Muckross Hotel this morning at eleven o'clock with a party of four gentlemen for the purpose of ascending Mangerton Mountain, they for the excursion, and I en route to Kenmare. There is a good road which turns off to the left shortly after you leave the hotel and leads up to the base of the mountain where the cars stop. Shortly after reaching this road we were overtaken by the man with the pony, or horse, I saw yesterday morning. We asked him how one horse would suffice for four men. He replied when one of us got tired he might ride. But suppose two became tired at the same time? This dilemma seemed to perplex him, though had he known the custom of the west country he could have answered we might two of us ride the horse, one behind the other. He proposed to charge so much for the pony, but nothing for himself. Poor animal! I wonder whether he would obtain any extra benefit? I turned and looked at the horse's head. It seemed, poor thing, to look so intelligent and to brighten up so, as if almost it understood the treaty, and were willing to undergo any work to serve its master. But after telling the man plainly that we intended to rely exclusively on our own legs he turned the horse's head and went back again. The views of the lakes and surrounding country to be obtained on this road up to the base of the mountain are very fine, and those who do not like the fatigue of going farther would act wisely if they came thus far either by car or on foot.

When we reached the car stand we encountered the mountain dew girls, who form quite a feature of the ascent of Mangerton. They carry a small can of goat's milk and a small bottle of whisky with a glass, with which they refresh the weary traveller. These two liquids mixed together in proportions according to taste bear the designation of mountain dew, and the purveyors are called mountain dew girls. Nothing less than sixpence will they condescend to receive. They were on this occasion six in number, including two sisters to my mind the prettiest, one eighteen and the younger one sixteen. So each of us had at least one belle to accompany up the mountain. Had choice directed I would have selected the eldest of the two sisters as being the prettier, but chance gave me as companion the younger. She, however, proved so faithful that I began to feel quite in love with her; for carrying a knapsack, and being fatigued from my hard day's work yesterday, I was obliged at the steeper part of the ascent to lag behind and sit down once or twice to rest. But this young girl instead of running on to her companions remained to keep me company, and refreshed by her with a glass of mountain dew, I after a while rejoined my companions. Our conversation was free, but for the most part innocent enough, though one or two of my fellow travellers were indulging in some double entendres which in the case of virtuous girls is a practice highly reprehensible; though my own question to the elder of the two sisters, whether she had many opportunities of changing her condition, passed perhaps the proper bounds of decorum.

I am offered more mountain dew, but decline on the ground that I intend to wait until I reach the Devil's Punch Bowl, being under the impression that there is a booth or hut there where I may obtain an ample supply. At length after some stiff walking we reach this place, which consists of a very small lake in a recess of the mountain, and bearing some resemblance to a punchbowl. Here, however, the spot is barren, there being no hut of any kind. There is what is called a well at this place of which it is deemed good luck to drink, and accordingly we do so. Then my fair young companion reminds me of my pledge to take some more mountain dew at the Devil's Punch Bowl. I state my interpretation of what I meant. It won't do, she says, she only came up so far on my account. As if indeed she would have left her sister and companions and gone back alone from the middle of the mountain. However, a promise is a promise, but I have nothing less than a sovereign. She will get change. I partake of more mountain dew. Then from her companions she obtains the change, for the most part in small coins. For form's sake I count. There is sixpence short. I call the girl's attention to the circumstance. With such a number of coins the slightest explanation would be satisfactory, but she says I had put the sixpence into my other hand. This I felt sure was not the case, so I count again. Still there is sixpence short. Then the young girl looks caught and guilty, and looking down is silent. Oh! what a contrast with the young widow of the Claddagh![3] I give the girl sixpence for the further supply of

[3] A woman to whom he gave twopence-halfpenny (1p) to buy potatoes for her children.

mountain dew, but I am not thus easily to escape from the hands of this impudent young hussy. She further demands threepence for giving change, though it had been done exclusively for her own benefit, on the ground that this charge is customary. As if in this wild spot money could have been changed often enough for any custom to become established in the matter. Nay, more, has any traveller been fool enough ever to change a sovereign here before? I doubt it. However, the young girl looked so flushed and pretty at my stern determination to resist such an unheard of, though small imposition, and my friends and her companions had gone on up the mountainside, leaving me alone engaged in this ridiculous dispute with a mere child, that at length I gave in and handed her a threepenny bit on the express understanding that we parted friends. No sooner was this dispute settled, than an elderly woman I had scarcely observed before, appeared and asked a gratuity, on the ground that she was keeper of the well, though she lived in a cottage at the foot of the mountain; but the request comparatively speaking was a reasonable one, so it was complied with. In the company of the young girl I then ascended the remainder of the mountainside, but it was clear that our reconciliation was a mere sham. She no longer stood before me the artless and innocent mountain girl, but like the rest of the world was 'of the earth, earthy'.[4] The rising good opinion was dashed aside, the opening confidence for ever destroyed. O virtue, how beautiful must be the reality when the semblance for a while can appear so charming! And yet this young girl had with her sister been to mass this very morning. Will she tell this little incident on the mountain to the priest at her next confession? I have my doubts. But before the ink is dry I begin to think I ought to be her father confessor, and conceal this little fault. At least I hope it is the first and last offence of the kind. If so, this young girl will have no reason to regret that the stranger counted his change at the Devil's Punch Bowl.

When I reached my friends we were joined by the owner of the mountain, Mr Herbert's keeper; and being now near the summit, I proposed to read out the account of Mangerton from Murray's Handbook, so we, mountain dew girls and all, sat down, and I read out the description from beginning to end. As I closed the book Mr Herbert's keeper said, 'Very good', but I fancied a shadow had come over the faces of the mountain dew girls, particularly that of the elder and prettiest of the two sisters. Had I given them pain? If so it may do them good, for by being a little less obtrusive they will evince more self-respect, and possessing natural attractions, will by the change, I think, wheedle more money out of the pockets of young gentlemen, and for the matter of that, of old gentlemen too.

4 1 Corinthians xv. 47.

We now stood on the very summit of Mangerton Mountain. The young girl still seemed determined to turn me to some account, for she asked one of my fellow travellers to take some mountain dew on the ground that the gentleman had taken it twice in the course of the ascent, but he excused himself, justly alleging that everyone might do as he pleased. Presently I wished my friends goodbye, and they left to descend the mountain on the other side. The mountain dew girls also departed. There was not a word of adieu to or from them, though when they were gone it seemed as if there had been an omission on one side or the other. I was now left alone with Mr Herbert's keeper, who was good enough to point out the different objects of interest, and I took a leisurely look at the surrounding scene. The general view from the top of Mangerton is certainly disappointing, and by no means equal to that from the Tomies. It does not either come up to the glowing descriptions contained in guidebooks and works of travel. And yet the day was charming, and the horizon most clear. I noted down what I really saw from the summit of Mangerton Mountain. Near at hand you see the Horse's Glen, Devil's Punch Bowl, and an expanse of country; then in the distance the lakes and surrounding district, and rising behind them the Torc and Purple Mountains, and Macgillicuddy's Reeks. The upper lake is seen very indistinctly, which I regretted, as beyond glimpses in the dark last night, and now today from afar, I had no regular opportunity of seeing this lake, which, according to some writers, is the most beautiful and charming of the three.

I now prepared to descend the mountain on the Kenmare side, and Mr Herbert's keeper very considerately advised me to accept the guidance of the three sheep boys, who were about to drive their little flocks to the village below. This advice I followed, and fortunately, for the path, if such it might be called, proved difficult, rugged, and not easy to keep to. For about an hour I continued gradually descending the mountainside, again and again losing the path, and again and again being directed to it by one or other of the sheep boys as he came within call from some distant walk on the mountain, driving before him a sheep or two. At length I reach the foot of the mountain near some houses, and am walking on unconsciously thinking the boys had not reached their destination, but not finding them following I turn back and discover that they go no further. I pause a little, but these small boys ask no gratuity, and apparently expect none; they merely guided me down the mountain out of courtesy. I give one of them sixpence to be divided between himself and his two companions, and this trifle appears quite satisfactory. On leaving them I could not help drawing a contrast between this and the other side of the mountain. At Killarney such a sum would be spurned by the smallest of boys like these as wholly inadequate.

Shortly after leaving the foot of the Mangerton Mountain I gained the high road and proceeded on my way to Kenmare. I passed through Kilgarvan and two or three other villages or hamlets, and the scenery is good. I reached Kenmare after nightfall, and put up at the Lansdowne Arms. This is a good and comfortable hotel, and convenient quarters for excursions to the country around. The waiter here tells me I am the first traveller he has known who has come here from Killarney over the Mangerton Mountain. He says there are wild deer on the mountain, but apart from such a contingency as an attack by them, I should not recommend this route. The descent to the Kenmare side of the mountain is more inaccessible and fatiguing than the ascent from Killarney. I was induced to come this way by the information of Lord Kenmare's gate-keeper, who said the adventurous traveller he mentioned stated he was about to take that route. Moreover, the gatekeeper professed to have some knowlege of his own on the subject. He said I should find Kenmare quite at my feet on descending the mountain, which proved deceptive. The distance from Muckross to the the top of Mangerton is about three miles, and from thence to Kenmare about ten miles.

Henry Chichester Hart
Dingle, County Kerry, and the south Wexford coast in 1883

[Henry Chichester Hart (1847–1908) was the son of Sir Andrew S. Hart, Provost of Trinity College. He was a brilliant botanist, and served as such on the British Polar Expedition of 1875; he was also a knowledgable geologist, and in 1883 took part in an important geological expedition to Palestine. The writer Standish O'Grady described him as 'the handsomest, noblest looking, most superbly formed Irishman of modern times'.[1] His great physical fitness and mountaineering skills allowed him to be the first botanist to access several wilderness mountain areas in Ireland, where he found and identified many new species. His strength and stamina became legendary amongst walkers, as did the prodigious nature of some of his excursions; in 1886, for a wager, he walked from Dublin to the summit of Lugnaquillia, Wicklow's highest mountain, and back, a distance of more than 75 miles, in under 24 hours.

In 1883 Hart embarked on foot on an extensive botanical exploration of the mountains and coasts of Ireland, upon which he wrote papers for the Royal Irish Academy; it is from these papers that I have selected excerpts which include modest comments on his finds, and laconic reports of

[1] Article by W. P. Hackett in the *Irish Monthly*, Vol. 41 (1913).

remarkable walking feats. I have omitted some of the long lists of plants and discussions of species to be found in the original notes to allow the accounts of his treks to be clearer. The first excerpts tells of his visit to the Dingle peninsula. For two weeks, sometimes in 'enduring and extraordinarily soaking rain', and experiencing 'abominable inconveniences' in places in which he stayed, he traversed the peninsula, walking over 300 miles of rough mountainous coastal country and climbing over 24,000 feet. Apart from his discovery of a number of hitherto unknown subspecies, his work confirmed that the number of species of flora on the peninsula was in excess of 510. In the second excerpt he describes part of an extensive tour along the 'changable' Wexford coast.]

THE DINGLE PENINSULA

The area of this mountainous peninsula is 138,996 acres, or about one-eighth part of the county Kerry. It possesses, perhaps, a greater variety of attractions and less accommodation for visitors than any other part of Ireland. There are to be seen here the most perfect Irish antiquities, whether pagan or early Christian. Its geology has been called the key to the geological structure of Ireland. Its peculiar position as the exteme west of Europe, its loneliness, the primitive simplicity of its inhabitants, the grandeur of its scenery, its exquisitely bracing atmosphere, and the many interesting features of its natural history, place it in the forefront ground for a summer's labours in many fields of research.

Its botany is especially interesting, and has drawn thither almost all who have paid attention to the subject in Ireland. Nevertheless, in consequence perhaps of the lack of roads and hotel accommodation, it required and still requires further examination . . .

The coastline is for the most part precipitous; the western and southern portion from Cloghane to Anniscaul almost entirely so. The rock formation of Brandon belongs to the Silurian group, and is chiefly composed of grits, slates and sandstones. The remainder of the extreme promontory consists of an upper series of rocks of a similar nature, known to geologists as the Dingle beds. The inner or eastern part of the peninsula is formed of Lower Carboniferous rocks, and here limestone is more frequently met with. The main part of the barony is unreclaimed, and cultivation is chiefly to be met with along the coast margin on the northern and south-western shores and in the valleys.

There have been several dubious and unverified records of plants from this promontory, both from the mountains and from the sea coast. With a hope to settle some of these, I walked the whole sea margin from Tralee to Castlemaine, as well as spending some days on and in the neighbourhood of Brandon. My chief headquarters were at Castlegregory, Cloghane, Ballynagall and Dingle. With the exception of Dingle, a visitor should make previous arrangements at these places, and I would recommend him to enter the promontory with a supply of provisions. At Ballynagall, a retired coastguard, who gave me clean accommodation, told me no visitor had been there except fish dealers since Du Noyer the geologist's time,[2] and I found this lonely spot, by the western flank of Brandon, the most delightful in the peninsula.

On the following day, July 5th, I traversed the mountains, Benooskey, Slievenagower, Slievenalacka, Slieveanea, and Connor Hill to Dingle. Benoosky is 2,715 feet, and reaches to alpine vegetation. The two commonest bona fide alpine species in Ireland occur from 300 feet below the summit upwards. These are *Salix Herbacea* and *Carex rigida*. *Armeria*[3] also occurs, and it is always surprising to meet this species at the summit and at the base of seacoast mountains while it does not occupy the middle distance. Slievemore in Achill gives a remarkable instance of this. *Saxifraga stellaris* and *sedum rhodiola*[4] accompanied the true alpines, and in this latitude they nearly deserve the same appellation . . . The district gone over today was varied and interesting, and many of the glens and lake shores would repay more elaborate research. I crossed habitats of Killarney fern and *Sibthorpia*,[5] but my labours were chiefly devoted to the higher ground. Towards night I sighted Dingle, and was fain to look for the hotel. Thinking I could telegraph to Castlegregory, I descended to the town, which looked so tempting in its lake-like bay. I had to remain the night, however, without sending word to my hospitable landlady, to the no small alarm of the Castlegregorians . . .

On the 10 July I finally left Cloghane. The mountains were enveloped in heavy cloud, more and more aqueous as I ascended. In order to avoid loss of time, I accepted the offer of a mountaineer I met on the way to accompany me and bring me the quickest way to the largest loughs under Brandon Peak to its east . . . I had put many leading questions to my companion, with a hope of extracting some reliable information on the natural history of the district, and I may be excused for repeating the following: 'In Lough Veagh, or the "white lake" (one of those which I had visited yesterday, but which, as is frequently the case, has a different name

---

[2] G. V. Du Noyer (1817–69) joined the Geological Survey in Ireland in 1848, and spent much of the year 1856 carrying out a survey of the Dingle peninsula.
[3] Dwarf willow; a sedge; thrift, which is more a sea cliff plant than an alpine species; it is rare on the tops of Irish mountains, but it is found commonly on the summits of some of the Scottish peaks.
[4] Star saxifrage; rosefoot.
[5] A member of the figwort family.

on the map), the people get pearl mussels. Three or four men went there lately with oilskins and dived for them. These come off an enormous animal called the "carrabuncle", which is often seen glittering like silver in the water at night. The animal has gold and jewels and precious stones hanging to it, and shells galore; the inside of the shells shines with gold. The divers hoped to have caught the "carrabuncle" himself.' This shining appearance in the water of the Kerry lakes is alluded to by Smith,[6] who gives it the same name, but without a full explanation like the present. It is to be hoped that the 'carrabuncle' will find its way to our new National Museum.

Turning a deaf ear to my cicerone's remonstrances, and telling him to meet me by what way he chose on the summit, I made my way into the cliffs by a somewhat dangerous gully, at about 1,600 feet above sea level. After a stiff climb for 300 feet, I came to the best alpine ground in Brandon, better than any on Macgillicuddy's Reeks . . . Having rounded the head of this glen above Coomaknock lakes, I came out on the ridge and followed it northwards by the head of the Feany valley . . . About a mile and an eighth north of the summit of Brandon along this ridge, and close to the ruins of an old signal tower,[7] I discovered *Polygonum viviparum*, a high alpine species, not known in Ireland south of Ben Bulben in Sligo. From here I struck down the west side of Brandon and walked into Dingle.

SOUTH WEXFORD

At Lady's Island I found a 'boycotted' publican; here I rested for an hour, and heard his side of the 'burning question'. I then made my way by the shores of the lake to the sea coast, almost to the point I left. I have already mentioned the distribution of *Diotis maritima*. Here the walking became very laborious, in soft, heavy sand, along the narrow strip between Tacumshin and the sea . . . After a while I was alone on a sandy waste, a high bank of shingle and sand forming a bar between the lake and the sea. I had gone a little way round the shore of this lake at first inland, but it was low, flat and muddy, and the long strip of sandy coast looked more promising. What was my horror, after about two hours' wearisome labour, to find a swift blue torrent, over a hundred yards across, foaming out of the lake into the surge of the sea. It was out of the question to go back. I

[6] Charles Smith, *The Antient and Present State of the County of Kerry*, 1756
[7] He would have had to cross the saddle to Massatiompan to reach the nearest signal tower, about 2.5 km from Brandon summit.

would have lost a whole day by doing so, and nothing would have induced me to face that sandy trudge again. There was neither boat nor human being in sight. I felt evilly disposed towards several persons who knew where I was bound for, and had not intelligence enough to warn me, especially towards the Ordnance map, which is quite out of date for this changable coast. On the map is marked a channel from Lady's Island Lake, and a continuous coast outside Tacumshin. The reverse is the true state of things. With some misgivings, I resolved to swim. This necessitated three journeys: one with my knapsack, which I emptied on the opposite side; one back with it empty, and a third with my clothes, boots, etc., in the knapsack. The knapsack floated bravely, and I towed it with a strap in my teeth. Each time I started about forty or fifty yards higher up the current than the point opposite; but on the third time, whether I was tired or the knapsack was very much heavier, I was carried well into the strength of the current at the bar, and began to wonder how far it was to Cardigan Bay. However, I accomplished the transport and resumed the journey. A few miles more brought me to a clean little inn at Kilmore.

Mary Banim (1874–1939)
The Aran Islands *c*.1887

[Mary Banim was the daughter of Michael Banim (1796–1884). She was a contributor to *Providence Sunday Journal* during the 1880s, and her *Here and There through Ireland*, an informal travelogue, was published in 1891. On Aranmore she stayed at the Atlantic Hotel, where a few years later Yeats would stay, and in 1898 J. M. Synge, on his first visit to the islands. She travelled to Aranmore by steamer, 'packed with a crowd of very ordinary pleasure seekers in ordinary European costume', who found the islanders 'as foreign-looking as if we were suddenly transported into the midst of the African in place of the Irish desert.' The selected extract from *Here and There Through Ireland* describes her first walk on Aranmore.]

Leaving behind us the Courthouse, with its little group of fishermen looking in at the open door, we set off briskly southwards, having the bay and a low white strand on the left of the road, the solid rocks of Aran on the right. But what rocks! Every seam, every tiny opening, gave forth its flower or fern. Tufts of the dark leaves that I knew meant scented violets – white violets, Mary said they were – the bright blue heather bell in quantities; primrose leaves; woodbine drooping through blackberry branches; hart's tongue, maidenhair, and spleenwort ferns; wreaths of which it grows one sheet of rosy bloom; the hoary rock rose; ox-eye daisies – flowers in every impossible spot. To look at those hard, cold stones, bare of any covering of earth, one could be at a loss to account for the existence of any plant, not to say of such luxuriance of blossoms as is rare in many a rich country. Whatever time, heat, or the work of the inhabitants in breaking up the surface of the rocks had made even a chink, there a seedling had taken root, had gone on, year after year, fertilising, with the decay of its own leaves, the narrow groove that sheltered the root, and so making a deposit of fine mould that sends out all this beauty, to transform each rugged stone into what the natives, with genuine poet's licence, call every division of their rocky territory – a garden.

The sands too proved full of inducements to stop now and again to enjoy what seems a pleasure to all, from childhood to old age – gathering the dainty little pink shells – cuni shells the people here call them. These, as well as other shells, are in quantities about the inner circle made by the waves at high tide.

We had been joined in our walk by a pretty, bright little girl, neat and clean, about ten years old, and quite ready to chat about everything she had ever seen in her life; quite ready, and able too, to spell the name of every object around us; not a word did she miss, and very few mistakes did she make in such small sums as – how many shells should she have left for herself, 'supposing' she brought home twelve and gave two each to her four little sisters? How many chickens would come out of a clutch of ten eggs, supposing two were bad to begin with and the thunder addled three more? As she answered me so frankly and intelligently, I thought that if this little child, in her simple island dress – a red petticoat, a little cotton frock pinned up like her mother's, and neat pampootys[1] on the tiny feet – were landed suddenly in some fine city drawingroom, amongst children of her own age, be-laced, be-velveted, and precocious in matters of worldly wisdom, how the spoilt young fashionables would stare and politely giggle at the little Irish peasant. Yet Kitty could speak two languages fluently and well, could spell and read better than ninety per cent of the children of advanced civilisation, and had those most attractive of manners – the naturally natural.

Continuing our walk, the road led us on under the stony hill, where, at

---

[1] Leather moccasins that were traditionally worn in the Aran Islands.

long intervals, could be seen the tiny patches of ground made by the hard toil of the people. Naturally, there is not a spot of earth on any of these islands; but the law of their owners, since the English gained possession of them, has been to exact from every tenant that a certain portion of the rock shall be broken up, sea sand and seaweed carried up, load by load, by the men and women, and thus gradually accumulated on the spot partially cleared of the upper crust of stone; but when this little patch of land is made, it is appraised by him who says he owns the stones, and the maker henceforth has the privilege of paying a smart rent for what the labour of his own and his children's hands has made. Of course these little spots of earth are but shallow layers on a solid stone foundation, so that a dry season means the total failure of the crop of potatoes or oats – almost the only crops grown. At the best of times it is just barely possible to meet the rent with the help of the kelp and fish, which at best do not bring in very much, but when the potatoes fail, every available penny is swallowed up by the rent; often it cannot be met at all, and then famine and eviction are the fate of the islanders.

A marvellous sight are the broad tables of solid flag that border the highway, and as we look up at the bare, shining hills of limestone, and see nothing but sand and stone and sea as far as the eye can reach, we find it almost impossible to realise that over three thousand human beings live on these island deserts, and, until quite recently, when the Land Commissioners made some much needed reductions in the rents, paid £3,000 per annum for permission to inhabit the place and use the bits of land they themselves had made. . . .

Here too, along either side of the road, are memorial crosses erected on this, the way to the cemetery, by the different families whose relatives lie in the burial ground about a mile and a half further on. These monuments are almost exactly similar to those to be found in Brittany, and are here very numerous. A square pillar, surmounted by a smaller square erection, in the face of which are inserted two slabs bearing the names of the persons to whose memory they are erected; the whole surmounted by a cross on which is, in some cases, a rudely carved Crucifixion. The monuments are in groups – sometimes three, sometimes six or more, and near them are cairns, or heaps of stones, piled up by those accompanying a funeral, each person at the funeral adding a stone to the heap . . . I stood on one flag beside a group of crosses and counted thirty different plants in full bloom, growing in wild luxuriance from out every crevice around my feet. If the islanders were only ethereal enough to be able to live on flowers, they could never know want – but, graceful and charming though they be, flowers will only fill the eye, and, from a practical point of view, the contrast between the plenteousness of hanging brambles, lace-like ferns, and bright blossoms, and the smallness and scarcity of the little patches of potatoes or corn, must at times strike sadly on the hearts of poor fathers and mothers with eight or ten little children to feed every day.

Many of those same poor fathers and mothers were to be seen about the village of Killeany, which lies about a mile to the south of Kilronan, and still on the eastern shore; a very poor village, chiefly inhabited by fishermen, whose trade scents the air less poetically than the flowers. But, as I said before, the people can't live on blossoms, and the bream and other fish which they dry here are the staple commerce of the fishermen, who take the dried fish in loads to Galway, getting about 5s[2] per hundred for them. The bream are prepared by the very simple process of splitting them open and drying them in the sun, and all round Killeany the stone walls are to be seen covered with the ugly, staring fish.

Very poor the people and very poor the houses are in Killeany, but, like all the Aran folk, the villagers are gentle and ready to oblige. One fine boy left a cabin to show us the way to another we were in search of, and both he and the baby he carried on his back were so bright and rosy I could not help asking what they lived on to get such rosy cheeks. Fish and potatoes, the child said. At the cabin sought for was one of the most wretched-looking poor women I have ever seen – not old, but aged from sickness, and pitiably ugly, partly idiotic from birth, deaf, deformed, and half blind. She had no relative in the world, I understood, whose duty it would be to provide for her, but 'of course, the neighbours cared for and helped her along out of the little they had.' Here was a practical lesson in charity. The previous year had been one of such continued drought on the islands that the entire crops had failed, and famine must have carried off half the people had not benevolence come to their assistance, yet this poor, helpless, useless creature had been cared for and watched over by her half-starving neighbours. There was no use in trying to speak with the poor creature, for, even were she not deaf, she knew no English. But it was not so with our next acquaintance; she had not much English, to be sure, but what she lacked was replaced by gestures so eloquent that there was little need of an interpreter. And here again I found an example of the Christian kindliness of the poor to each other. This old woman had buried all her children; her husband had died in their young days; she could no longer work, for old age and rheumatism had made her almost a cripple, yet she too was the adopted of the poor, and never was left without the day's food. She was not from this part of the island, but from the other end where the chapel stands, and one of her sorrows was that she could never again go such a distance to hear mass on Sundays. But, sure as the Sunday was fine, she dragged her old limbs up to the holy Mass Rock and

[2] 25p in today's money.

the blessed well above there on the hill. Never in her whole life had she been away from the Aran Islands – never farther from home than the South Island, and that was many a long day ago. The poor old woman was highly pleased to have a talk, and came to sit by the water's edge close to the ruined Fort of Ardkin. . . .

Being now sufficiently rested, we resumed our explorings by beginning the ascent of the hill right in front of us. When about half way up we came suddenly on a spot such as I could never have dreamt of seeing in this stony region – an emerald belt of land, carpeted by a soft, rich grass that felt like velvet under our feet. This narrow, verdant plateau continues for a space to wind along the side of the hill; above and below are the eternal rocks, but rocks so richly decorated with wild flowers that even their rugged faces began to grow lovely in my eyes, so tenderly did the graceful vines and blossoms seem to encircle them with love and beauty.

Certainly there is a strange charm about the whole place – a charm that seems gradually to throw a kind of fascination over the mind, and that makes one almost feel as if in some enchanted land. The clear and balmy air; the quiet of the people, who have something of the stillness of a lonely place in their ways and manners, yet have nothing whatever approaching to sadness in either; the beauties of sea, of sky, of bold, rugged cliff scenery which nature has lavished around, as if to divert the eye and mind away from the awful sterility of the islands themselves. All combine to make what the saints of old appear to have found the Aran Isles: happy and peaceful retreats from the cares and temptations of the world.

'This is the Angels' Walk,' said Mary, as we stood upon the soft green sward, 'an' it's here the Guardian Angels of Aran come, of a summer's night, to take their diversion.' It is a sweet spot the angels have chosen, this long path of velvety turf, whereon they may walk, side by side, and look abroad over the wide moonlit bay until they come to the old Mass Rock and the holy well of St Enda (or St Aeny), which terminates this veritable oasis in the desert of stone. The Mass Rock is a rude stone altar, covered with a large slab; standing upright at the back of the altar table is a smaller slab on which is traced a cross; beside this a holy well, whose waters are clear and limpid, is roofed in with a long flag, the whole wreathed above and around with trailing briars, woodbine, wild vines, and drooping ferns. Here, in former days, mass was said, and here the people still come to offer up their prayers and take a draught of the blessed waters of St Aeny's well, a shell for this use lying on the altar stone. I thought a lovelier church in which to worship the Creator of this beautiful world could scarcely be found than this lonely spot, hallowed by so many sacred memories.

From the 'Angels' Walk' and St Enda's Well we climbed the remainder of the rocky hill, our path leading zigzag hither and thither over the flags and through the curious stone walls until we reached, on the highest point of the island, 'Teampull Benain',[3] the ruin of what is said to be one of the oldest Christian churches in Western Europe; a very small and simple structure, of the early order of Christian architecture. A peculiarity of this little oratory is that it lies north and south, contrary to the almost universal custom observed in the building of churches. The gables and walls of Teampull Benain are still in a good state of preservation; in one of the side walls – the western – is a stone curiously large in proportion with the size of the building; this stone measures four feet by four, while the entire length of the church is but fifteen feet one inch.

Immediately behind Teampull Benain are the remains of a house supposed to have been the dwelling of St Benignus, and to have been built in the fifth century. It is a strong stone building, with portions of the walls of small square cells adjoining. In the shelter of this dwelling we sat down to gaze on the lovely view spread around and to have a good chat with our guide about whatever should come to our minds, for I found that the only way to learn anything of the real thoughts and feelings of the people was just to let subjects come of themselves, and leave catechizings alone. So we rested in the shade of the old house that had seen so many centuries come and go, and looked out on the very same scenes that had charmed the eyes of the warlike Firbolgs three thousand years ago, of the Christian recluses of the earliest days of Christianity in Ireland, and of the many generations of Celts inhabiting these curious islands up to this very hour. The wide Atlantic rolled in and in, and, foaming and beating along by the farthest of the islands, dashed in feathery spray high up the walls of the Cliffs of Moher opposite. Far to south – faint outlines on the horizon – we could just discern the Brandon Hill in Kerry, so named after St Brendan the Navigator, whose oratory is still to be seen on the summit of that mountain from whose base the saint embarked on his famous seven years' voyage on the Atlantic Ocean. To the west the long line of sea, every wave sparkling in the brilliant sunlight; to the east, the Bay of Galway stretched in between the high headlands of Clare on one hand and the low Connemara and Galway shores on the other. All around us were the ruins that spoke of ages past, while below at our feet the quiet life of the primitive Aran people went on – much as it had gone on during those same centuries – dividing our attention, as the way of life is, between majestic scenery, remains of a far-away time that brought thoughts of an existence almost mystic in its holy isolation, and the simple everyday comings and goings in the hamlet below . . . While we rested in this lovely spot a most beautiful appearance on the sea – the effect of the sun on a passing shower

[3] Benain or Benignus was a follower of St Patrick, and his successor.

some miles off – brought to our minds 'Hy Brasail',[4] the enchanted land seen from the north-west extremity of the island, as Mary assured us. As we watched it seemed to us as if a flood of rose-coloured oil covered a part of the sea; this rosy colour moved along, then slowly arose, like a cloud in the air, turning, after a few minutes, to a brilliant green, and so moved onwards until it neared the Cliffs of Moher, when it again settled down on the waters and once more spread out like a crimson flood.

An tAthair Pádraig Ó Dúinnín (1860–1934)
Incheelagh[1] and Gougane Barra, County Cork, *c*.1895

[Born in County Kerry, Pádraig Ó Duinnin entered the Jesuit order in 1880 and went on to study at UCD, where his Latin tutor was Gerard Manley Hopkins. He taught at Mungret College in Limerick and Clongowes Wood, County Kildare, joined the Gaelic League and knew Douglas Hyde and Padraig Pearse. He began to write fiction and poetry around 1900, and in 1904 he produced a comprehensive English–Irish dictionary. In 1902 he wrote a little-known travelogue of Killarney and surrounding area entitled *Cill Áirne*, which was published by Conradh na Gaeilge. I have selected an excerpt from this work which describes walking in the mountains near Gougane Barra in County Cork. The excerpt was translated by Jim O'Malley of Killarney, who drew my attention to it.]

Even though Gougane is a considerable distance from Killarney, I feel that there is no other place in Ireland more similar to the environs of Killarney, which we have already described, than that beautiful lake that lies beneath the dark and melancholy hills. For this reason I wish to give an account of a trip that I made some time ago to Incheelagh and Gougane. It was a day at the end of autumn. A storm, accompanied by rain, filled the rivers and the lakes, which it made difficult to travel the road, and the streams cascaded noisily from the mountain tops.

4 Hy Brasil was a mysterious island, neither land nor sea, and hovering always between night and day. It was thought to lie far out to sea at the same latitude as Ireland, and it appeared on medieval maps under several names. The Aran Islanders claimed that it became visible every seven years.
1 Inchigeelagh.

The train brought me to Macroom. It was almost 5.30 in the evening when it reached the station. It was still bright and I felt energetic. I was told that Incheelagh was about eight miles away and that there were no beautiful sights until one reached Incheelagh. I began my walk in a lively fashion. But within an hour night fell with dark clouds all around and a misty rain enveloped me from every side to such an extent that I could not see my hand. I had never previously walked this road; dark and chilling thoughts assailed me as I tried to make out the hills around through a blanket of fog – what shape had they, what age were they and so forth? Were they covered in great masses of heather? I had no answers. At times the lonely sound of the streams resounded in my ears as it raced over rocks in the stillness of the night. But soon the rain fell unrelentingly and I was drowned wet when I reached Incheelagh.

The deluge lasted all night. Despite my weariness and the comfort of sleep, I could hear the violent clatter of rain pounding the roof and the nearby lakes with a fierce noise.

I awoke early in the morning. I was most eager to see the scenery along the way from Incheelagh to Gougane at my ease. But the rain had not ceased. One would have thought that it had rained abundantly during the night without persisting in the morning. But it poured more than ever and grew in intensity as the hours passed.

My patience had exhausted itself. I grew tired of waiting and I set out despite the downpour. The river Lee runs alongside the road from Ballingeary to Incheelagh and just at about the halfway point it expands into a series of lakes, known as Lough Allua. However, the rain could not last forever. Shortly afterwards the rain ceased and the sun shone brightly. It was wonderful to behold the sparkling sunbeams after such a terrible storm. It lit up the slopes of the rugged hills and the water sparkled like clear glass. Once the rain and mist had cleared one could see the outline of every mountain and the bulk of every rock along the road. The volume of rainwater had flooded the road, making it difficult to walk, and the streams intensified by the moment. As I approached Gougane the mountains on either side grew taller and wilder and the river raced along in a violent torrent releasing itself from the overhead hills. Due to the level of the water it was difficult to cross to the island in Gougane that night. It had become a real island.

On the following morning the flood had subsided and the sun vividly lit up the ridges of the hills; I walked west to Coomroe – a rugged narrow valley in the mountains – and even though the heather was very wet I climbed the peak close to Maoulagh (Maolach). When I reached the top, I looked down at the spot that I had left. The lonely lake nestled under the bare hills and the fragrant isle in its solitude appeared to be a sanctuary for the celestial angels. The lake was silent – not even the chirp of birds in the sky, and the great hills casting a giant shadow over its waters. The valley resounded with the roar of streams cascading violently from the mountain tops.

It was a sight to behold – such unruly, angry streams flowing, dancing, revelling, at times hiding in masses of heather, at other times forming loughs from which waterfalls fell noisily to earth. They exploded violently on reaching the gound, dispersing their volume into many channels and then racing in a torrent to the lake. It was wonderful to observe, from the shoulder of Maoulagh, the fury of the flood dissolving itself into a crispy white foam amongst the rocks. It was a wonder to gaze at the shadows of the tall mountains casting their reflections over the surface of the lake.

Coomroe lay lonely and sullen down below me. To the north I saw a most unusual view of the two Paps and the hills east of Caherbarnagh and the Reeks extending to Beara. They resembled giants vividly exposing their rugged features over sea and land.

Perhaps the cool breeze, blowing across the hills, bestirring the clumps of heather or playing with the blue waves, or bending the branches of the willows on the islet or sighing in the streams of Coomroe – perhaps it tells the tale of great deeds that occurred here in the distant past; of the conflict between O'Sullivan Beara[2] and Carew, of the watchfulness of the O'Sullivans from the mountains over the alien sea, looking to see if a Spanish armada was coming to their assistance. Perhaps it sings again the music of the bards and poets that held sway in this mountain fortress, the music that was recalled by the fireside for generations, that both delighted and grieved the tribe of the Gael.

Some time after the walk described above I revisited Gougane. It was quite wet but the rain could not defeat my determination, and my companion, Dr Lynch from Ballyvourney, was equally determined. The road from Ballyvourney to Ballingeary is rugged and demanding and the hills were shrouded in a fog, which meant that we had no views of the peaks along the way. From Ballingeary we walked to Keimaneigh. As we reached the entrance to the Pass, the rain poured down in a torrent, but we persisted steadily to the far end of the Pass.

It is difficult to describe the features of this way as it lay before us beneath a mantle of fog and rain. Not only did it inspire awe and desolation but one felt that the place cast a spell over the dark blue cliff faces all around, over the dark rocks hanging far above, over the great clouds of fog that had settled on the dense forests of heather, and even over the rain that sent streams hurtling down every cliff and left the road heavily flooded beneath our feet. At times I thought that I was passing through the rooms

[2] Donal Cam O'Sullivan Beare: see page 179.

of an enchanted castle by the ocean where a spring tide was filling with all its might to swallow me in its maw. The Pass revealed many different aspects of itself as every part of it grew more wonderful and beautiful, and there is a variety of vegetation along the faces of the cliffs. On our return journey through the Pass the day brightened and the heather and bushes gleamed brightly in the sunshine.

Stephen Gwynn (1864–1950)
County Donegal in 1899

[Stephen Gwynn was born in Dublin and reared in Donegal. After attending Oxford University, he had a full and varied career in literature and politics, and in spite of being aged fifty at the outbreak, served with distinction in the Connaught Rangers during the First World War.

The following extracts are taken from *Highways and Byways of Donegal and Antrim*, published in 1899, a travelogue of the northern coastal counties of Ireland, as fresh today as the day it was written. The bicycle was at the height of its early popularity in the 1890s, and Gwynn cycled a meandering route through the two counties, leaving his 'machine' and taking to shank's mare when only walking was possible. One of these places was Slieve League, where the mountains of south Donegal drop dramatically and abruptly into the sea; this is the subject of the first excerpt. In the second excerpt Gwynn tells of a walk in the valley of Glencolmcille and up across the cliffs to the Sturrell Point, with a local man named Gillespie as a guide.

His descriptions of the flora and fauna of the area have a sense of having been written only yesterday, and together with his account of the riches of antiquarian interest inspire one immediately to visit the place.]

SLIEVE LEAGUE

To see Slieve League is possible by the use of a boat, a pony, or your legs: not by bicycle. I recommend a boat for all this cliff scenery, time and weather permitting. There is said to be a cave of extraordinary dimensions in the Slieve League cliff, but I must describe the thing as I saw it from on foot.

Leaving the hotel, one walks down a road which follows the swift and rocky course of the Glen River seawards for about two miles; then a track turns off to the right up which ponies can carry a lady almost to the very top. A few hundred yards further on a road branches away also to the right, towards what simply appears to be a very high mountain with a sharply serrated ridge defined against the sky. The other side of that mountain is a precipitous cliff varying from 1,000 to 2,000 feet, and part of the serrated ridge is the One Man's Path. All the water you can see from here is the estuary winding down to Teelin Harbour, and beyond that the mouth of Donegal Bay with the Sligo mountains showing blue on the far side.

The road goes on for a considerable way and turns into a path up which a donkey can travel; I made the journey in company with a man who was going up to cut turf. Here in Glen Columbkille parish they get their firing free, but they have to go a far way for it in some cases. A few of the more fortunate can cut on their own farms; my companion had to ascend at least a thousand feet before he reached his own particular bog; yet there are plenty less lucky than he, for they have not all donkeys to carry the sods. He was a fisherman by trade and belonged to the crew of a yawl, one of the rowboats which go out to fish for cod, ling, and mackerel off this rocky coast. They never go far from Teelin, as it is the only safe place to run to. Most of the fish caught in this way is sold to cadgers or travelling hawkers; the Congested Districts Board[1] make no objection to this trade provided the price given is at least sixpence a dozen above what they give at their curing station. For instance, if the Board's price is 5s a dozen for ling, the men who deal with them must not sell ling to the cadgers under 5s 6d a dozen. My friend seemed to envy the more fortunate crews of smacks who take to the nets and go round to Galway Bay or Downings Bay in Sheephaven; but he had 'an old father and mother that had no other son but him', and they objected to these protracted and risky cruises. On every smack is a crew of eight; six Irish, and with them two Scotchmen, who are regularly retained by the Board at a fixed wage to teach the others how and where to shoot their nets and how to mend and keep them. It is a school of technical education and one sorely needed, for the Irish have never at any time used the sea for peace or war, and the men seem to take to it. I saw a gang of a dozen tramping in from Malin More and Glen Columbkille to a day's net mending, after which they must tramp back the eight Irish miles, for there is no place in Malin More or Glen where a smack can find refuge, and even rowboats, if there be any ground swell, are hard set to it to get in without a shattering. These details, I confess,

[1] The Congested Districts Board was established in 1891 to encourage agriculture and industry in poor parts of the country.

seemed to me more interesting than scenery, and when my acquaintance broke off to show me a slab called the Giant's Grave with some old wives' story attached to it, I headed him off antiquities.

But when one reached the cliff edge and saw the sea a thousand feet below and the Connaught coast stretching away in its interminable line, one felt there was something to be said for scenery. Carrigan Head is below on the left, where stands one of the old signal towers,[2] which communicates with Malin Beg, that with Glen Head, and so on. From this brow the grassy path runs level for a bit along the cliff edge till you come to the side of Bunglass – a sort of horseshoe bend or bight in the three miles of cliff – and from this you see Slieve League in all its glory. About a thousand feet below you is the blue water, bright green round the rock base, and breaking upon what seems to be smooth fine sand, but really consists of water-worn pebbles big as your two fists. About a thousand feet higher than you stand rises the cliff on the far side of the bay, and its seaward front shows a singular variety, red and yellow in streaks, beside the greys and browns, for Slieve League is not granite. But the extraordinary beauty of the scene was given by a sight which must be common at that point. It was blowing half a gale, the bay was full of spindrift, and the sun striking on this made a rainbow right below us, arched against sea and cliff. I never realised what intensity of colour was before.

From this point you begin a really stiff climb, following the edge of the cliff in its upward winding. The stiffest of the actual climb is over when you get to the One Man's Path. Here the cliff top is literally a narrow edge of stone about two feet across, mounting very steep for about fifteen yards. It must be done on hands and knees. On your right inland is a very steep slope running down towards a tarn;[3] on the seaward side is practically a straight drop, but only over a heathery slope. It is my opinion that if you fell off the One Man's Path on the landside you would roll down with little damage, and that if you fell off on the seaward side you would be able to stop yourself by clinging to the heather. My guide – for I took the gentleman with the ass as a guide – was of a very different opinion; and there is no doubt that although the cliffs here are not absolutely plumb – as they are at Glen Head and Horn Head – you could toboggan down them with every certainty of a speedy run to the bottom. But the One Man's Path is nothing to be afraid of. Your guide, if you have one, will industriously try to frighten you, and then flatter you when you have got across. All I can say for mine is that he was genuinely afraid, for he

---

[2] One of a series of signal towers built and manned around the coast during the Napoleonic Wars to give early warning of a French invasion.
[3] Lough Agh.

declined to carry my macintosh over the place, on the ground that his boots were bad, and I had to wear it, which gave me an insight into the difficulties of cliff work for ladies. The path can be circumvented on the inner side, and with a strong wind may be an ugly spot enough to cross. Oddly enough, the day I was there some eddy of wind protected it from blasts, though a little further up one could hardly stand.

Further on a little, one sees the Chimneys – some not very interesting pinnacles of rock – halfway down the cliff, but the view from the top is wonderful. The whole of Donegal Bay and the Sligo coast is spread out to the south and south-west; inland are the mountains from Lough Erne to the Glen Beagh range, and north-east you see Glen Bay and Glen Head, and the coast away up by Ardara and Glenties. West and north-west stretches the limitless Atlantic. On a bright sunny day, with wind about one, that place gives the sense of immense space more strongly than I ever experienced it before. On a ship you have sea all about you – perhaps nothing but sea – but you are not looking straight over ocean and land at once from a height of two thousand feet.

Coming back is an easy affair. You will see the pony track in the valley below you, and it will take you back to the road; an hour's very fast walking brings you to the hotel. The whole thing should take an active man four or five hours. Tourists should be careful to believe what they are told about the dangers of Slieve League when it is capped with mist. Under these conditions a guide is indispensable. Anyone who wishes to walk back across the mountain will find it rough work, and possibly dangerous, even on a clear day, to people who do not understand bogs. In a short cut which I took I saw several very nasty-looking places. The mountain is full of hares, which add a charm of wildlife to it, and everywhere one is haunted by the pretty little snow buntings, a bird strange to English eyes.

GLENCOLMCILLE AND THE STURRELL POINT

As we went up the Glen I marvelled more than ever at the flowers; blue-bells everywhere – saw even some white ones; marsh marigolds; orchises bright purple or pale and livid; white pignuts; a few surviving primroses, and a few early flag irises; I saw even one foxglove that day – May 29 – but it was at Carrick. There were all the vetches, from the tiny yellow lady's finger to the taller purple kinds; a handsome purple thornless thistle; bog cotton, of course, and the fragrant bog myrtle on boggy heather slopes, and a queer little fleshy pink flower, almost like a great lichen in its leaf, whose name I have forgot. In the ditches were purple bog violets with their picturesque mottled leaf; and above all, by the little river which runs up the Glen – as also by the Carrick River – quantities of *Osmunda*[4] growing already to a lordly height. It reaches six or seven feet. The valley is full of a swamp, a great place for snipe, Gillespie told me; a great place also for otters, which abound in this region both in sea and rivers. In the grey stony face of Craig Beevna, which overhangs the valley, badgers abound, and there are foxes on the hills. Of this wildlife I saw no trace, but there were numerous birds of the bunting order which were strange to me, and I could not put names to them. Altogether it should be a good camping ground for a naturalist.

One of the most interesting things in the Glen – more interesting even than the crosses or Columbkille's ruined chapel on the hillside[5] – is a cave in the cemetery of the Protestant church which was discovered by chance by men digging a grave not long ago. It is an artificial underground passage leading between two underground rooms. The roof is constructed of immense transverse slabs of stone. A precisely similar cave is found in a field at Ardrummon on Lough Swilly, and is always said to have been one door of a passage communicating with Killydonnell Abbey, a mile or so away. No doubt they were built as places of refuge. But perhaps still more interesting are the old remains of huts, roofed in likewise with huge stones, somewhat on the plan of cromlechs. These buildings a little way up the valley on the left occur in a regular group. One of these, alas! is, by a utilitarian generation, converted into a pigsty. One has a fern growing in luxuriant grace across its doorway. What they were for, what species of hermits lived in them – whether St Columba's mysterious sect of the Culdees[6] or others – is matter for conjecture. My guide set them down as pagan.

The day was misty, as I have said, but Gillespie observed that I might never be there again, so up the head he took me to the Sturrell or Spire Point. After a stiffish climb we came to the cliff brow. On the way up my companion discoursed of many things, the praise of the Congested Districts Board chiefly. What they have done for the fisheries was not news to me. He was of the opinion, also, that the homespun industry was a real source of profit to the peasants, and if this last year was not as bad as the early eighties, that was thanks to a potato spraying system that the Board had introduced. The Irish Industries Association, too, had done

[4] Royal Fern, a hardy fern which thrives in damp places.
[5] Saint Colmcille was born about AD 520, and founded important monasteries all over Ireland, including Glencolmcille, before founding the monastic settlement at Iona in Scotland, from where missionaries were sent out to evangelize the Scots and the Britons. He is also known as St Columba.
[6] From the Gaelic *Celí Dé*, 'companions of God', an ascetic sect which flourished from the eighth century to the tenth.

good work; had helped homespinning, distributed looms, and started lace-making. But what hurt them was the American tariff, for America had once, it seems, been a good market.

Discussing these things, we got to the brow of the cliff. Eight hundred feet sheer below, one could see through the mist a sort of ghost of the surf – a very impressive sight. Just by us was the ruin of an old signal tower. Gillespie had known an old man who remembered having wrought at it in the days of Napoleonic war. It was just off here, near Malin Head, that Sir John Warren sighted Bonepart's invading squadron in 1798, on board of which was Wolfe Tone.[7] But that story has to be told when we get to Rathmullen, as the story of Columba must be when we get to his birth-place at Gartan.

We plunged along the cliff front in the driving mist, and ultimately struck a road leading out to the Sturrell[8] itself, which is a high conical piece of rock, with a limitless drop below it. At this point the youths of that side of the Glen are in the habit of climbing down the cliff face in search of strayed sheep. From the Sturrell there should be a view of the Rosses and Aranmore, far away north; but this day we could not even see Tormore, the island a couple of miles out, famous for a wonderful gathering of seabirds in the breeding season, ill-reputed for a recent fatal boating accident. Having seen, we came down, passing Columbkille's holy well, which is not a place where cures are wrought, but merely a religious centre where folk go for penance and add their tribute to a great cairn of stones. As we were there and were tasting the water, I thoughtlessly asked Gillespie if he had ever seen Doon well.[9] 'Once,' he said with a curious intonation, and I knew instantly what I might have guessed: that he must have been taken there in hopes of a cure . . . He hurt his knee at hurling, or hockey playing, from a blow of the hard wooden ball, and is very lame indeed. To that circumstance, no doubt, he owes an exceptional taste for education. I was surprised to find how interested he was over the fact that Lord Leighton had stayed in Malin More a few years back; and indeed there were few things that did not seem to interest him, for he had the temper that makes of so many Irishmen either scholars or wanderers, though living in this out-of-the-world place.

Cashel, the village in the valley, is, however, in the stream of affairs compared with the townland of Beevna, where Columbkille's chapel

---

[7] Wolfe Tone (1763–98) was an Irish revolutionary and is held by some to be the founder of Irish Nationalism.
[8] An unusual name for the area, but probably from the Gaelic 'staighre aill' or 'cliff of the stairs', referring to the tight, steep terracing formed by grazing sheep.
[9] Doon Well is a famed holy well in north Donegal, near St Colmcille's birthplace at Gartan.

stands. It is separated from the rest of the glen by the river and the marsh, over which runs a causeway, and constantly in winter, and sometimes even in summer, tide covers this; thus, the folk of Beevna who have no boats, have no way of communicating with society at all, except by a journey over the top of Sturrell or Craig Beevna and round by the head of the glen. Altogether I felt that I had learnt much from my day, though the dense mist prevented sightseeing, and we concluded with a dissertation on the theory of rundale,[10] which was illustrated by reference to one or two plots in the glen. It appears that in Kilcar, three miles from Carrick, there is a whole townland where the farms have never been 'squared', and the land is still held in rundale . . .

I had tea – very good – at the little public house, took my machine, wheeled it laboriously up a mile or so of hill; found a level of a mile at top, then a generous descent of about four miles, the whole of which to the hotel may be coasted, and it is barely needful to pedal again even once. This is all very well when the road is dry and clean, but whizzing down among stones and on a muddy surface I was thankful to escape a sideslip. I ran also into a flock of sheep – but gently; and there is always the losing hazard of a pig or a cow. That is why coasting is hardly safe in Donegal: the reader may take the warning.

Nora Tynan O'Mahony (1866–1954)
The Foothills of the Dublin Mountains in 1908

[Nora Tynan O'Mahony was the younger sister of Katherine Tynan, journalist, novelist and poet. Katherine had kept her maiden name when she married barrister and writer Henry Hinkson out of reverence for her father, Andrew Cullen Tynan; it is said that Nora kept the name because she wished to be recognized as Katherine's sister. The Tynan home, an eighteenth-century farmhouse called Whitehall near Tallaght in County Dublin, was a *genius loci* of the Irish literary revival in the final decades of the nineteenth century, when on Sundays young nationalists and literati such as W.B. Yeats, George Russell, Douglas Hyde, and the Fenian John O'Leary would while the evening away in discussion of poetry, literature and politics. Nora married

---

[10] Rundale is a term for joint occupation of detached strips of farming land that was common agricultural practice in the Middle Ages.

John O'Mahony, a barrister and journalist, in 1895, but he died of heart disease in 1904 at the age of 34.

Nora Tynan O'Mahony wrote occasional essays and poetry in The *Irish Monthly* magazine, and after her husband's death wrote romantic pieces about mountain walks, extracts from which appear below. *The Irish Monthly* was a religious journal which spanned the years 1873 to 1954; it was at its best at the end of the nineteenth century when it published pieces by Oscar Wilde and W.B. Yeats.

The essay I have selected describes walking in the Dublin foothills in 1908 and refers to the changing rural world in County Dublin at the beginning of the twentieth century.]

On Killinarden Hill

It was early yet to go a-picnicking, but a week of bright sunshine and genial spring warmth in the middle of February encouraged us to anticipate already the joys of a later season, and set out for a long, life-giving, breezy day on the hills. As we were not the happy possessors of a pony and trap, or even a modest donkey-chaise, and had, moreover, some short-legged little people of our company, our choice naturally fell on the hill most easy of access, Killinarden, 'the Church (or Wood?) of the Little Height', at whose very feet, lapped by the singing streams of Jobstown, the midday tram of the Dublin and Blessington Company obligingly deposited us, entirely fresh and ready for the steady climb upwards.

The Hill of Killinarden, the theme of poets more than one, had long indeed been a favourite resort of ours; many a happy day had we spent there, visiting old friends in its kindly, hospitable farmhouses, or blackberry-picking in its thorny brakes, or gathering ferns and primroses, foxgloves and rowan berries, through its winding boreens, still teeming with such treasures despite the frequent forages of professional fern-pickers and flower-gatherers from town, to whom, of all Dublin dwellers, Killinarden seems most intimately known.

As remembered long ago, the hill was a vastly pleasant and prosperous place, dotted all over with happy homesteads sheltering under the wing of kindly and comfortable parents a group of young men and maidens, all seemingly without care. The light-hearted songs of the haymakers or harvesters were heard in the fields day by day, the notes of the fiddle or the flute set many willing feet a-jig on the kitchen floors by night; while on Sunday evenings the neighbours came down from the hills and up from the valleys to make the rafters ring with song and laughter and dance, till at last, mayhap, grey-headed old Phil the Ploughman, greatest among step-dancers, would be brought in to put all the younger men to shame by the magic and infinite variety of his steps.

Today, by comparison, the hill seems, to one person at least, a lonely and saddened place, with the old folks gone, the farmhouses largely deserted, and a poor tramp on the roadside, or a barefooted child, shy-eyed and finger-in-mouth by his mother's doorstep, about all one may now see of humanity. This very afternoon, indeed, it is part of our project to call and say goodbye to an old friend and neighbour – pretty well the last on the hill, as far as we are concerned – she, too, bids farewell to the old, beloved, memory-haunted place. The long, low farmhouse, nestling close to the heart of the hill, looks down from its many window-eyes on the fairest of prospects, wide and far reaching over three smiling counties. Its well-stocked garden and orchard of knarled old apple trees, even the elaborate, planned haggard[1] and out-offices, bespeak both taste and neat-ness; the homely sitting rooms, with their solid mahogany furnishing and old engravings on the walls; the wide, hospitable kitchen with the antlers over the fireplace, and the pewter platters and trenchers, which had been buried in the days of the Rebellion lest they should be converted into bullets by the yeomanry, still lining the shelves of the long dresser: all tell of many generations reared here in comfort and prosperity. But now, with the hillside deserted, for one solitary woman bereft by death of all that made life worth living, one may well imagine an existence here, whether in the dark winter nights or the long lonely evenings of summer, to have become a very epitome of desolation.

Halfway up the hill we sit down on a sunny bank, and discuss the luncheon of chicken and ham and bread-and-butter with milk and home-made cake, which we had wisely brought with us, with such hungry appetites that a king might very well envy. Then off again up the steep ascent, past the brake of furze and thorn bushes with the little watercress stream running through it, in which we had so often gathered baskets of great luscious juicy blackberries; and crossways to the right, by a boreen made to 'break the hill', then straight up again till on looking behind we find the world grown a very big place indeed, full of blueness and distance and windswept space, with the dear familiar landmarks all drawing close in under our feet, and the great high hills, Mount Pelier and Feather Bed and the rest, settling down as it were to sleep in the valley below on our right.

Higher up again, and a little 'blown' from the long pull upwards, we discover ourselves shut in on both sides by tall banks of already blos-soming furze – what must it be in May, with the foxglove in flower, and the gorse in full bloom? – a perfumed blaze of gold against blue, blotting out all but one little gilt-framed bit of the world below, a world of tiny

[1] A stackyard.

houses of a myriad intersecting walls and hedges that map out each lilli-putian field and holding into a fine mosaic of blue-green squares and triangles. The little mountain sheep browse quietly by the edge of the road, 'the lark in the clear air' trills his first ecstasy to the sun, and 'the rest is silence'.[2] Yet even here, though we do not meet them, there are other human beings, as is evident by the smoking chimney of a little thatched house[3] set at the far end of the private and begated boreen which seems an indispensable appendage of each mountain dwelling, however small.

Soon we know by the brisk cool wind blowing down in our faces that we must be very near the summit, and lo! all at once we find ourselves on top, nay, on the other side of the hill, fronting a great, broad breezy plateau stretching away to the skirts of Kippure and its sister hills, and holding like a shining jewel in its bosom a wide sweep of water, the veri-table lake which I remember being told in my childhood lay like a magical fairy thing on Killinarden's crest. Here it is all wild moorland, boggy brown turf of a velvety softness clothed in furze and heather and bracken, with little narrow paths worn by the sheep in their rambles, and the blue sky reflected roughly in the wind-stirred water, and the misty mountains standing all around – a place to lift up one's head and one's heart, to draw in a long, deep, wholesome breath, to feel like children, 'just glad to be alive'.

Doubtless it is the wonderful sense of freedom, of 'wide, illimitable space', that induces us in a spirit of adventure to come home by another route than that by which we had come. So, straight as the crow flies, we race along the heathery sheep tracks – it were vain to think of mere walking in this invigorating atmosphere – cross a rock-built wall or two, and presently find ourselves flying, with the children a long way in front, down the boggy side of a steep hill. A woman comes to look wide-eyed after us from the door of a cottage brown as the turf about it (we had often noticed this same cottage, high against the skyline, from our miles-away home in the valley below).[4] A long-limbed lad at work in its garden rests his spade a moment to watch us in wonderment. The young ones, flying before us and hardly waiting to pick themselves up when they fall head-over-heels in their flight, wait for a moment at odd corners to disappear again in a flash like elfin mountain sprites, as soon as they catch sight of us on the crest above them. Now we are back in the road, and knowing our

---

[2] Songtitle; *Hamlet*, v. ii. 363.

[3] Malachi Horan's cottage; see George A. Little's *Malachi Horan Remembers*, M.H. Gill, 1943.

[4] Nora Tynan O'Mahony lived at the time near Tallaght in County Dublin.

way, we try to circumvent them by taking cuts crossways over the fields, but without success; till at last like homing birds, our hurried, headlong flight ends at the very gate of our lonely, leave-taking friend.

Here, as ever before, we are treated to a dish of delicious tea and home-made cake, and given a few flowers from the garden, primroses and snowdrops, the first, rare, early flowers of spring. Then, as our time grows short, we bid goodbye and Godspeed to our kind friend, and hurry down the rest of the hill, gathering bunches of fragrant coltsfoot on our way, while someone expresses the opinion that it is not the climbing up of the hills but the 'stumping down them' that makes one really tired.

Congratulating ourselves, however, on having had a splendid time, and on having inhaled enough pure, fresh air to last us at least for a week, we cross the stream at Jobstown just five minutes before the steam tram comes puffing and snorting through the leafless trees to bear us back, with the shadows already falling, to the warmth and welcoming lights of home.

Joseph Campbell (1879-1944)
Donegal *c*.1911

[Joseph Campbell was born and educated in Belfast. He was inspired by the Irish literary revival and published a number of volumes of verse early in the twentieth century, before moving to Wicklow in 1912 and becoming involved in the Irish Volunteers, and subsequently the Easter Rising. He took the Republican side in the Civil War, and after eighteen months of intern-ment in the Curragh, he emigrated to the United States. He founded the School of Irish Studies in New York in 1925, and after lecturing at Fordham University for ten years returned to Ireland and settled in Wicklow. The excerpt I have chosen is from *Mearing Stones*, a travelogue published in 1911; in it he describes a walk with his sister in west Donegal, in which he comes across both poverty and industry, and experiences the friendliness of the people.]

Bearing south by the Owenwee river from Maghery, we strike up through Maum gorge. Outside Maghery we come upon two men, one of them a thin, wizened fellow with no teeth, the other a youngish man, very raggedly dressed, with dark hair and features like an Italian. The old man tells us in Irish (which we don't follow very clearly) to keep up by the riverbed, and we can't possibly lose our direction. A quarter of a mile further on we meet another man. He bids us the time of day in passably good English. I answer in Irish, telling him that we are on the road for Glen Columcille, and asking him the easiest way over the hills. He repeats what the old man told us, viz., to keep to the river bottom, and to cut up then by the fall at the head of Maum to Laguna, a cluster of poor houses in the mountain under Crockuna. 'When you get there,' he says, 'you cannot lose your road.' He comes a bit of the way with us, and then we leave him at a point where the track ends in the heather, and where a squad of navvies is engaged laying down a foundation of brushwood and stones to carry it further into the hills. It gives us a shock, in a way, to come on this squad of wild-looking men in so lonely and desolate a place. We are now well into the gorge, and a wild place it is! Halfway up we come on a house – if one could call it such – with a reek of blue smoke threading out of a hole in the thatch. No other sign of life is visible. The walls of the gorge close in darkly on every side except the north. On that side is the sea, white on Maghery strand, and stretching away, a dull copper-green colour, into the sailless horizon beyond. Hearing the voices, a young man comes out from between two boulders serving as a sort of gateway to the house. His face is tanned with sun and exposure and he is in his bare feet. We greet him in Irish and he answers – a little surprised, no doubt, at hearing the language from strangers. Then another man comes forward – a brother, if his looks don't belie him. He is in his bare feet also, and hatless, with a great glib of black hair falling over his eyes. 'You have the Irish?' he says. 'It's newance to hear it from townsfolk.' We talk for a while, enquiring further as to our direction over the hill, and then we push on. Near the head of the gorge we sit down to have a rest, sitting on a rock over the stream, and bathing our hands and faces in the brown, flooded water. All the rivers of Donegal are brownish in colour, and the Owenwee (recte *Abhainn bhuidhe*, 'yellow river') is no exception. The water stains everything it touches, and I have no doubt but that the dark colour of the people's skin is due, partly, to their washing themselves in it. Coming through one's boots, even, it will stain the soles of the feet.

We resume our journey, and after some rough and steep climbing reach the plateau head. Loch Nalughraman, a deep pool of mountain water, lies to the east of us, shimmering in the grey morning light. All around is bogland, of a dull red colour, and soaking with rain. We make through this, jumping from tuft to tuft, and from hummock to hummock, as best we can, going over the shoe-mouth occasionally in slush. In an hour or so we come on a bridle path of white limestones, set on their flat in the spongy turf. We follow this for a while, and in time reach the poor village of Laguna.

Entering into one of the houses I greet the *bean a' ti*[1] in Irish. She rises quickly from her seat by the hearth where she has been spinning, a crowd of very young children clinging to her skirts. She is a dark woman, with mellow breasts and fine eyes and teeth. She is barefooted, as usual, and wears the coloured headdress of her kind, curtseying to me modestly as I approach. She answers me in Irish – the only language she knows – and bids me come in. '*Beir isteach*,' she says. A young man of five-and-twenty or thereabouts is weaving in the room beyond. (I recognised the heavy click-clack, click-clack, click-clack of the loom as I entered). Hearing my enquiry he rises up from his seat, drops his setting-stick and offers to guide us as far as the southern edge of the hill. 'You will see the Glen road below you,' he says, coming out in his bare feet into the open, and speaking volubly, like one used to good speech. 'Look at it beyond,' he says, 'winding from the Carrick side. Keep south, and you will strike it after two miles of a descent.' The woman brings a bowl of goat's milk to my sister. She drinks it readily, for she is thirsty after her climb. Then, thanking the poor people for their hospitality, we say, '*Slán agaibh*,' and press forward on our journey to Glen Columcille.

We reach the high road in about half an hour, near a schoolhouse, shining white in the sun, and busy with the hum of children singing over their lessons. Things look more familiar now. We pass many houses, with fleeces of dyed wool – green and blue and madder – drying on bushes outside the doors, and men busy stacking turf and thatching. Here and there on the road flocks of geese lie sunning themselves, head-under-wing. As we draw near they get up and face us with protruding necks, hissing viciously. Dogs bark at us occasionally, but not often. (I had heard ill accounts of the Donegal dogs from travellers, but on the whole, my experience of them has not been quite so bad as I had been led to expect.) Slieve League rises on our left, a dark, shadowy bulk of mountain, shutting off the view to the south. All around is moorland, with a stream in spate foaming through a depression in it, and little patches of tilled land here and there, and the inevitable brown-thatched cabin and the peat-reek over it. After some miles' travelling we come on a little folk shop by the road – a shop where one might buy anything from a clay pipe or a lemon to Napoleon's Book of Fate. The window looks tempting, so we go in. The shopkeeper is a quiet-mannered little man, not very old, I would think, but with greyish hair, and eyes that look as if they were bound round with red tape – burnt out of his head with snuff and peat smoke. We ask him has he any buttermilk to sell. He hasn't any, unfortunately – he is just run out of it – so we content ourselves with Derry biscuits, made up in penny

[1] 'Woman of the house'.

cartons, and half a dozen hen eggs to suck on the way. Some people may shiver at the idea of it, but raw eggs are as sustaining a thing as one could take on a journey! We pay our score, and get under way again. At a bridge where the road forks we sit down and eat our simple repast. A bridge has always a peculiar fascination for me – especially in an open country like this where one's horizon is not limited by trees and hedges, and I could spend hours dawdling over it, watching the play of sun and shadow on the water as it foams away under the arches. Here there is a delightful sense of space and quietness. The heather ale is in our hearts, the water sings and the wind blows, and one ceases to trouble about time and the multitude of petty vexations that worry the townsman out of happiness. Did I say one ceases to trouble about time? Even here it comes, starting one like a guilty thing. We reach Meenacross post office at 4.30 p.m., and an hour later see the Atlantic tumbling through rain on the age-worn strand of Glen Columcille.

Revd William P. Hackett (1878–1954)
The Dublin Mountains in 1912

[Born in Kilkenny, William Hackett was educated at Clongowes College and entered the Society of Jesus in 1895. He studied Philosophy in Le Puy, France, where one summer he walked with a few companions to the shrine of St Francis at La Louvesc and back, a distance of 120 miles, in three days. On his return to Ireland he taught in Clongowes College, and was ordained in 1912.

He explored the Dublin Mountains on foot over the next few years, and wrote a series of articles in the *Irish Monthly* magazine in praise of walking. After the First World War, many Irish Jesuits were sent to Australia to address the need for priests there, and in 1922 Hackett also, reluctantly, went to take up a post in Melbourne. There he had a distinguished career as a college rector, and he founded the Melbourne Central Catholic Library, modelled on that in Merrion Square in Dublin. He became a close friend of Archbishop Mannix and they frequently holidayed together. The archbishop preached the sermon at his funeral after he was killed in a motor accident in July 1954.

Hackett's brother was the writer Francis Hackett, author of *The Green Lion*, which was banned in Ireland in 1936. His sister Florence was also a writer, and is probably best known for *With Benefit of Clergy* (1924), a novel about a problem marriage.]

Everyone admits that walking is a healthy exercise. Many are ignorant of how pleasant it may be under suitable conditions. Around Dublin in particular, there are many exquisite walks for the hardy pedestrian. The roads are good, and if one is suitably clad, the weather is not so terrifying. The timid are often deterred from setting out on a long walk because the day breaks gloomily. The following brief extract from a diary gives an account of what we saw from the top of Seahan on a day that seemed most unpropitious. You may say that Seahan has no meaning for you. Suppressing well-found amazement, I supply the following topographical information. Do you know where Rathfarnham lies? A road from the end of the village follows the Dodder to Glenasmole. The splendid mountain bluff that overhangs the lake on the right is Seahan. It is over 2,000 feet high, and on cold days in winter is nearly always covered with snow. Three of us climbed this mountain in mid December. The following is the record of what we saw from the top of Seahan.

When we were about 1,400 feet up, the advance guard of a large mass of cloud that held the summit swept rapidly down to meet us. Soon everything about us grew grey and spectral. The wraiths of advancing mists cut off the view that had but a moment ago charmed us. We kept resolutely on our way. As we mounted, the clouds above us thickened. We were glad to strike an ascending path, as else it would have been difficult to keep on true to our course. At 1,800 feet our path entered a small gully. Here we sheltered from the damp wind that hurtled across the gully with wild shrieks. We lunched. We emerged into a bog. There was fog around us, below us, above us. However, the dark summit of the mountain appeared above, gloomily, vaguely. We attempted to reach it over a morass. Though wet, it was not treacherous, and soon we drew near. Around were piles of stones, grey, red and black. They yield under the boot. Relics of remote antiquity, they retain nothing of their former existence save their deceitful appearance.[2] The wind howled on the summit. It was cold. It was damp. We had attained our end, but yet we were baulked. Grey mist had buried the valleys. The wind was keening for the dead. Gloomily we descended. We faced north. The slope was steep but easy. Three hundred feet from the summit the fog grew thin. Another hundred and we were on a level with the roof of fog that vaulted the valley.

The immediate vicinity was still full of laggard wraiths of mist, but, for

---

[1] Seahan (648 m) is one of the western outliers of the Dublin Mountains.
[2] A large neolithic cairn and a smaller bronze age burial monument can be found on the summit.

an instant, miles away to the north the sunlit plain could be seen. It was fair, strikingly fair. Fifty feet lower found us free from all scurrying cloud. Then the scene that met us was most ample and splendid, exciting even in its beauty. The overhanging dome of fog, a few feet over our heads, extended out beyond the neighbouring hills and valleys which thus lay in dense shadow. Beyond the furthest hill the belt of shadow could be plainly traced along the plain, a dark pendant of the gloomy hills. On the east a wall of murky hill cut off the view of the plain, but beyond this gloomy line of hills and beyond the shaded plain extended an unlimited extent of country illuminated with unbroken sunlight that lit up town and country, and made spire and steeple glitter. The monument in the Phoenix Park stood out conspicuously, and Maynooth spire was prominent in the plain. The eyes easily swept over all the intervening country. The Hill of Lyons lay beneath us beyond the Hills of Tallaght, which were still in gloom; beyond Lyons could be seen the plain of Kildare extending to the Hill of Allen, which lay like a pumpkin on the horizon. In front was the whole County Dublin, and the plain still rolled on to where the vision got lost amid the hills of County Meath. Everywhere unbroken sunshine lit up hamlet and field, while here and there the glitter of a silvery thread betrayed the swollen Dodder or the Liffey as they hurried to the sea.

On all that lay to the left the dome of mist still cast its shadow. Hence the tints were purpureal sinking into black. The mountains were all decapitated by the fog, but the gloom on the one side heightened the beauty of the brilliant sunlight on the other.

John Herman Rice (1876–19??)
Counties Waterford, Tipperary and Wicklow, c.1913

[John Herman Rice, son of a Crown Solicitor, was a barrister by profession, and was appointed District Justice for East Mayo by the Free State in 1924. He retired in 1942.

Rice was an intrepid walker, yachtsman and traveller who, when free of the gravity of his busy professional life, enjoyed writing poems, short plays and graphic discourses about his travels in Ireland and abroad. He also wrote about long walking tours with a group of companions of Unionist and Nationalist backgrounds, all good singers, drinkers, and great exponents of political argument. Rice walked for the relaxation and enjoyment it afforded, the joy of being with 'upstanding companions', the singing and the drinking all intertwined with the thrill of achieving, with studied nonchalance, considerable physical feats.

The following excerpts are from *Moonbeams*, a slim volume published in 1917. In the first Rice describes a trek from the sea coast of Waterford to the Galtee Mountains and in the second a walk in County Wicklow.

ACROSS THE KNOCKMEALDOWNS AND THE GALTEES

Ned Foley's yacht, *The Seagull*, lay at the mouth of the Blackwater, waiting for the rise of the tide to help her over the bar. The sun was now touching the horizon, and, as he slowly sank, the outline of a distant mountain showed itself clearly against his ruddy face.

'By Jove!' exclaimed Jeremiah Slattery, 'Galteemore looks well tonight: I suppose it's fully forty miles from here.'

'Every inch of it as the crow flies,' said Charlie Stanley. 'Just the walk for you, Bob!'

'Well,' replied Bob Bible, 'I'll bet anyone a fiver I get there within thirty-six hours from tomorrow morning.'

'Done,' shouted Dick Geary, 'and I'll go with you to see you lose.'

The water had now risen sufficiently to allow us to glide over the bar, and in a few moments we were on shore. During the evening the money was lodged with Richard Carey, while several additional bets were also made on the result of the issue. I suddenly decided to accompany the travellers, for at least a portion of the journey; so, at seven o'clock next morning, we started from the 'Devonshire Arms', accompanied by several who were financially interested in the contest. Soon clearing the long and straggling town of Youghal, we reached the Turig Bridge,[1] which separates the counties of Cork and Waterford. Here our attendant band bade us farewell, when, having decided to go by Tallow[2] instead of Ballintrae, we commenced a long and sharp ascent towards the northwest, following the course of the Turig, and leaving the Blackwater behind.

The view seawards soon became extremely pretty; the Blackwater, from here, appearing to form a large lake, environed by an amphitheatre of verdant and gently sloping hills, which terminate abruptly in the two bold and picturesque eminences of Knockvarry and Blackball Head. Quickly we passed from this view, and mile after mile of bleak and monotonous country took its place, relieved alone by the striking outline of the Knockmealdowns, standing on the confines of Tipperary county. Having passed the twelfth milestone and come in sight of Tallow, the general appearance of the scene became greatly improved; and when, at length,

---

[1] This is today called Rinecrew Bridge, and is a short distance south-west of Youghal Bridge, which today takes the N25 across the Blackwater river.

[2] The westernmost town in County Waterford.

we reached Joyce's well-known establishment[3] our appetites for breakfast would not have helped to make the fortune of any hotel proprietor.

We afterwards visited some leading politicians (of which the town is full, and for which it is famed); then for a short time watched an angler's fruitless but untiring efforts on the banks of the winding Bride.

Strolling quietly along by the old road, we soon crossed the intervening hills, and reached Lismore before three o'clock. Knowing well the danger of delay in this town, Bible expressed his determination to start for Clogheen at four sharp. As, of course, Geary and I were merely his attendants on the journey, we were forced to share his will; yet it was with rebellious spirits, but well loaded pockets, that we crossed the Blackwater at the hour named. Anyone who cares for sylvan scenery and who has not as yet visited Lismore, ought to take the first opportunity of doing so. I know of nothing more gently beautiful than the surroundings of this ancient seat of learning; more especially along by the Glen, which we were now traversing.

Having enjoyed the leafy shades for two or three miles, we emerged on the rugged mountain road, and immediately, on Geary's suggestion, paused for refreshment. Bible sagely remarked that the halt was opportune, but should not be repeated too often until 'Dawson's Table'[4] was reached. Thereupon we decided on a double allowance at each stoppage, as it was absolutely necessary to lighten the loads which weighted our pockets. Before arriving at the mountain barrack I was beginning to feel the effects of the long tramp; but Bible, showing a bold front, refused to stop; and Geary, as he struggled in desperation after his leader, breathlessly informed me that I would find them in Clogheen. Using language appropriate to the situation, I sat down on a mossy bank and momentarily retired from the contest, but after a smoke I resumed the journey, and reached Baylough just before sunset.

Here, to my astonishment, I descried Geary and Bible seated upon a rock, and pretending that their goodness of heart alone had prompted them to wait for me. The evening was fine and calm, one which among the mountains generates meditation. Often before had I lingered in this self-same spot, and as often had the same thoughts come surging though my mind. What reminiscences do these old encircling hills awaken? Through all the varying vicissitudes of time they alone have passed unchanged. How many cycles has this dark, dismal lake, nestling under the shadow of Knocknacomitas, outlived? How many shall it survive? Age after age may pass away; strange races may flourish or may fade; but these old hills will,

[3] A hotel, public house and grocery now called the Devonshire Arms.
[4] An outcrop of rock on the summit of Galteemore.

year after year, grow young with the coming of the spring, as they have ever done since those far-off days when the parricide Parthalon first set foot upon our shores. And then, again, in that single word, Knocknacomitas, do we not get a glimpse of those beautiful and poetic, yet simple, expressions contained in the Irish tongue: Knocknacomitas – the wrestling, or vieing, mountain, which stands as it were in eternal rivalry with the loftier Slievecua across the pass.[5]

The chill caused by the setting of the sun soon interrupted these thoughts, and reminded us that it was time to depart; so, slowly we descended from the rocky heights, and soon afterwards found ourselves enjoying a strong appetizer, seasoned with a mild political lecture, under the hospitable roof of Dr Tom Hennessy.

Having reached Clogheen, we ordered dinner. This, when it arrived, consisted of a boiled leg of mutton, to which full justice was done. When the repast was at an end, Geary, as is customary, rang for hot water, sugar and a lemon. Curious to relate, simultaneously with these there arrived in the room two distinguished gentlemen from Cahir, Mr Michael Keating and Mr Patrick Brett. The soothing effects of the sugar and lemon soon produced feelings of fraternity, so that before long we were in the midst of a discussion on all the more important topics of the day. Brett's prowess as a wag was never better displayed, and it was a pleasure to observe Keating's demonstations of joy at his drolleries, as he scored time after time off the irrepressible Bible. However, the thirty miles which we had negotiated since morning now began to tell its tale, so we prepared to retire to slumber, having left instructions to be aroused with the lark.

At the foot of the staircase an acrimonious discussion took place between Bible and Brett regarding the merits of a local political society, of which Dr Hennessy was the leading ornament. The argument having grown warm and personal, Keating gave vent to his feelings by muttering '*in vino verita*', as he looked with amused forbearance towards the disputants.

'Perhaps, sir,' remarked Brett, sarcastically, 'you mean *in vino veritas.*'

'By no means, sir,' replied Keating; 'are you unaware that the last "s" is not pronounced in French?'

The morrow found us early astir, and we were soon ready for the day's campaign. It was an ideal morning as we decided to proceed along the Ballyporeen road, before making up our minds at what point to assail the great mountain range which looked so formidable across the valley. This we accordingly did for about two miles, when meeting that prince of sportsmen, James Phelan of Lisfuncheon, and acting on his instructions,

[5] Neither of the names Knocknacomitas or Slievecua are in use today.

we entered a boreen leading to the right, and soon found ourselves stranded in an open field. Having crossed a few ditches we arrived on the banks of a rivulet,[6] where Geary insisted on a halt for refreshments. Bible and I considered it was somewhat early, but Geary convinced us without much difficulty that our idea was fallacious. The warmth of the air, the beauty of the spot, in fact everything conduced to detain us here for a time; Bible, however, was adamantine, and sternly urged the resumption of the journey. Thus coerced, we waded across the stream, and trudged ahead until we discovered ourselves on the Cahir–Mitchelstown Road.

The mountains here frowned down in a threatening attitude, as if defying us to attempt the passage, but we had no intention of doing so at present as we strolled calmly along towards Skeagnarinka.[7] I had by this time made up my mind as to the point where we should begin the crossing, and both Geary and Bible, who knew little of this portion of the range, gave me *carte blanche* as far as my leadership was concerned. Close to Skeagnarinka, where the County Limerick touches Tipperary, the outer range of the Galtees slopes downward in crescent form, exactly in front of Galteemore, presenting a unique and most delightful picture. It was here that we left the road and commenced our struggle with the passive but mighty forces of nature.

Having gone along through the fields for about half a mile, we began to gradually ascend and soon commenced a zigzag course, following the windings of a goat track up the steep incline. The height of this hill was not great – not more than 600 feet – yet our temperatures had reached boiling point when we arrived at the top, and we sorely needed the stimulants which Geary produced. From the road it had appeared as if Galteemore rose directly behind this hill, but we now found confronting us, across a shallow valley, another range, thickly wooded, and of about the same height as that upon which we stood. Without waste of time we crossed the hollow and entered amid the shady trees on the opposite side. Considering the heat of the day, this proved to be of the greatest relief, so much so that we were in no hurry to expose ourselves again to the warm embraces of King Sol.

The woods here resounded with the diversified notes of Nature's feathered musicians, and for the second time Bible's threats were necessary to urge Geary and myself to advance. Very soon we surmounted the crest, to find, with sadness, that we had reached the limit of the verdant foliage. As we emerged from the green shade of the wood, a fine scene presented

---

[6] Probably the Shanbally river.
[7] Called today Skeheenaranky.

itself before us. Here the valley was deep, and of considerable extent, and the great mountain appeared to fall back from the gurgling, rushing brook which hurried past its base. Crossing the little stream by a primitive wooden bridge, we soon afterwards came upon a hidden glade where we disturbed a flock of grazing sheep, who received us with great astonishment. This lovely spot held us captive for a time; but soon we proceeded, amid huge fragments of rock which had fallen down from the lofty heights above, and passed slowly upwards through a picturesque dell, as we began the great ascent.

Quickly the character of the scenery changed, romantic loveliness giving way to majestic grandeur. The dale suddenly contracted; vast cliffs, rugged and uneven, towered upwards to a great height; the little stream, pent up within its narrow bounds, rushed onward with noisy tumult; then we came out upon the bare and open mountain, and advanced without difficulty up the long and gentle slope. The heat was now very great, and our progress became, in consequence, extremely slow. But there was no hurry, and the warm breast of the mountain invited repose. Futhermore, the gradually enlarging view behind us grew at every step more striking, while the soft blue ether above, undisturbed by fleeting fleecy clouds, seemed to benignly bless the earth beneath.

Thus surveying the ever-extending landscape, we leisurely pursued our upward course, and revelled in the belief that life was worth living after all. When, at length, we reached a point which appeared to place us on a level with the distant summit of Knocknacomitas, we had a long halt for 'dinner', which passed off in a most successful manner. It was after four o'clock when we left here, and another hour flitted by ere we found ourselves in a position to overlook Slievecua. Soon afterwards, as we surpassed Cronagh (the second greatest of the Galtees), Geary commenced to make the pace hot. It was only then that Bible and I thought of a wager which we had made the night before about being 'first up'. After a short but strenuous effort I saw my chance of victory was hopeless, so forthwith handed in my checks, surveying the race from the rear. As they appeared to near the summit Geary also retired, then Bible, going on alone, soon passed out of sight.

Not long afterwards we found him stretched on the grass, close to Dawson's Table, reviewing the magnificent panorama which lay revealed. We had reached an altitude of 3,015 feet, the fourth highest point in the Emerald Isle. Galteemore is the most impressive of the great mountains of Ireland. Its summit is undulating, and of considerable extent, from the midst of which bubbles up a delightful crystal spring.

It would be impossible to enumerate *in toto* the surprisingly splendid views which radiate from here towards every point. The wondrous beauty of the prospect was heightened in effect by the circumstances under which it appeared to us. As we gazed upon the scene, sunset was fast approaching, and a delicate haze, which brightened into a rich amber colour, overspread the empurpled hills around us, and the waving woods across the valley. The Glen of Aherlow was veiling itself in sombre shadow, but all above was gleaming with light, and the declining sun, as he sank gradually in the western heavens, shed a soft radiance upon the landscape, and tipped with golden hue the naked cliffs and the fringe of foliage that hung upon their brows, displaying an illumination which no pencil or pen could imitate or describe.

It was now time to commence the descent, and I was glad to find that the realization of the fact that the Glen and the Sliev-na-mucks still lay between them and the town of Tipperary, scarcely affected the good humour of my comrades, which all things had combined in producing. At the northern side of the summit there is a sheer precipitous drop of over 1,000 feet into the calm little circular lake of Diheen, which St Patrick is reputed to have made the prison of the last of the dragons. Not wishing for the society of the latter, we passed along by the left shoulder of the mountain, where the passage is very steep and not easily negotiated. Soon, however, the gradient became modified, and, keeping well to the left all the time, we advanced with rapidity. Darkness was now quickly approaching, but this caused us no apprehension as the full moon was high in the sky and already illuminating herself. Soon we turned towards the right, describing a semicircle; then, as we reached a lake[8] close to the bottom of the valley, we saw the last signs of twilight vanishing in the wake of the sun. Here we lit our pipes as we sat down by the water's edge, knowing that the assistance of the nocturnal traveller's friend was near at hand.

It was like a scene in fairyland to watch the shadows chase each other from the ever lightening dell, as, in expectation, we awaited the advent of the Queen of the Night. Our vigil had not lasted long when, suddenly, the valley was flooded with silver light, and every little wavelet in the dark waters at our feet displayed its shining crest; then glancing upwards we beheld Phoebus in unclouded splendour rising majestically above the mighty mass of Galteemore. It was a gorgeous sight; one, indeed, to be long remembered. By the aid of the soft but brilliant light we had little difficulty in resuming our journey, for although our path was flanked by lofty heights, yet none directly barred our progress, and a downward walk of less than two miles saw us clear of the mountain barrier, and on a road once more.

Soon afterwards we came to a house, from which loud sounds of revelry

[8] Lough Curra.

burst forth. Geary knocked at the door, and explained that we were lost sheep, far from home. The hospitality of the Glen of Aherlow was immediately extended towards us, and before very long Bible was installed in the position of Master of Ceremonies. Through his instrumentality the uproarious fun of the night caused the hands of the clock to scamper round its face in undignified haste, so that before we knew what had happened the blushing dawn was peeping through the windows.

Geary now counselled the resumption of the tour; when, with sadness, we forced ourselves from the gay and hospitable scene. Loud cheers pursued us on our journey, which we responded to amid the rousing echoes of the resounding mountains.

The sun had risen as we crossed the Slieve-na-mucks, and not long afterwards three beds groaned beneath the weight of the weary wanderers at Dobbyn's Hotel.

A RAMBLE IN THE GARDEN OF ERIN

It was on a pleasant September evening that I met two distinguished men strolling along the Kingstown pier. One of them, Stephen J. O'Mahony, was almost as well known in New York as he was in Dublin; while his companion, Michael O'Callaghan, hailed from the County Cork, but generally resided for choice in the metropolis. Both gentlemen were politicians of the extreme type, and both were on the same side; but, as so frequently happens in Irish public life, they differed on minor points, one taking his leader in Belfast, and the other from Cork; with the result that, although close personal friends, they were irreconcilable political enemies. However, as I arrived on the scene, all was calmness, as they were peaceably discussing a walking tour in the County Wicklow, which they contemplated commencing next day. Asked if I would accompany them, I readily assented; when it was ultimately agreed to enter the Garden of Ireland by the north-west, instead of the north-east, starting from Terenure at an early hour in the morning.

I was at the appointed spot in good time, and in a few moments O'Callaghan arrived. To my dismay he informed me that O'Mahony and himself had just had a serious row with regard to the political situation, brought about through a speech delivered by Mr William O'Brien[9] the previous day in Macroom, in consequence of which O'Mahony had returned to the city in a state of indignation, and that it was useless to

---

[9] William O'Brien (1852–1928), MP for North-east Cork and Mallow, and for Cork City 1883–1918.

expect him to turn up. 'Anyhow,' said O'Callaghan, 'two is company, three is none.' I felt compelled to totally disagree with him in this, pointing out that by no stretch of the imagination could I come to regard him as a bouncing damsel of sweet seventeen! Eventually, however, we decided to start, and by the time Templeogue came in sight O'Mahony had been completely forgotten by the versatile Corkman.

It was a gloriously fresh morning, so putting up a rapid pace, we quickly arrived at the historic village of Tallaght – the necropolis of the Partholan race.[10] Here we naturally paused to pay a visit to Fox's renowned hostelry,[11] where O'Callaghan was well known and respected. We refreshed ourselves judiciously, and were preparing to proceed on our journey when a stout gentleman sitting on a barrel close by, asked us to assist him in the consumption of 'another round'. His request being acceded to, he then informed us that he was walking to Poulaphouca. O'Callaghan thereupon told him of our desire to reach the same place, so it was naturally decided to join forces on the march. To my astonishment I soon found out that our new acquaintance was an old schoolfellow of mine, who came from the County Limerick, and whose name was Norman.

The onward tramp was now resumed, but at this moment a wildly driven cab hove in sight, out of the window of which a shouting and gesticulating figure appeared. We awaited its arrival, when, from its recesses, O'Mahony emerged. He completely ignored O'Callaghan, but greeted me effusively and made Norman's acquaintance with enthusiasm. A further delay now necessarily ensued before Tallaght was finally left behind. From here to Jobstown there is a gradual rise, but after passing the latter the ascent becomes much steeper, consequently the view is a continually enlarging one, until at length there is a panorama extending from the distant Cairn of Crimthan[12] on the one hand to the counties of Meath and Kildare on the other. Our next stoppage was at the Embankment,[13] close to the village of Saggart, where we weighed ourselves in the yard of the hotel; Norman exceeded my weight by five stone, and nearly equalled that of O'Mahony and O'Callaghan combined.

[10] The name 'Tallaght', meaning 'Plague Grave', is derived from the legend that the Parthalonians, early colonizers of Ireland, settled in this area but were eventually wiped out by plague .
[11] This public house, much extended, is still extant in Main Street, Tallaght, and is now called The Foxes Covert.
[12] This location of this landmark is unclear, but the only hilltop with a cairn that would have been visible from the Blessington Road at that point would have been Knockaniller, now covered in forestry which hides the cairn.
[13] The Embankment, then a hotel and today a public house, takes its name from the section of nearby earthen fortification that marked the boundary of Dublin's Pale.

On leaving this place we walked steadily along admiring the scenery around. On the right hand side flowed a charming brook called, I believe, after Dean Swift, who owned some property in this neighbourhood; while, on the left, we passed the curious Brittas Ponds, which are used in connection with large paper mills close by. Soon after this the County Dublin was evacuated, and Wicklow entered.

Having reached the well-known 'Lamb',[14] we came in sight of Blackamore Hill, famous as the Irish encampment in 1798. It was here that Norman finally decided to accompany us on our campaign among the mountains. There now appeared a beautiful avenue of overhanging trees, which presented a pleasant picture as it stretched away before our view; but like all things it came to an end, and as it did so, we entered the suburbs of Blessington. Here, I must confess, I used all my endeavours to induce my comrades to make a prolonged halt, but Norman and O'Mahony were unwilling, so after a smoke and some refreshment at the hotel, we again pressed forward. The pace was necessarily not now as rapid as it had been, so none of us were very sorry when the sharp ears of O'Callaghan detected a sound which he declared to be the waterfall. He was right, and in a few moments the 'commando' stood on the handsome bridge which spans the 'phouca's den'. At this exact spot the counties of Kildare and Wicklow meet. Making our way to the really pretty little hotel, no time was lost in ordering the best repast which could be obtained, while in the interval much-needed stimulant was partaken of in the bar. Twenty-three miles had been accomplished.

Having left very little of an excellent dinner, we lit our pipes and reviewed the political situation; but soon, the subject becoming a trifle warm, and O'Mahony still refusing to become reconciled to O'Callaghan, Norman suggested a walk to Hollywood, which he said was an old haunt of his. When four men go for a stroll on a beautiful evening after a good dinner, it is only natural that one or other of them should burst into occasional song, but this nearly proved to be our undoing, as Norman's ditties belonged to that order usually associated with the 12th of July, while O'Callaghan's had all a flavour of '98. They soon resorted to violent personal abuse, and as we reached Hollywood the situation was critical. Entering the local hostelry I displayed great diplomacy; first on insisting on O'Mahony abandoning his attitude of reserve towards O'Callaghan, and then persuading the latter to sing 'Limerick it is beautiful as everybody knows.' Overcome by this flattery, Norman made a spirited attempt to respond with Cork's national anthem, 'The Rakes of Mallow', after

[14] The Lamb was a horse-changing station on the coach road between Dublin and Blessington.

which O'Callaghan shook him warmly by the hand, and peace was restored.

Almost immediately afterwards an acquaintance of Norman's entered the establishment, and was quickly introduced to us as Mr Reuben Dodd, the famous motor cyclist. This gentleman's advent added considerably to the conviviality of the fleeting hour, as whenever his turn for a song arrived he invariably responded gamely with a step-dance.

On our way back we passed a police barrack, outside which stood four constables; one of them evidently objected to the song with which O'Mahony was passing the time – 'The Peeler and the Goat' – and wanted to know what we meant 'be brakin de pace uv de night'. A few soothing words from Norman, however, caused his rage to abate; then as we left we raised a lusty cheer for nothing in particular, which was enthusiastically responded to by the officers of the law. On arrival at the hotel, Norman complained of an abnormal thirst; O'Callaghan suggested a pint of stout; Norman pleaded that he had never attempted such a plebeian drink in his life. He had five that night. Next morning he and I found a deep secluded spot in the river, where we had a most refreshing dip, while the other two helped the waitress to make sandwiches for our journey. Dispensing with breakfast we strolled forth, O'Callaghan's person presenting a rounded appearance from the large consignments of liquid and solid ammunition concealed thereon. Hollywood was on the line of march, and here we halted. Sixteen miles between us and the 'Seven Churches', so we took more provisions on board; also a tin whistle and a Jew's harp.

Now began a sharp ascent, and gradually civilisation was left behind. The day was very warm, yet Norman's twenty stone affected him not in the least, and he led the way at a rattling pace. We made it a rule that a stop for refreshments was permissible every hour. The second of these occasions found us at crossroads. In our uncertainty it was decided to hazard our future on the toss of a penny: the coin directed us to take the road to the right, and this was done without question. Soon we began to ascend, and next passed across a considerable stream, which is known as the King's River. The road now became miserably bad, but it was determined to proceed. Suddenly Norman, who was ahead, discovered a hovel well up on the mountain, at the door of which stood an old man. The latter gave us the joyful tidings that we had come five miles out of our way, but that there was a ford about two miles further down by which we might cross the river and regain the road. We could not find the ford, but discovered a single crazy stick across the water, which was here about five feet deep. O'Callaghan's agility helped him to easily negotiate the stick, but Norman, O'Mahony and I hesitated. At length O'Callaghan suggested that he would carry our clothes across, which he successfully did, while we swam the stream. When this interesting performance had been accomplished, the provision store rapidly diminished, and after a stiff climb we found ourselves on the correct road once more.

We had expected to reach Glendalough at six o'clock. It was now five; we were at the bottom of a great valley, and dark clouds were gathering around us. Another hour passed, and then a man cheered us up by telling us that we were still four Irish miles from Wicklow Gap. Soon began our ascent towards the famous pass. The mists became heavy, the road rough, and our tempers very bad. Norman, also, showed signs of fatigue, while O'Callaghan's gaiety of heart had flown. O'Mahony and I were a considerable distance ahead when, suddenly, the mists cleared; consequently, being now about 1,000 feet up, we had a grand view in the twilight of the great stretch of country behind us, the road which we had travelled winding away like a silver thread into the dim distance. Several times I was confident that the summit was at hand, and was as often disappointed, but at length all doubt vanished as I beheld the shadowy appearance of Lough Nahanagan[15] glistening in the darkness on the right-hand side. This celebrated pass is the only means of communication between north and south Wicklow for many miles, lofty mountains barring all progress elsewhere. Loud cheers announced our position to our colleagues, still labouring up the mountain side. In about twenty minutes they arrived, and cast themselves down exhausted on the wet grass.

Then an extraordinary and unexpected incident occurred. Norman, having recovered his breath, commenced humming 'The Boyne Water' with complacency and contentment. Slowly, and with great deliberation, O'Mahony placed his glasses on his nose and glared over them at the perspiring Norman. 'Sir,' he said, as he dramatically waved his hand towards O'Callaghan and myself, 'my friends and I were born with a craving for liberty in our hearts; you, who since your tenderest years have been nourished on orange lilies, alone blast our patriotic hopes: the moment for vengeance has come.' 'What means this?' exclaimed Norman, springing to his feet, 'There is assassination in the air.' O'Mahony fell back a step or two, and then, as the opponents stood facing each other in the darkness, I thought I had never seen anything so truly tragic. But the tableau lasted only for a second, as O'Callaghan's inconsiderate laughter burst the bubble; when, after explanations, a kind of harmony was quickly re-established. Norman, however, insisted as a safeguard that O'Mahony should march ahead, which the latter consented to do, to the stirring note of 'The Gallant Tipperary Boys', excellently performed by O'Callaghan on the Jew's harp.

[15] Today Lough Nahanagan is the lower reservoir of the Electricity Supply Board's Turlough Hill power station.

The Gap is 1,600 feet in height, and the gradient on this side being nearly one in eight, our progress was rapid. When about halfway down, the valley appeared to become more and more restricted, fantastic shapes approached and receded, while bright light sprang up around us on all sides. It was a really weird scene, and all Norman's exhortations and arguments about 'will o' the wisps' and glow-worms were required to urge O'Callaghan to continue the journey. He certainly would not have done so had any alternative presented itself, while O'Mahony and I were practically struck dumb by the sight of so many ghosts. The experience was a never-to-be-forgotten one. It was after nine when we sighted the lights of the Glendalough Hotel, and a few minutes later were discussing the incidents of the day in the smokeroom. . . .

Next morning being Sunday, those of us who went to our devotions had a walk of six miles before breakfast. On returning, Norman informed us that he had made arrangements for the ascent of Lugnaquilla, but that before anything was done O'Callaghan would have to shave himself. As that gentleman was unable to do so, Norman offered his services as a barber. All went well for a moment or two, until the soap fell on the ground, when Norman slipped on it with most disastrous results, which included the gapping of the razor. This finished the shaving, O'Callaghan still retaining two-thirds of the bristles.

At eleven o'clock, accompanied by Herr Anderson and a reliable guide, we mounted a sidecar and an inside pony trap, which had been requisitioned for the day, and proceeded towards the great mountain; but to get to its base many hills and dales had to be negotiated. Naturally our poor beasts of burden were soon distressed and we had to walk a considerable portion of the way, so that when the real climb commenced we were not in the pink of condition. When about a quarter of the way up, we became enveloped in a thick cloud, which had a drowsy effect, but in a few minutes it passed away and the atmosphere was again clear. Up to this we had really no trouble, but now the low furze made its appearance, and, as it was wringing wet the climb became decidedly unpleasant. Despite this we struggled gallantly forward, gradually approaching the goal of our ambition. O'Callaghan and the Dane now became almost done up, while to make matters worse another dense fog and mist came on. Before this had cleared away we were wet through, so that when the top was at length reached, our joy, though great, was not extravagant.

The summit reminded me a good deal of Knocknacomitas, but it occupies a far greater space and is almost flat. It is covered with a green sward of velvet softness, in striking contrast to the heathery side up which we had just tramped. Lugnaquilla reaches a height of 3,039 feet, depriving Galteemore of third place among the mountains of Ireland by a few inches. The view from here is one of superior magnificence, which rapidly restored our good humour. Close by, the fine mountain of Slievemaan rears its head, while the unrivalled Glenmalure stretches away for miles towards the north-east. Here also can be discerned the widely celebrated Glens of Imaile and Aghavannagh, lying to the west and south. The mountains in this locality do not form extended chains, but are assembled in lofty groups, separated by narrow and precipitous ravines.

As the day was now far advanced we commenced the descent, which did not prove as easy as had been anticipated. It was dusk when we arrived at the bottom of the decline and shortly before ten o'clock reached Drumgoff. After supper we again ventured on a political argument, in which our host, who was a vigorous opponent of most existing laws, took part. As none of us held identical views, the arguments were varied, and, I am sure, brilliant. It is to be regretted that I cannot recollect them for the benefit of future generations.

John W. Healy (1895-1975)
The Dublin and Wicklow Mountains, 1914-16

[Born in Dublin's south suburbs, John Healy was inspired as a schoolboy by the sight of Djouce Mountain shining with snow on a sunny day. He started walking with great enthusiasm in the nearby Dublin and Wicklow mountains in 1912, when he was 17 years of age. He wrote an account of each of his walks in his diary, noting the miles covered. He studied medicine; graduating in October 1918, he went to England the following month to take up a temporary commission with the RAF, which allowed him to extend his hill-walking and climbing experience to the mountains of Wales and Cumberland. He never married, and his annual holidays were almost exclusively devoted to mountain climbing, in which activity he quickly became an expert. By 1923 he was familiarizing himself with the Alps, by 1924 he was traversing the Matterhorn massif, and by 1925 he had climbed Mont Blanc. He was elected a member of the Alpine Club in 1934, and was a founding member of the Irish Mountaineering Club.

The following pieces are excerpts from the diaries he kept of his excursions into the Dublin and Wicklow Mountains. The first excerpt describes the attempt, at the age of nineteen, to climb Lugnaquillia, the highest summit in the Wicklow Mountains, while the second describes a trek across the high moorlands of the Dublin Mountains and a meeting with a strange band.]

Tuesday 17th March 1914

We rose at 6.45a.m.,[1] breakfasted at 7.25 and started for 8.30 mass at Greenan at 7.50a.m., arriving somewhat late. I walked back with O'Duffy; McWeeney cycling. We started from the hotel equipped for the ascent of 'Lug' at 11 a.m. We followed the road till opposite the Carrowaystick Brook and followed the zigzag path which brought us up the steep side of Glenmalure about 500 feet. The slope then eased somewhat and we left the path, keeping well up on a ridge to the right to avoid a bog. We continued high up on the side of this ridge following the direction of the Carrowaystick Brook. Then meeting a more massive spur to the right, thinking it to be part of the great ridge of Lug, we followed it up. It was very slow, heavy work as we had passed the snow line (2000 feet approx). The slope was steep and the ground was rough. We halted here and had bananas and chocolate. The cold here was about the most intense I have ever experienced. Our discomfort was increased by the very strong wind which blew us sideways. Having no gloves, my hands soon became numb and lost all sensation. I took a photo with great difficulty but do not expect success.

We then resumed our march and soon reached a cairn finding ourselves on the summit of Cloghernagh Mountain (2,621 feet), and seeing the main cone of Lug looking most sinister and awe-inspiring upwards of two miles away on our left, towering above us. It was completely covered with snow. We took shelter behind the cairn on Cloghernagh and had some of our provisions. The others determined to descend and I to make an attempt to reach the summit of Lug and rejoin them at the hotel. I took some provisions and lightened myself of the camera and tripod, taking O'Duffy's stick instead of latter.

There was a long slope up to the main cone, being the rounded back of a great ridge. This was covered with snow but I passed over it easily, being only inconvenienced by the wind which obliged me to hold on to the stick with both hands. I had borrowed McWeeney's spare pair of stockings to protect my hands and found them a great relief. I should probably have reached the top but for the mist which began to come down over the mountain, and also driven snow. On this I turned and followed almost the same route down the mountain reaching the hotel in a little more than two hours later, before the others who returned by a roundabout way.

We had tea together and then O'Duffy cycled to Rathdrum and took the mail home. McWeeney and myself, knowing we would be too late for any passenger trains up to Dublin, determined to return by the night

[1] They had stayed the night at the Glenmalure Hotel.

goods from Shillelagh. We reached Rathdrum in some two hours from the hotel being completely drenched by torrential rain *en route*. On arriving at the station we had tea at the stationmaster's house and dried ourselves as well as possible. The night goods came in about 11 p.m. and the guards allowed us a passage without any hesitation. We left at 11.30 p.m. and got on to Wicklow about midnight, doing a lot of shunting there and on the way. We had the rest of our provisions in the brake van with the guards, who gave us hot tea. We were very comfortable and dried ourselves more at the red-hot stove in the van. We reached Greystones before 2 a.m. on Wednesday and travelled from there into town on the footplate of the locomotive. It was a wonderful experience, especially passing through the tunnels. From Bray in we travelled at a good speed with only one stop and arrived at Harcourt Street at 3.40 a.m. Then I walked home, arriving about 4 a.m. and had five hours' rest (3½ hours' sleep) before rising later on to go to lectures.

[Undaunted, the companions returned again to the valley of Glenmalure the following September and climbed Lugnaquillia in three hours and ten minutes, returning to the hotel in one hour and fifty minutes. The arrival at the summit was a fine moment for Healy, as his description tells.]

The view from the summit of Lug was of enormous extent and quite came up to our expectations. We seemed to be above the whole of the visible world. To the east, south and especially the north we had a panorama of the great Wicklow ranges and their chief summits, some smooth domes of green or brown, others cut up and scratched by denudation, all were below us now, even the lofty Mullacleevaun, Tonelagee and Kippure, giants which we might have thought of as peerless before, though now the horizon has climbed beyond them. Strange to see old friends like Seechon and Djouce at so great a distance and from such an elevation; they seem small and distorted from here though Djouce still retains much of his old majesty. Turning to the west a vast plain seems to spring almost from one's feet, so abruptly does the great mountain rise from it, and gradually loses its clear definition of fields, hedges and rivers as the eye travels farther away, until at length it melts into a haze from which arise distant mysterious giants, the Slieve Bloom and the Galtees.

Sunday January 30th 1916
Met W. Dunn at end of lane at about 9.15 a.m. Left in his bike and we set

off with Rücksac[2] to try Kippure a second time. We walked to Rathfarnham and on to Ballyboden. Here we turned to right over B's bridge[3] and at the first turn to the left halted so that I could get on my puttees. We climbed up the hill so well known to me and when we were emerging from the Kilakee Woods we were struck by mist and saw it clouding the pine woods ahead. I had to get off the R.sac to put on my coat and then to force on the sac again almost choking myself. No sooner had we made these preparations for the worst than the mist cleared off. It was close under the trees but when we emerged on to the Feather Bed[4] it became cool. The upper part of Seechon was covered with mist and when we saw the whole Kippure chain in the throes of black clouds, we began to suspect that Kippure would slip out of our reach again. A very definite line demarcated the region of the mist from the valley below. The latter looked very clear and sharp in details.

The Military road[5] was in very bad condition. When approaching the top of the pass we were surprised to hear the sound of a brass band. Soon we came in sight of it on a bend of the road beyond and below us, and it was accompanied by a long line of dark figures behind. Such an appearance in the mountain solitudes, together with the unearthly sounds of the band which were interrupted and modified by the gust of wind, might well have been regarded as a supernatural visitation. It was like a bit of one of Poe's tales (a Tale of the Rugged Mountain?). On passing this awe-inspiring battalion we found that it consisted of the young criminals of Glencree Reformatory. After this event we turned our attention to Kippure. We advanced a little way along a turf track, meaning to strike the ridge leading from the cliff above Lough Bray. But now, however, the aspect of the mountain was so savage, and as the clouds became blacker and denser, we decided it was better to abandon it and instead cross the mountain to Glencullen. We retraced our steps to the road. Here we were greeted by a tall and weatherbeaten stranger from whom we parted after some comments on the weather and the mountains.

[2] Healy uses the original spelling, with umlaut and capital, for this piece of equipment, of which he was very proud. It seems at this time the two companions shared a single 'Rücksac'.

[3] Billy's Bridge, over the Owendoher near Stocking Lane, a name that appears on few maps and seems to have died out in the 1950s.

[4] A high moorland plateau straddling the Wicklow–Dublin border, so named for the extensive growth of *Eriophoretum* (Bog Cotton) that covered the bogs here before they were extensively harvested for peat in the twentieth century.

[5] A road constructed in the early 1800s to facilitate quick access into Wicklow by the military in case of rebellions; it leads out of County Dublin southwards for 40 miles to Aghavannagh.

As the blowing band and fiendish cohort had turned and was now bearing down upon us, we made haste to leave the road for the mountain on the east side. We struck up a misty ridge in front, finding the ground very wet in places. After a toilsome pull we reached the skyline of the ridge and were pleased to find that we had no more to climb and that we were on the plateau between Glendoo Mountain and Prince William.[6] During the climb the martial sounds of the spectral band accompanied us and as we penetrated the wastes it became more and more incongruous with our surroundings. After reaching the plateau we cast about for a sheltered place to devour our grub. A small stream overlapped by a turfy bank was selected and we ate and drank standing, leaning against the sodden bank. The hot tea from the thermos was welcome.

After the feed, I borrowed B's[7] pipe and enjoyed it to the full as we crossed the plateau obliquely. I felt so good that I wanted to climb Prince William. This passed, however, and suddenly 'a feeling of sadness came over me that my soul could not resist.' I collapsed on the edge of the quagmire and had some of our fruit in this unpleasant place. Having received energy from the rest, we went on, and having crossed an endless series of works[8] we arrived at a valley leading down to the Glencullen valley below. We followed this down for some distance and found ourselves on the steep grass slopes beside the gamekeeper's plantation and overlooking the Glencullen valley. Here we rested for a bit, the weather having turned out fine. On our way down to the bottom of the valley I had a few falls. We crossed the stream and made our way across the barren, half-reclaimed land beyond until we met the road.

We traversed the valley as far as Glencullen village where we turned up the hill to the left and passed through Ballyedmunduff and Barnacullia. Just outside a house we stopped to listen to a gramophone reproducing a song from one of the Italian operas. We took the Ticknock road and followed the usual route to Rathfarnham. On the way back when passing pine trees we frequently smelt a heavy scent like fine flowers. At Rathfarnham we had to force our way through a recruiting meeting to reach the tram. Total about twenty-two miles.

[6] Prince William's Seat, a small outcrop of granite where it is said that Prince William, son of George IV, rested a while on a walk during the monarch's visit to Ireland in the 1820s.

[7] Since he started out with 'W Dunn' it is not clear whose pipe he means.

[8] Presumably peat cuttings.

Herbert Fitzgerald (1894–1919)
The Dublin Mountains in 1917

[Herbert Gerald Fitzgerald was born in Dublin, and on finishing school in Belvedere College, he entered Trinity College to study Law. In Trinity he involved himself in the Swimming Club and the Historical Society and produced articles and poetry for TCD, the college magazine, for which he was assistant editor in 1917. There is little doubt that his love of the outdoors, his active lifestyle, and his love of the mountains in particular would have ensured that, had he survived, we would have heard a lot more from him, but his health was poor, and he died in 1919 at the age of twenty-five. Like both Wall and Malone,[1] Fitzgerald appears to have been much influenced by Belloc, and some of his prose has a distinct ring of that writer, particularly when describing the slightly ridiculous.

The following excerpts, which describe strolls in the Dublin and Wicklow foothills, are from a slim collected volume of his works, mainly from TCD magazine, called *Rambles, Rhymes and Reminiscences*, published in Dublin in 1920. The first excerpt describes a walk to Laragh, near Glendalough; Herbert Fitzgerald was no Henry Hart,[2] but for someone who did not enjoy good health, this was indeed a marathon journey. Assuming he started at Tallaght, having taken the steam tram from Terenure, he would have climbed a total of 3,000 feet and covered 25 miles in his twelve-hour hike. For those who know Kilmashogue, it is difficult to believe that over eighty years have elapsed since the second excerpt was written, because, with the exception of the recent construction of a motorway, and the fact that the last laundry in the area closed its doors half a century ago, there is little change in the route Fitzgerald describes, part of which (the steep hill up Kilmashogue) is today the beginning of the Wicklow Way, Ireland's most popular way-marked trail.]

TWELVE HOURS

Turning my back on the city, I sat on a low fence, recovered my breath after the hill, and lit my pipe. Then I stood up and, looking down on Dublin, smiled, for it was a Saturday morning, and a time when it is good for a man to be alone. Taking up my stick, I walked towards the south.

The Feather Bed Pass[3] is like an introduction to a Shavian play. If you like it you will probably like what follows, unless you are too tired to go

[1] Pages 137 and 144 respectively.
[2] Page 83.
[3] See page 146.

on. So also there is a great deal on either side of the main thread (which thread in the case of the Feather Bed is of course the road)[4] that you can ignore if you are in a hurry or feast upon if you like that sort of thing; and, further, unless you are moderately skilful in finding your way through bogs you will get lost, or at least, very tired, if you get off the road.

Personally, however, I find it easier to cross the Feather Bed Pass than to read a Shavian introduction, unless, indeed, in a snowstorm, when it is easier to read Shaw (provided the fire is good). When I reached the highest point of the road I put one foot in Dublin and the other in Wicklow, and sang that song called 'I'm going to be married on Sunday'; then remembering I was singing on a Saturday I thanked God there was no truth, as far as I was concerned, in what the maiden said, and whistling '*La donna è mobile*' (quite flat, no doubt), I went along to Glencree. Sitting down where the Enniskerry Road starts off with its irritating twist, I drew a picture of the Glencree Valley, which the Editor is too poor to reproduce, and which, if he did, you would not understand; because when I cannot draw a particular object I write down what it is, where it should be, and this view is full of such things. Art being satisfied, I toiled up the road until I was able to look down on Lough Bray; then I discovered a female person painting, and to her I raised my hat, saying, 'It is a fine day.' Without taking her cigarette (for she was smoking) out of her mouth she replied, 'It is'. Then knowing that she was neither a lady nor an artist, I pointed two fingers at her lest she was a witch, and walked away, coming in due time to the first bridge on the Liffey. Here, as was proper, I went down to the stream and drank some water, making a cup out of my hands in a way I had been shown by a man whose name is of no consequence at all. Having eaten half the bread I brought with me, I took the road again, with my briar reeking pleasantly and my head full of foolish thoughts about bridges and what Belloc says of them. Being for practical purposes an Irishman, it was natural that I should think of O'Connell Bridge, which is as wide as it is long; and that made me think of the very narrow people who cross that bridge every day; so feeling great pity for them I turned round and, facing Dublin (which was nearly fifteen miles away), recited, after the manner of Martin Harvey, 'The Wreck of the Hesperus', one line of which, you will remember, goes 'And his teeth were as white as the Clontarf Baths that ope in the month of May'.[5]

At three o'clock I came to Sally Gap, which is an intersection of two roads on the Watershed, and having passed by that road which leads to the

[4] The Military Road.
[5] Not, of course, from Longfellow's 'Wreck', this quote is presumably from a popular Dublin version. Longfellow's lines read 'And her bosom white as the hawthorn buds that open in the month of May'.

most beautiful lake in the world,[6] I sat down and gazed about. I was well satisfied for I had covered half my journey, and the hills around me were very beautiful; my mood was no less buoyant. The stillness of the hills rested on my mind, and the four twisting roads filled me with wonder. I rose slowly and resumed my journey. The road grew worse and in places was quite overgrown, with but the three lines cut in it which show the passage of an occasional cart. Mile on mile I walked (in little mood for singing, for my thoughts were on serious matters and my body was becoming tired). I passed some men carting stones out of a quarry, who saluted me with more respect than I deserved; so giving all of them God's blessing, which was the most valuable thing I could, and which a man can always give when he leaves civilisation behind him, I marched on with a firm, swinging stride until I crossed the Cloghoge river.

The road became better but I was tiring and I had some twelve miles still in front of me. Its twisting and doubling irritated, and the silence of the hills seemed cynical at my weariness. I passed over bridges that spanned ridiculous little streams across which a flea could jump, but I did not rest until I came in sight of the waterfall in the Glenmacnass Valley. Making my way to the river, I drank out of it and finished my bread. Then, lying on the grass, I smoked a pipe. Stiff with every joint but with a great sense of satisfaction, I returned to the road and stumbled down the hill in gathering dusk.

The road soon lost its wildness. It was level and well-kept and trees stood up against the dark sky and between their branches the stars twinkled. Then I reached Laragh.

SONGS IN THE SNOW

On the night of November the 17th snow first fell, and being great lovers of the hills, it seemed natural that The Other One[7] and Myself should journey to them immediately, so that we might sing their praises and report to our soft-footed friends who were shivering in the city, that Kilmashogue was covered with dry, hard snow, and that it looked very fine from the Whitechurch Road. Therefore, we hurried towards Rathfarnham early in the morning, having broken our fast at dawn, and in no time were striding through Willbrook, where we saw the first wonder of the day.

[6] Lough Tay; see John B. Malone, page 145.
[7] His frequently referred to, but not identified, walking companion.

'A sparrowhawk!' exclaimed The Other One, 'and we are not five miles from Nelson's Pillar'.

And then we met some ribald laundry girls. So I echoed: 'We are not five miles from Nelson's Pillar.'

Passing the Moravian cemetery,[8] I made the customary remark: 'There is no necessity to ask from what direction the wind usually blows.' And The Other One, replying properly, said, 'No, indeed.' And should you not understand that remark, I can only tell you to go and see for yourself.

Soon we were climbing the boreen up the side of Kilmashogue. Here we met a jovial fellow, who cried out to us, 'Ah-ha, gentlemen, 'tis a fine hardy morning!' So we replied together: 'It is indeed, thank God.' And after that we met no one for many hours, until we came upon a maid and her lover kissing in a dark lane.

The hill up Kilmashogue is very steep, but eventually you come to a wooden gate on your right, over which it is good to lean, for you can look down on Dublin from it. And, indeed, if you keep very still you can hear, if the wind be right, the roar of the city, and that is a wonderful thing to hear.

Standing on the lowest bar of the gate so that our feet were out of the snow, we wiped the perspiration off our foreheads and recovered our breath. Then we marched on under the larch trees, and, leaving the road, fared along until at length we came to a lane which comes from nowhere in particular and goes to nowhere at all.

Having eaten some snow, we were filled with the fury of winter, so we rushed along the lane in the direction of nowhere in particular singing, The Other One about a wholly impossible woman, and I a strange song about creation.

And now, as you are beginning to yawn, I shall only tell that it was several hours afterwards, when we were on the road to Rathfarnham, that The Other One said, because I had been silent for a long time, 'Damn you, you might be sociable.' But he was unjust, for I was composing verse, and here is what I composed:

> When snows are white on Kilmashogue
> And noses in Dublin are red,
> We two fine fellows, with staff and brogue,
> Light of foot and light of head,

---

[8] A community of Moravians from Bohemia were given asylum in Dublin about 1750; their numbers dwindled in the early twentieth century.

Set out with the joys of youth in our blood
To find secret paths in the Hills,
And singing the songs that wise men should,
We forget all human ills.

And the ills we forget, set out in rhyme,
Are the fivefold ills of man –
Death, Woman, and Passion, Ambition, and Time –
Which worry our fitful span.
But the fivefold joys the balance keep,
And with them our memory fills –
The smile on the face of a Child, and Sleep,
Friendship, the Sea, and Hills.

And when we go home we'll eat, if you please,
Great slices of roasted lamb,
And blackberry dumpling, and Gruyère cheese,
Then smoke our pipes, and damn
Ourselves like men if we've ever known
A better dinner or day,
And thank the Lord for having shown
Us joy in a simple way.

Now I do not wish you to think that I regard this as very fine poetry; but
let me tell you that it is much easier to criticise my verse than to compose
it, and it is much easier to compose it than to undergo the hardships and
hunger that inspired it. Therefore, before you criticise it, go and do as I
did, and then see if you can write better. And if you cannot, keep silence;
and if you can, it is no great credit to you.

John Gibbons
County Galway in 1929

[John Gibbons fought in the First World War and after the armistice worked
as a London newspaper correspondent. He began writing unassuming travelogues, from the perspective of the pedestrian, with a book called *Tramping
to Lourdes* in the late 1920s. His next book was *Tramping through Ireland*,
published in 1930, from which the chosen excerpts have been taken. G. K.
Chesterton wrote the foreword to a later work, *Afoot in Portugal*.

Tramping through Ireland is based on his experiences when he was sent by his newspaper to Ireland seeking stories from the new Free State. In Dublin, a journalist contact recommended that he go to Lough Derg, 'the most Irish thing in all Ireland'. Gibbons was a Catholic, and although he did not regard himself as devout as a pilgrim might be, he decided he would like to see the place, and took a train to the town of Athlone, which he regarded as the centre of Ireland, from where he decided to walk to Lough Derg. The excerpt I have chosen describes the walk from Athlone to Athenry, in County Galway.]

As walking westwards one slowly crosses the great central plain of Ireland one experiences at first a sense of absolute loneliness. When I started it was raining. Not hard rain like it does at home, but with a soft, gentle downpour that before many minutes had sodden even the straps of the pack on my back. The road was good enough for anything; very nearly as good it was as our best in England, and with next to no traffic on it, one could safely take its very centre. But it was the desolation that worried me. Hour after hour and one would pass perhaps one ass-cart with a load of turf. Far to the south and west one could see through the rain the hazy outlines of some mountains, but for miles around my road the monotone of the mist stretched almost unbroken. There did not seem to be even fields in our sense, and next to none of the cheerful red brick of the English farmhouse. Every few hours a grazier's limewashed cottage would loom up in the distance, and that was all. Even the miniature hillocks of turf, stacked brick-fashion as it had been cut from the bog, took on almost the aspect of mountains in that desert of rainy loneliness.

'The Emerald Isle' they call it! It was the greyest world that the mind could conceive. You cannot miss the way of course, but it is about the only blessing. The roads are signposted even better than in England, but there are no milestones. And the next day will be about the same as the first.

Then gradually, as you get used to it, you will begin to see things. You are not of course in the Gaeltacht, where they really speak Gaelic; but even the English does not mean quite the same as it does at home. The chemist's shop somehow becomes a 'Medical Hall', and a 'victualler' means a butcher. On the other hand, a public house is generally a 'grocery', and it was with a little thrill of pleasure that I first heard of a 'grocer's curate' as the most delightful of euphemisms for a bartender. What on earth a barmaid would be I do not know. But then they generally do not have any. Even the writing is changing a little. It is generally in Gaelic with the English underneath, but as often as not a shop sign will have Roman characters in as near the shorthand-like curves of the Celtic as may be. You can see how the change is coming. Shops to English notions are oddly unspecialized, with a few shirts and perhaps a toy hurley-stick all mixed up with a row of devotional books. Once I saw a sign that advertised its owner as 'Grocery, Greengrocery, and Fruiterer, Wine and Spirit Merchant, and Funerals provided', and once I saw a rosary which might have cost fourpence hanging up forlornly as second-hand. And wherever the shop could possibly manage it every mortal thing would be advertised as 'Irish', from the gramophone records to maps. The Free State must, one imagines, be the world's most economically-patriotic country. Someone told me how they admired the Prince of Wales as a true Sinn Feiner. 'Buy British', it comes in all his speeches. Only of course we don't. But these Irish people *were* buying Irish. 'Burn everything English that comes into Ireland, except the coal': that used to be the old cry. Now it is no longer needed, for they do buy Irish.

So one by one, and ever so slowly, the little towns began to succeed one another: Ballinasloe, Kilcullogh, Athenry, Oranmore, and the rest. And it was not a little bit like I expected. According to guidebooks I have read they should have been dirty, squalid places, with ragged children playing on the filthy stones outside each tumbledown cabin door. There ought to have been hordes of beggars pursuing the Saxon stranger with whining lies. But it was all wrong. I think my guidebooks must have been old-fash-ioned. Really, when you come to a place like, say, Ballinasloe, you find a wide street of houses at least as solid as any in my own London suburban road, pavements swept perfectly clean, very few people visible at all and certainly no beggars, and a general atmosphere of virtuous respectability that strikes one as almost oppressive. After, in fact, a very long day's hard walking in the rain, it will presently dawn upon the Saxon stranger that if there is anyone thoroughly dirty in the town it is himself. The guidebook, I think, must have forgotten to correct a legend a century or so out of date.

So the townlets passed, and by and by as I grew, so to speak, more into tune with the place, each one began to provide its incident or so. It was in Athenry, I think, that I saw my first Feast. It is a tiny town with some simply enormous ruins, a castle and an abbey and bits of some city walls. There was a battle there that I never heard of, but a man who shaved me in a little shop knew all about it, dates and all. And in the very middle of the place stand the remains of a medieval stone Calvary. You leave it behind you, and bearing straight on pass on the right where the boys were playing fives[1] against the huge derelict chancel of the abbey. And a wonderful fives court it must have made. Then you pass a stone where someone has cut in letters meant to outlast the ages his imperishable

---

[1] A ball game similar to squash but played with bats or the hands.

convictions of 'Up Duffy', and a hundred yards farther on you can begin to see the thing.

There was a ridge in the distance, and outlined on it against the skyline I could see an endless procession. Not all together, but in ones and twos and threes, all making unhurriedly for the same goal. Then as I got nearer still I could see other columns radiating from other points of the compass, with here and there a jaunting car picking its slow way over the field roads, or even a motor bumping painfully over the stones and ruts. Closer still and I was actually amongst the people. Quite ordinary folk they were – little family parties, couples, mothers with babies, single young men, and all with the same set look of cheerful solemnity. And most of them as they passed each other would exchange a word of low-voiced greeting. Even for the stranger there was a salutation. From the men, that is. For the women would look gravely down upon the road. And I noticed the same thing all through Ireland.

So in another minute or so I was at the place itself – a little hollow with three or four trees in the swampy ground beside a stream, and in the centre one tree growing from a pool. And this was the Holy Well itself, the very life and being of the whole Feast. Now, whether or not there ever was an apparition here is officially unsettled. This was no Lourdes, and the Church had made no pronouncement, but left it free to individual faith to believe or not to believe. Only for miles round they did believe. And for miles round scores of other holy wells up and down all Ireland they were believing too. Only this was the first that I had ever seen.

Around were the jaunting cars, their horses freed from the shafts and taking their ease with a forkful of hay. There were half a dozen two-seaters and a good many glittering cycles with flannelled young men who at home would have been playing tennis. There were girls in frocks as smart as any in London, and with them old women in long, heavy, green skirts and huge enveloping shawls and no hats. There was a booth or two with lemonade and cakes and jujubes for the children and a Free State policeman (only they call them 'Guards') looking on, and a woman with a basket selling rosaries and little medals. As she took my coppers she wished me a good station and profitable to my soul. It was all most peculiar.

The whole general atmosphere, indeed, was extraordinary. There was neither the awed piety that at home we keep for in church, nor the flippancy that goes with out of church. These people were somehow just gravely cheerful. All of them had either just done something or else were just going to do it. Girls to one side, men to the other, they were taking off or putting on boots and stockings, and as each was ready without giggling or self-consciousness they found a place in the line of people perpetually encircling the well. I did not go myself. I simply did not dare. This is

Ireland and I am a foreigner here. This is not an international Lourdes, and the people would only see an impertinent tourist playing at the thing as he intruded upon their devotions. And I can think of heaps more reasons like that. And at the very end, if you really want to know, I did not go because I did not think myself good enough to go with those people.

What I did do was to peep shamefacedly for a moment within the circle round the well. There was a low wall of whitewashed stones, broken only at one point. It was there that you could see the Well itself. There was not very much to see. A shabby little picture of Our Lady, a rough shelf with some vases of the jam jar variety filled with flowers (fresh flowers), and half a dozen rosaries and trifles hung in the tree above the pool as thank-offerings for favours granted or prayed for. And that was all. Only round and round the people were going with their prayers, barefooted on the pebbly track. Some indeed were doing it on their bare knees. Fifteen times it was that they went round. Some of them were in little family parties. There was one plus-foured, estate-agent-looking father encouraging two small sons to keep it up. I watched them as they drove away afterwards in the two-seater, the man and his smiling wife in front and the two peculiarly chirpy children in the dicky seat behind. Most extraordinary it all was.

And the thing was that I had not meant to write about it at all. Back in Fleet Street they had warned me to keep well off politics and religion. They are both of course best left alone when talking about Ireland. And then I had done it. Only I do not see how to talk about Ireland without talking about religion. In a country where every drover on a country fair day will stop the harrying of his beasts to bless himself at the ringing of the bell for the Angelus, and where every man inside a bus will raise his hat as he passes a church door, it is a trifle difficult to ignore the subject. Once later on, I know, down in Waterford, I saw a street of people suddenly burst into a jog trot. I have seen the same thing in our Rochdale back in the old times of mill-hours, and I have seen it in my own suburb in the days when we used to catch steam trains, but never till I went to Ireland had I seen grown-ups running for fear of being late at church. As I say, it is a little hard in Ireland to write as though it were England.

Claude Wall (1904–1992)
Mweelrea, County Mayo in 1932

[Claude Wall was born in Dublin. After attending school at Belvedere College, he qualified as an accountant and spent most of his career in the insurance industry. His great passions were hill-walking and music, and in 1923, at the age of nineteen, he began to keep a diary of his travels and climbs, which formed the basis of newspaper articles he wrote during the 1930s. In 1939 he wrote *Mountaineering in Ireland*, the first hill-walkers' guide book dealing solely with the mountains of Ireland.

Wall was a founder member of the Irish Mountaineering Club in 1948, and was elected president of that body in 1953. His retirement in 1968 gave him more opportunities to indulge in music and walking, and in old age he still enjoyed outings into the hills, always celebrating his birthday with a climb.

His diaries are fresh and artless, and like J.B. Malone's,[1] beautifully hand-written, and filled with his passion for exploration and his hunger for knowlege of everything he saw. One of the early entries reads:

> This summer Frank O'Flanagan and I decided to go out every Sunday for the day and to make weekend trips in future, instead of wasting our time about town. The idea of keeping a diary did not occur to me until one day on the road to Wicklow we met a little man on a bicycle, who had been riding for the past forty years. In the course of our conversation he suggested that we should keep a diary of our travels. It is a pity I did not start at the beginning, as I have already had some remarkable experiences, including an impromptu dip in the Salmon Leap at Leixlip while endeavouring to cross it by means of stepping stones. However, it is better late than never.

The excerpt selected from his diaries tells of an exciting climb on Mweelrea, the highest mountain in the province of Connaught, which will ring true to all who have conquered it.]

'It's nice to get up in the morning but it's nicer to stay in bed', sings Harry Lauder and certainly his words are applicable to the soft and misty West. Our time of rising on holiday varies from 9.30 to 10 a.m. and in spite of the importance of this particular morning, I was not out of my bed until before half past nine. To me at all events, this was the most important day of the holiday. Failure in the attempt on Mweelrea would be a hard knock and success meant a successful holiday, whatever might follow.

I looked out the window eagerly. Across Killary the clouds were sweeping along the hills but it was dry and fairly bright; the outlook was

[1] See page 144.

good. It was that type of morning that generally presages a fine day. Mr King[2] informed me that my old friend Walsh of Bundorragha no longer crosses the ferry, due, he stated, to old age. He sent us to a nearby cottage and the owner took us over from the Harbour, quite close to McKeown's Hotel.[3] The Killary is wider at this point than at Bundorragha and with the water freshened by a strong westerly breeze, we took about twenty minutes to cross.

The clouds were still trailing along Leenane mountain but I noticed with delight that the Devil's Mother[4] was clear although Ben Gorm and Mweelrea were heavily veiled. A walk of about a mile and a half along the opposite shore brought us to Bundorragha, bringing back memories of a weary, drenched traveller and a grand Mayo welcome six years ago. The Mweelrea mountains form roughly a horseshoe enclosing a deep glen, down which rushes the Owenagloch river. Commencing at the southern ridge Bundorragha Hill rises sharply to a height of 1,259 feet. Then follows a bold spur of Mweelrea (1,623 feet), the main summit (2,688) followed by Benbury (2,610) and Ben Lugmore (2,616). The latter sweeps down steeply to Fin Lough near Delphi, scarcely two miles from Bundorragha. It can be seen that the whole group could be swept in one walk, given suitable conditions, as ridges of varying heights connect the summits. The quickest way to climb Mweelrea is to proceed up the Owenagloch valley, but we decided to attempt the chain.

It was after 12 when we tackled Bundorragha Hill, which was now free from cloud. It was a stiff little climb and took about forty minutes. Hugh Gately spurted early and led the way but soon falling back, reached the top last. Having gasped back our breath we took stock of our surroundings. Fin Lough and Delphi lay at our feet. At the opposite side of the valley, Ben Creggan and Ben Gorm rose proudly to their full height free from mist. The upper end of the Killary wound its way up to the Devil's Mother. Across the waters the clouds still swept the Twelve Bens and the wild Maamturks. Due north, clouds came and went from Ben Lugmore and Benbury, while straight ahead was the black mass of Mweelrea clinging to his white veil obstinately, but I was in striking distance now and nothing but an accident was going to stop me.

A steep descent over broken ground brought us to the lowest part of the ridge below Mweelrea. Hugh and I bore to the left thinking we might

[2] They were staying at King's Hotel in Leenane, where the night before they had been treated to a 'rough but wholesome meal'.

[3] Mweelrea is on the northern shores of Killary Harbour, and Leenane on the south; today there are no ferries and the approach is normally made by the road to Delphi.

[4] A plateau-topped mountain east of Leenane (see page 218).

circumvent the sharp spur before us, but Bill went straight for his objective and proved to be right as he quickly established a lead of a few hundred yards. The dark King of Connaught now towered in front and perhaps realising the game was up condescended to brush aside the veil from his squat head.

I started on Mweelrea proper at five minutes to one. I was now last in the party and although I frequently deprecate the practice of gruelling oneself in climbs it was unthinkable that I should not stand on the lonely summit first so I went at it with a will. There was another reason. With the weather conditions so uncertain it was well to push ahead rapidly. Bill went straight at the southern spur while Hugh and I kept to the inland flank closer to the main summit. This slope was very severe. We were sheltered from the wind and it was very sultry. The ground was broken up at times approaching the perpendicular.

I was very anxious concerning the camera which I was carrying. The hands had to be used occasionally and a slip would probably mean a few hundred feet journey for our 'Brownie', if not for myself. In addition to all this, it was evident that a grim struggle for mastery was taking place between the three of us. Bill was out of sight while Hugh and I struggled along silently to the neck between the southern spur and the summit. As far as ability to do the deed was concerned, there was nothing between us but I depended on the enthusiasm within me to carry the day eventually.

We now sighted Bill ahead with his lead considerably reduced but still sufficient to carry him home an easy winner if he kept on full steam. I did not slacken, but drawing away from Hugh, crossed the short boggy plateau in pursuit. Mists were again clinging to the crevices near the top while two little lakes showed far below in the deep Owenagloch valley. On the southern side the view was magnificent. The mouth of the Killary was now laid bare and the great inlet stretched in for its full length like a great snake burrowing into the mountains, while behind rose the most picturesque chain in the west, the Twelve Bens of Connemara.

Bill was slowing up and I gradually overhauled him on the last steep slope although my head was throbbing away, my legs weary and I had bellows to mend. Bill spurted again but the experience was telling and I cut off the corners and began to lead him by taking a more direct route. He stuck it manfully for a while; I saw him climbing a naked rock in his path though I shouted to him to desist. Eventually he slackened, probably realising I would keep on until I 'bust' and I gained the eminence alone.

The fog had now come down heavily and as I turned to the right for the final stretch, I was enveloped in cloud. It was about twenty minutes from here to the top. The slope was easy over a number of minor eminences and along the edges of tremendous cliffs. I saw the first one in its full length plunging down perpendicularly into the valley below. The others just disappeared in the swirling mists. It was a wonderful moment when a tiny cairn loomed ahead and I squelched out over the rank grass to the top of Connaught. I consulted my watch: it was ten past two. I liked to be alone for a while, alone with Mweelrea and the clouds.

Eleven years ago I had first passed by and looked at Mweelrea indifferently. Five years later I had waited at the foot to climb the King of Connaught and had turned away regretfully but determined to return – now Mweelrea was beneath my feet. I was robbed of the view it must be. Mweelrea had yielded hard and knew that I must return again for that marvellous sight from Nephin to Slyne Head and the great ocean with its chain of islands. And indeed Mweelrea still had something up his sleeve, of which more anon. The others arrived in about ten minutes asking me what about the view that was to reward their labours, but I knew that they were satisfied although they will hardly come again for the view.

Mweelrea is sometimes spelled Muilrea. P.W. Joyce writes: 'There is a well-known mountain over the Killaries in Connaught called Muilrea, and this characterises its outline, compared with the surrounding hills, when seen from a moderate distance: *mael reidh*, smooth, flat mountain.' The general translation given, which the local people confirm, is *maol riogh*, 'the bare or bald king'. The latter name is more poetic but not any more descriptive than the former. Mweelrea barely achieves the kingship of Connaught and is but forty-two feet higher than Nephin, 2,688 to 2,648 feet. Benlugmore and Benbury are both over 2,600 feet, while Croagh Patrick, Thievummera and Clashcame, all adjacent mountains of Murrish, are within 200 feet. I had now ascended the highest mountains in the four provinces of Ireland, and Mweelrea comes lowest on the list:

Munster:	Carrauntoohil, 3,414 feet
Leinster:	Lugnaquillia, 3,039 feet
Ulster:	Donard, 2,796 feet
Connaught:	Mweelrea, 2,688 feet

The clouds lifted partly in patches before we left and we saw Achill, Clare Island, Caher and Inisturk, as well as bewildering glimpses of lesser peaks about. The clearest view was at our feet, the coastline revealing some tempting white strands hidden away from the roads and traffic. The strong, mist-laden breeze soon moved us from the summit. Needless to state, we did not attempt to continue to Benbury; the conditions were now against us and there was real danger not only of losing our way but of serious accident if we carried on.

We commenced to descend more to the south as I had formed a foolish notion that there was a road at the foot along the northern shore of Killary. Further, I had stupidly allowed the party to set out without lunch, as we reckoned to be back to dinner at four. During the descent we got some maginficent views of the south and I left the others to gain advantage points for 'snaps'. Now followed the greatest gruelling I have ever gone through on a mountain and which I sincerely hope I will never have occasion to face again.

Descending to the south, I did not notice that I was leaving the others. My descent was slow and painful. It was all very wet and steep; several times I had to make wide detours to avoid sheer rocks. Misfortune commenced early. I laid down the camera to refresh myself at a brook, when, suddenly hearing a bump, I was horrified to see the precious 'Brownie' hopping down the hillside. Away it went, taking a bigger bounce each time and clearing the rocks with great bounds, until with a final leap of several yards it came to rest. I watched, fascinated, and luckily had the presence of mind to watch its course rather than following. It must have descended more than a hundred feet before it stopped.

I now descended at breakneck speed to the area in which it had fallen. Having called and shouted to the others without eliciting a response I commenced a search among the rocks and marshes. In and out and round about I wandered, prodding with my stick in the rain. I retraced my steps several times and came down by different routes. When I had almost finally despaired I found it. Having sat down to recover after an extremely bad half hour, I slung the camera over my shoulders with a piece of cord and continued my downward journey. It was soon pretty evident that there was no road along the foot of Mweelrea but I went on, hoping that I might be able to get around by the shore.

I soon realised that there was little chance of this, as the shore was mainly broken and rocky with nothing in the nature of a beach, and I commenced to move along the steep mountainside in the direction of Bundorragha. The mountainside was not unlike the lower slopes of Bray Head and I had to ascend frequently to get across awkward cliffs. The clouds descended lower, so to re-ascend was inadvisable. As I rounded each rugged bluff slowly, another appeared some distance on. I had no food and but for the frequent drinks of water I doubt if I could have kept going. One particularly steep series of smooth rocks brought me to a halt and I sat down dismally. I was really alarmed now. If the fog descended any further I would have had to sit still until assistance came from the water. I shook off my feeling of depression and ascended the mountainside again until I was high enough to pass along in safety.

At last I spied a lonely house in front and this cheered me up considerably as I thought that I must be near Bundorragha. When I reached it I found it was deserted and I had to plug along again by the mountainside. The short path leading from the house soon lost itself in marshes, and the interminable bays and cliffs came on again. I was now out of danger as I was some hundreds of feet above the sea; the steeper portions of the hill-side were lower down. I was very tired and hungry and did not mind how wet I became; I frequently went up to my knees in the marshes. At last I heard the distant barking of a dog and it was never more welcome. Crossing the next bluff I saw the ferryman's cottage about a mile ahead and what a relief it was!

This gave me new energy and I pushed ahead eagerly but it seemed a long time before I reached the rugged boreen leading to Walshe's home. It was now after 6 o'clock. I knocked eagerly at the little cottage door. The old woman opened the door but did not recognise me. When I mentioned my name she pulled me in and soon the kettle was singing on the fire and two or three eggs were having the jolliest set-to imaginable in a fat saucepan.

It was a grand Mayo welcome but a sad one. Her son, the fine dark-haired young man who had served under Kilroy, was dead. It was sad news. He had some trouble with his teeth, and went to Dublin to have them taken out. Complications set in and he was dead in a few days. The old man was still in the land of the living while a nephew, returned from America, sat in the corner. The old man was not at home but the *bean a' tí* was indignant when I told her about the ferry. She said that he still rows his curach across, but the hotel people spread the story that he had given it up to benefit their own men.

I would have liked to have stayed but I knew that a search party would be out soon if I did not move. After a tremendous feed, I made an offer of payment which was promptly refused. The nephew from America brought out the rowlocks, and we soon shot out into the Killary. They told me that Smith and Gately had passed along the road two hours earlier. The nephew was very dark with high cheekbones and a sensitive, rather wild face. He made short work of the journey; it was grand to be in the noble old curach compared to the ordinary rowing boat in which I had crossed.

When we landed on the opposite shore, he refused payment. He said the old woman would kill him if he took anything. I pressed him, saying that she need not know. His eyes flashed angrily but then he smiled and shook his head decisively. I asked him to come into Leenane for a drink but he declined ruefully, remarking that he was carried home last week; whenever he tasted it he went mad. There was a little boy with him and I managed to give him a couple of shillings.

I met a man on the road into Leenane and passing Begley's I was hailed by Frank and Bill, Mr and Mrs Begley. The other two had also got into some difficulty, but thought I was in front of them. I went on to the hotel to allay anxiety and then returned to Begley's for another feed and a very pleasant evening.

We returned to the hotel at a late hour in a downpour but I did not mind. Across the water the dim outline of Mweelrea showed through the mist, conquered but having a grim laugh up his fat sleeve. We will try conclusions again, and next time I intend to get a great view from the summit and there won't be any mistake about the descent!

J. B. Malone (1914–90)
Dublin and Wicklow Mountains, 1933 and 1939

[J. B. Malone was one of Ireland's best-known hillwalkers. The low, rounded summits of the mountains that he glimpsed from his home as a young man in the southern suburbs of Dublin beckoned to him, and he began to explore them methodically, summit by summit. From the beginning, he kept meticulous records of his explorations, his 'marches' as he called them, set down in a fine hand in a series of hard-backed notebooks that span the years 1932 to 1945. While he did walk in most parts of Ireland, Malone's main interest was his own Dublin and Wicklow range, and over the years he came to know every hill, summit, valley and riverbank there. He was forever exploring, forever seeking out the hidden places; this sense of exploration, of pioneering, comes strongly through in his journals in phrases like 'I went forward' and 'I reached the Feather Bed, where desolation begins', or in the comment on 'the awful emptiness between Glencree and Sally Gap'. There is no scarcity in his journals of colourful comments about inclement weather. Caught out on one occasion on the shelterless Feather Bed plateau in the Dublin mountains, he looked back and saw 'how the wind had veered to WNW and a heavy rainstorm was coming on in black fury. At the most exposed part of the road, the last straight mile into the Glencree, the rain began, and continued until I was beyond Curtlestown, a steady, soaking downpour. The peak of misery was when, at the bend of the road at Barnamire, the rainsodden bag of grub burst, as I dragged it from my pocket, and my last sandwich fell in the mud.'

In 1938 the *Evening Herald* commissioned Malone to write a regular column about hillwalking, and he subsequently wrote a number of guide-books for walkers. He is, however, best known for his central role in the establishment of Ireland's way-marked walking trails, and in particular, the most popular of these routes, the Wicklow Way

The following are excerpts from his journals describing in detail, complete with basic compass bearings, the routes he followed on his early mountain explorations.]

30/4/33

Enniskerry – Tinnehinch – Glencree – Lough Bray – Sally Gap – Luggala – Togher – Long Hill – Enniskerry

Wind, east, north east. Cloudy, rain threatening, visibility fair to poor. Made this march with Radigand Barden.[1] We had only the 1 inch OS Dublin District and Macready's half-inch map. All the way up Glencree the rain kept threatening. After lunch at McGuirks,[2] we struck south for Sally Gap, and noticed the clouds down on Kippure summit, and on the butt of Gravale. After Liffey head, we were no longer on the 1 inch map, and we got a glimpse of the woods before us, as we went down the Ballycorrigan Road. It must have been after 6 p.m. when we were at Luggala. The clouds lifted a little and the sun began to set, and below us we saw Lough Tay. Some things can be described, but Lough Tay seen after marching through the high bogs of Sally Gap, cannot be. The deep woods were round it, and little flukes of wind ruffled the surface, reflecting the first break in the sky. 'If this be earth, what is Heaven?' is all one can say about such things. And when we came to the high pass, where the road turns east to run down into Togher, we were well lost. We saw the Vartrey Extension[3] before us, which Macready doesn't mark, and with mists hiding the far side of it we took it for the sea, and expected to be in Enniskerry in two hours. But there were twelve miles ahead of us, and that included the nine miles up the longest road in the world, the cursed Calary road. We marched, and it grew dark, and we still marched, and it grew darker. We could no longer read the maps and we still marched, until at last we saw the flash of the Baily[4] – only then we sang. Even then, we started up the Killoge road in error, and but for Radigard Barden's remembering that we had not come out by that road, we might be wandering yet. Back through the dark woods of Tinnehinch and up again out of the Dargle – and only by running did we catch the last bus, with twenty-eight and a half miles behind us.

[1] Radigand Barden was Malone's cousin.
[2] McGuirks was a popular teahouse adjoining the Military Road at Glencree which opened during the 1880s and operated almost continuously until the 1990s. A visitors' book was kept over most of that period in which those who stopped for refreshments signed, some of them writing comments and poems, and others leaving drawings. Malone's and Barden's signatures appear under 30.4.33.
[3] One of the reservoirs serving Dublin city; it did not exist when Macready made his map.
[4] The Baily is a lighthouse at the tip of Howth Head, the northern portal to Dublin Bay.

Bohernabreena Chapel – Annmount – Glassamucky – Boundary Ridge – Glencree Reformatory – N bank track to Ballycoyle Wood – Ballyross Wood – Sward – Onaghagh – Seskin Plank – Lacken House – Annacrevy – Kilmalin – Glencullen Cross – Kiltiernan – Stepaside (bus).

Wind ENE, Cloudy, (at 1600/3000), clearing later. Visibility good. With Frank Hitchcock. 12.30 – 9.30 p.m.

This midweek walk was designed to gather information re the NE approach to Kippure, and to enjoy the beauties of Glencree.

From the bus, we went up Glenasmole by Annmount, turning off by the boreen between the schoolhouses to see the grand view of the upper lake, then coming back to push on S, swinging left to take the mountain road above Cunard and Castlekelly.

Here, when the last trees lay behind us, and the bare mountain sloped away on every side, we were favoured with a modern miracle. There, upon our right, on the road margin, loosely wrapped in the *Irish Times*, lay a half-full bottle of sherry, in splendid isolation.

Neither had this miraculous wine passed through the hands of middlemen, but still bore its original label, which proclaimed with majestic Castilian simplicity, *Amontillado, Jerez de la Frontera*. Our suspicious sniffs soon gave way to sipping, then as we threw our heads back, and let it gurgle down, the world was bathed in a golden glow, while through our veins coursed the spirit that fired the *campadores*. Catalina de Erredo, with her 'horses and weapons of steel, and the high protection of God' had nothing on us – as we strode upon the roof of Wicklow, upon a soft boreen, while over beyond the glen rose the Six Mountains, and high above, the clouds moved fast through the upper air.

With the last of the magic sherry we laced our milk supplies, carrying the bottle still to convince stay-at-home sceptics. By this time we had come to the turn left up to the Feather Bed, which we left alone, keeping straight on S by the old turf-cutter's road. This was in surprisingly good condition, and led us almost all the way up on to the Boundary Ridge. On gaining this, we turned right, heading SSW along the other turf road, which, however, ceases after a half mile, at an abandoned bog cutting. Beyond this, we pushed our reconnaissance still SSW for about a quarter mile further, finding the Boundary to be a double mearing traced across rough boggy moorland. Some way beyond the beginning of the dip to Mareen's Brook we turned back, halting when again on the ancient track. Here, while the larks sang strongly, we lay basking, watching the swift flying clouds leaping up from behind Killakee. Peculiar mists lay upon

Cloughnagowan, and writhed into the Onaghagh hollow in the Glencree Mountains, but left Kippure quite clear.

We started again by heading SE across the ridge, while the mists in Glencree dissolved before us (another miracle), as we traversed a B2 area,[5] with many moss clumps and small pools of green slime. Gradually more and more of Glencree came into view, first just the crests of the surrounding mountains, then a relevation of the hidden depths of the glen, the rivers and forests, all that makes it the loveliest of Wicklow's valleys. Before us now opened a modern turf bog, into the workings of which we marched, striking a fine bog road which enabled us to keep exactly to our SE trend, and led us out onto the Military Road just above the Reformatory, to which we cut down straight across the fields. After a chat with a returned Texan priest, we set off down the north road for about a mile. But we missed the turn off the track S to Ballycoyle Wood, so had to strike down across lush meadows and briars, at length finding the wide remains of the old road. From here, Tonduff towered above us S, while westward, the Eagle's Crag came frowning above the Lough Bray hollow. Haze in the dim distance made photos hopeless, but never spoilt our enjoyment. Everywhere enchanting glimpses opened. There were the pathetic ruins W of the Ballycoyle track, then the countless views of Maulin from the track itself, before we plunged into the jungle of ash saplings, as we turned left at every forking of the path.

This led us at last to the open river bank and the wooden bridge previously seen by me. Across this we halted, enjoyed the last echoes of the sherry, bathed our feet, then set off again by the fine path through bracken, ESE towards Ballyross.

The finest view here was of Big Sugar Loaf appearing in the gap between Lacken Wood and Ballyross Wood. After this, we followed the track on through Ballyross Wood, but somehow kept too much N for the crossing of the Ballyross or Ballycoyle stream, finding ourselves forced to follow the bank a little downhill before getting across, which left us in the 'Magic Carpet' meadow N of the wood. Fortunately the field had been cut, for there is no kind of path across it. Emerging at the cottage, we turned S and climbed up the zigzag to the south road, noting some evidence of an opening S of the barred gap, into the Ballyross wood, which probably cuts the corner, and rejoins the bracken track some way W.

On the south road we headed E for Onaghagh corrie, turning up too soon from the road, however, which we had left at the Forestry Fire warning, where the path is too overgrown by bracken. We had admired

[5] Malone's own code for terrain.

the gradual revelation of Maulin's majesty, which we discovered to be due not least to the fact that the forest flanks consist of minature trees as yet, and when anything appears on the mountain, even a sheep or a man high up on the Stripped Blaze,[6] the illusion of enormous height mostly vanishes.

Into the Onaghagh corrie we went then again, striking off SE over the softish flat floor (rather drier than previously experienced) and noting that a small green tree (ash?) among the dark pine marks the point to turn off left from the wall. When across the Ballyreagh Brook, we followed the sheep track up S, till slightly below the left shelf of the rock. Here we halted for grub, listening to the rhythmic rise and fall of the sound of the cascades, and on getting off again, made back down to Ballyreagh Bridge. But by some trick of the light, the NE ridge dividing the two branches of the Ballyreagh was made much clearer this day, and it was with some reluctant glances that we turned our backs on climbing problems, and headed N for home.

From Ballyreagh Bridge we turned off N for Seskin Plank Bridge, but were misled again at the gates N of the 'rath', where one *must head NW to the left corner of the field giving the rath a wide berth on the right*. We thus came to Seskin Wood much too much E of the Plank, swung W along by the stone wall, which we crossed at an inviting but delusive gap, and found ourselves in 'another part of the wood'. Any enchantment, however, soon vanished upon clumping into black sludge streams (sewage from farms draining into the Glencree river?) and on having the insteps ripped off us by hidden briars. We followed the riverbank along W in desperation till at last the Plank appeared. Here we took photos, and headed up for Lacken House, uneventfully save that I got a wet bootful at the mud splash three-quarters way up.

I don't remember whether we turned left or right on regaining the Knockree boreen, but my rough note mentions 'Curtlestown', which would have added three unnecessary miles to us! However, we left Enniskerry alone and by the long rise to Ballybrew made the Devil's Elbow in the gloaming, having looked back from the crest to see mists again rolling over Djouce and the upper Dargle. Past Foxes[7] we reached Kiltiernan in due course, and with a good weariness on us, trudged on the odd mile to Stepaside, where we waited 10–15 minutes in the dark before the bus came.

[6] Malone gave specific topographical features his own descriptive names.
[7] Foxes Pub in Glencullen is still there.

[At the age of 21 J B Malone penned this lament for a loved raincoat that was stolen; the extreme cruelty of the fate he wishes upon the stealer of the coat can only hint as how attached he was to it.]

Lament for a Raincoat
Purchased Clery's Bargain Basement 1933
Stolen in Rathgar Chapel 1935

I marched him down the deeps of many glens,
With him I climbed the crests of mighty hills –
O dear dark coat! Your wandering is done –
Never again to see the summer sun,
Never to take the southern road
Nor feel the keen teeth of the icy blast
Scourging the naked slopes of great Seecon,
Never again to see the Golden Hill
To come to Mooney's pub beside Kilbride
Where all the tumbled walls of well-hewn stones
Are thick with lichen, like the green sea slime.
The wastes of Calary and far Lough Dan,
The flukes of wind that ruffle fair Lough Tay,
Kippure's dark buttock, beetling over Lough Bray –
Never again these will be seen by you!

Some lousy scut has stolen you – well then
Upon him may these heavy curses fall!
May all the travail that that coat has borne
And ten times trebled fall upon his head!
May all his life one ruddy route march be,
Filled with the troubles of a thousand tramps –
The utter loneliness of wild Glenbride
The thirsty miles, from Lisheens to the bus
May all the maps mislead him – may his plans
Miscarry always, and let weather foul
Follow his footsteps, where so'er he goes
And may hard hunger, sweat and weariness,
March on beside him while the wretched man
Shall struggles forward – he shall never know
The happy glory of a safe return.

Aye, may his home be desolate and drear,
As full of comfort as Mullaghroe,
May all his brats be girls, so that his name

Shall perish from the earth, and may each one
Come to a shameful end, or take to gin.
And when old age at last shall strike him down
May he die roaring, with his feet in air! –
No graceful growing old – no, let him be
A frowsy, blear-eyed, drooling , 'down and out',
Dying in a ditch unshriven and unknown

Envoi

Old coat that I loved, beside the Annamoe,
Where are you now, alas, where are you now?
'The best of friends must part' – so runs the song
But we may hope to meet again some day,
When lost things shall be found, when there shall be
A steady south wind blowing, and the spring
Shall know no ending – then perhaps shall we
Take once again the southward road we know,
Old coat I loved, beside the Annamoe.

Nora Laverock Lees
Connemara *c.*1935

[In spite of many enquiries, I failed to discover more about Ms Laverock Lees other than that she took a walking holiday in the Connemara area in the 1930s before travelling to Waterford and taking a steamship passage back to England, where she presumably lived. She wrote of her experiences in a book called *Bogs and Blarney*, which was published in 1936.

After visiting the Aran Islands, she sailed by Galway hooker from Inish Oirr to the south Galway coast; the excerpt I have selected deals with her journey from Kilkieran to Letterfrack. Ms Laverock Lees conjures up a delightful picture of Connemara in the 1930s, and her descriptions of the places, the people, and in particular the conversations, are wonderfully well observed.]

CONNEMARA

Wandering up the straggling village I met a postman and asked him if he knew of any place where I could stay the night. He told me of a Mrs

Walsh down the road who might be able to give me a bed. Off I went to see Mrs Walsh, who came to the door and, drying her hands on the corner of her apron, listened to the tale of my homelessness. 'Musha, 'tis not much room we have, but sure you're welcome, indeed you are; come in now and I'll do me best for you,' she said. 'Is it off a turf boat you say you're after coming? Oh, glory be to God, and was it terrible sick you were?'

She stirred the fire, and talking away the whole time, busied herself getting tea and boiling eggs. My face, after its lashing with wind and salt spray, stung and burned with the warmth of the kitchen, and as I got up and walked over to the table, the floor swayed and rocked under my seafaring feet.

After tea, I walked out along the road to see the sunset. Ambling leisurely along in the middle of the road, I was watching a pig trying to poke a smudgy pink snout under the closed door of a whitewashed cabin, when suddenly there was a loud hoot behind me and I had to jump into the ditch to allow a ramshackle old car to pass – a noisy reminder that I was back in the world once more.

Poverty stalks more openly through the mainland here than on the Aran Islands. The cabins are ruder, life seems sterner. Even the cattle look small and stunted, black mountain cattle they are mostly. 'Aye, 'tis poor they are, very poor,' said a man I talked to as he came along walking beside an aged, moth-eaten donkey. 'Sure there does be no grazing in among them rocks and bogs.'

I told him about the fine cattle I had seen on Aran.

'Oh, musha that's the place now. All the good that's in it; sure many's the time we do be sending cows over from here to give them a couple of weeks out there on Aran, and faith you wouldn't know them when they'd be coming back, they'd be fat and strong looking.'

Sitting by the kitchen fire for a few minutes before going to bed, I was chatting with Mrs Walsh when a 'piper of the ashes' suddenly began to chirp a little thin song from the back of the hearth.

'It's a long time since I've heard a cricket,' I said to her.

'Well, indeed now, and 'tis only lately they've come back to the house again,' she said, 'for they left a twelvemonth ago when himself died, and sure it was that lonesome without them; but they always leave a house when there's a death in it. Isn't it a strange thing now, wouldn't you wonder how they'd be finding out? But they're queer things altogether. Would you believe now that if you were to kill one of them, the others would come and do something bad on you. 'Tis true. Faith it is, and I seen it happen meself, for there was one day when himself was here and he put his foot on one of them, and what do you think did they do, but that night they came and eat a pair of socks that was hanging up here be the fire to dry, and the next morning when he went to get them, it was only a few crumbs of wool that was left.'

Bidding her goodnight, I went off to bed. The bedroom door, I discovered, would not stay shut without the assistance of a chair, for the latch had come off and was now used to prop the window open.

Next morning it was pouring as I started out on my tramp towards the mountains. I stopped for a moment at the one village store to see if they had a pair of woollen socks which, I thought, might make the road seem softer. The men in this part of the world must be barge-footed, for the six pairs of socks in the shop were all too long by several inches, and my feet are not of the daintiest. As I could get no socks, I bought a pair of oranges instead, which I stuffed into my rucksack as a contribution towards my lunch.

It was a good-natured little shop, where bacon stood peacefully side by side with paraffin oil, rounds of butter nestled up to pairs of stout boots, while on the shelf at my elbow was a square tin labelled 'Peril Barley'. The woman told me she thought 't'would be a grand day later on', so bidding her good day, I hoped she would be right, and went on my way.

There is a glorious feeling in stepping out along the highway in the freshness of a young day, even it be a wet one, with a full day's adventures in front of you and no definite idea of where, tired and sore, you may put up for the night. I was plodding along thoroughly enjoying myself when a car whizzed past, then slowed down, and a man called out to know if I would like a seat to Carna. I thanked him and said I would rather walk, which sounded an absurd lie, I suppose, with such torrents of rain; but walking, I glowed with warmth, whereas sitting in a car with soaking wet clothes I would be frozen.

Soon the rain settled down to a thin mist. Beside a clean, neat cottage I met a tall, fine-looking girl with silk stockings and a sprigged cotton overall over a dress. In her hand she carried a pail of milk. It was all very puzzling until she spoke, and then her American accent explained everything. She was a girl whose travels had spoilt none of her simple ways. She told me of her life in America and of the number of Irish girls there were near her, so that it felt just like being at home. She said it was fine to be able to speak amongst themselves in Irish when they did not want others to know what they were saying.

As we stood talking, her mother came out of the cottage and joined us. Her face was very old and wrinkled, but whenever she looked over at her daughter, her dull eyes lit up and the tired expression of her face freshened. She said it was at Carna I should have been this morning to see all the grand processions, and I told her that I had just refused a lift there in a car.

'Faith,' she said, 'and you should have taken it; was it afraid you were for the two men that was in it?'

'No,' I replied, 'it wasn't that.'

'Because,' she went on, "tis no fear of anyone you need have round these parts, for they're all good people, indeed they are.'

I asked her if the people living round about here felt much difference under the Free State Government.

'Well now, in some ways 'tis better off we are, and in some ways maybe 'twas better before,' she replied. 'I'll tell you now something that makes a big difference to us. In the old days when a man or a woman died in the workhouse, they were just nailed down in an ould plain bit of a wooden box and buried in the workhouse cemetery, the craturs. But, musha now when they die in the workhouse, they're put into a grand coffin with brass and all on it, and they're brought to the village they came from and given a decent burial in the cemetery, like you'd think it was not poor they were at all, God help them.'

The daughter went into the cottage and reappeared a few minutes later with a glass of creamy milk standing on a gleaming white gold-rimmed saucer.

'I guess you're thirsty with the walking,' she said as she handed it to me.

She disappeared again to see about the hens' food, and her mother took that opportunity of telling me what a good girl her daughter was, and how unlike she was to most of the young people these days.

'For,' she said, 'the young people is not as religious as they were. Sure you never see them fasting at Lent like they used to, and them living on a quarter of a pound of dry bread a day and not even a dropeen of milk through their tea; and wasn't it the grand strong people they were then, able to get up at four or maybe five itself, to see would they see the sun and it dancin'. 'Tis a great pity, indeed it is, for there's nothing in the world that's any good to anyone but only religion. And,' she went on 'I don't know as how it matters a whole lot whether 'tis a Catholic or a Protestant you are, for it's all one, so long as the heart is good. It's the heart that matters. There used to be a Protestant gentleman living in these parts, and sure twas a lovely man he was and he as good to all the poor people, sure I never seen the likes of him.'

The daughter joined us again, and after some more talk I shook hands, and with injunctions to be sure and look in on them if I was passing that way again, and a kindly 'God speed you', I left them.

I don't think I have ever met so many flocks of geese anywhere as I did walking along that stretch of road to Carna. And I hate geese. Of all hostile, unfriendly, spiteful characters, they are the worst. As I tramped along, they rose up from the side of the road, shaking their pure white wings; then, long necks craning with hatred, they waddled towards me and hissed their horrid thoughts at my feet. In vain I tried to retaliate by whispering that evil word, 'Christmas', to them.

Turning a corner I met a woman coming along barefoot in a bulging red petticoat, with an enormous sack of something on her broad back. She was bursting with effusiveness when we met, and, sliding the sack to the ground, looked at me as if I was her long-lost sister – also, poor thing, with a load on my back. Then stretching out her hand sideways, so that it met mine with a smack, she shook hands with such vigour that mine felt like crushed pulp when I got it back. And all this without a single word. I was so taken aback that I said nothing either, and before I could recover, she had shouldered her sack and was off down the road while I stared after her in blank astonishment.

The President was expected at the hotel in Carna that afternoon, and those who were not away at the religious ceremony which was being held that day, were in a flutter of excitement watching for him to arrive. Perhaps that was why, in the whole of Carna, I could find nothing to buy for my lunch.

Thinking of the luncheon table bristling with knives and forks set ready for the President, I turned sorrowfully away, and with muddy shoes plodded out of the village to consult with a fingerpost at the crossroads.

The next village was four miles off, and the road stretching away towards it led across a deserted bog. Just as I was standing underneath its yellow fingers, wondering whether I could curb my appetite for another four miles, a girl came out of a cottage across the road and smiled at me so pleasantly that I unburdened my troubles to her and asked if she could possibly make me up a few slices of bread to take with me.

'Sure of course I could,' she said, beaming reassuringly; 'you'd get none in the village, I know, because the people all bake their own bread. Sit down there now and I'll cut it for you. Will you take a sup of milk while you're waiting?'

She was horrified when, getting up to go, I produced my purse.

'And do you think I'd be taking anything for a few bits of bread like that?' she said indignantly. However, I pointed out that I should never have thought of asking her had I known that. No, she would take nothing. I looked out into the garden where her little daughter was stooping down picking up fallen fuchsia blossoms.

'All right,' she said, still reluctantly. 'I'll take it to buy something for her. But mind, you're more than welcome to it, and I don't like to be taking it at all.'

The white road, stretching out across the bog towards the mountains, looked so different from the road to Carna. It seemed to lead right out of the world. There was not a cabin, not a cow, not a sign of a human being for miles, and it felt glorious to tramp along and break the still silence with a rhythmic crunch, crunch on the hard road.

Coming to a little reedy lake, I turned off and sat down on a rock by its margin to eat my lunch. The brown, peaty water gently lapped the rock, and a lonely curlew called from the bog nearby. In places the heathery, rolling surface was broken by a dark brown cutting, its sides marked with a neat herringbone pattern left by the spade that had sliced out the sods, and beside the cutting stood the heaps of lighter brown turf, stacked up and left to dry.

As I finished the last thick slices of bread, ate my orange and started off again, I felt sorry, after all, for the President; sorry for anyone who was not at that moment tramping along with this gentle, fresh breeze blowing in his face. Can any breeze in the world be purer and more satisfying than one that comes softly over the sea, plays about the tops of heathery mountains, and then lilts gently over a stretch of wild, lonely bogland, catching up the perfume of bog myrtle on its way, till, laden with fragrance, it is like smooth mellowed wine; and as you stand still and drink it in, a flood of pure happiness surges over you. Oh, it is good to be drunk with that headiest of all air – bogland breezes.

Drifting mists covered the mountains with clinging cobweb veils, but sometimes the wind, breathing gently round them, lifted a corner of the veil and revealed the sloping sides of green mountains. The flat bogs on either side of the road sank often into little lakes on whose quiet surface water lilies lay dreaming among their flat, green leaves. I have always had a secret longing to hold one of these purest of white flowers in my hand and touch its cool, wax-like petals; but, with myriads of them there to pick just for the stretching out of a hand, I could not pick one.

On I tramped through the quiet solitude, alternately putting on and taking off my waterproof as shower after shower drifted over and passed. At last I passed a few stray cottages and thought I must be nearing Glinsk, but there was no sign of a village; instead, another long, lonely stretch of bogland lay ahead, and round a bend of the road a straggling arm of the sea stretched lazily across the lumpy ground. I had thought of staying at Glinsk for the night, as, on the map, it looked a fair-sized place. Having walked on another couple of miles, I met a postman on a bicycle.

'Can you tell me how much further it is to Glinsk?' I asked him.

'Is it Glinsk? Sure, glory be to God, you're after passing Glinsk two mile back.'

'Is it those few cottages you mean?'

'Musha, it is now; that's Glinsk all right.'

I hated the place from that moment, and steadfastly turning my back on it I faced the open road, and asked the man if he thought there might be anyone further on who could put me up for the night.

'There's not many in it has room for a stranger,' he said, 'two rooms is all the most of them has; but if you ask at that one you see away down the road there, they might be able to do something for you.'

On I went and, coming to the cottage, knocked at the door and asked if they knew anyone about here who could put me up for the night.

'Musha, I do not now. The houses is all too small. Sure, I'd have put you up meself only I have a sister staying with me. But is it travelling you are?' she said, eyeing my rucksack, 'faith and you'd better come in and have a drink so.' I sat by the fire and steamed, while she made some tea. 'I'm afraid 'tis on to Cashel you'll have to go,' she said; 'there's nowhere nearer, and there's a hotel itself there.'

Sitting at the kitchen table drinking hot tea, the thought of footing it on for another three or four miles began to feel possible. It became more and more possible until, as I shook hands at the door, I felt almost fresh.

'God speed you,' said the woman of the house. 'God bless you,' my heart sang as I thanked her and went on my way.

I thought ruefully of the lift I had scorned in the morning. No car passed me this time, only a donkey laden with panniers of turf and an old man in a faded yellow bawneen, who said, through the drifts of rain, 'That's a fine evening, thank God.'

That evening, instead of sitting down to bacon and cabbage, and sharing a thatched roof with homely faces and friendly hens, I walked into the company of people who bath, and trying to forget my old tweed skirt with its baggy knees, and wishing my muddy shoes would sink just a little further into the thick carpets, I went over and sat down to a young banquet. All around me, English voices talked of twelve-pounders, of gillies, of flies, while I sat and ate pale pink salmon trout.

What civilisation! My bedroom window that night had ropes, and stayed open when I pushed it up; instead of pigs in the yard outside, there were shining de luxe cars and not a sign of a hen, and the bedroom walls were so thick that no snore came through them from the adjoining room. Next morning I lay in bed and chuckled as I saw my poor old shoes come in, clean and with as much polish as their wrinkled damp toes would take.

But in spite of all that, I was in Ireland still; for when, after breakfast, I went to see the manageress, she said she could only charge for my food seeing the little back room was so small where, being absolutely full up, she had, out of kindness, erected a bed. I thought of other hotels where you pay nobly for the privilege of sleeping in the bath when they are full up. She and her husband were far more interested in hearing where I walked from the day before, and where I thought of going to that day, than they were in the bill. It was raining, and they said if I cared to wait an hour or two they were sending a car through the valley to Kylemore, and I could have a lift in it if I liked, or if I really would rather walk, then I must wait and they would have some sandwiches made up for me.

At a small shop near the hotel I managed to buy a pair of woollen socks – big, but not impossible – and sitting down I put them on and turned the long legs down and down until my ankles looked like advertisements for balloon tyres.

The fishers had all gone forth to fish when I trudged down the wide path and out on to the hard road again. It wound in and out, following the curves of narrow armlets of the sea; armlets, whose low-tide fringe of bright saffron-coloured weed was their sole relationship with the wild, noisy Atlantic. On the other side of the road, the green slopes climbed up to a pointed peak. The heather was saturated with all the recent rain, and here and there a mountain torrent tumbled, sometimes sheer down a rock face, then it tore along under a bridge and out to the inlet. Clumps of honeysuckle hung, heavy and wet, by the wayside.

Coming to where a wide, dark brown river swirled down, and did its best, with the cramped inlet at its disposal, to make an important exit, I turned and followed it up towards Ballynahinch. It was a river sacred to fishermen, and moored to the bank were small boats painted battleship grey. It all looked very solemn, very serious. I only saw one fisherman, at the reach just below Ballynahinch station. He, too, looked very serious, as he sat in a boat, in the rain, while a bored gillie moved the water gently with his oars. Enormous granite boulders stuck out of the water here and there, making the hurrying stream foam with rage until it looked like an eddy of brown stout topped with a frothing head.

At Ballynahinch the signal was down and there seemed every hope of a train,[1] though there was nobody except the stationmaster to take any interest in it; but then there is nobody at Ballynahinch, it is not even a village. At last it came fussing along, a funny little train with two carriages. I bundled into a compartment, and there in front of me sat the Perfect Hiker and his wife.

They both looked as if Mr Gamage or Mr Lillywhite[2] had just that moment bowed them out, having removed the price ticket from shoes, rucksack, socks, waterproofs – everything. I *might* be wringing wet, my men's socks might look a bit funny, my shoe might gape in a hole at the side, but anyhow, I thought, as I got out my sandwiches and ate them, I *have* walked.

The rain had stopped by the time we got to Clifden but the surrounding hills were still woolly with mist. As these were the first proper shops I had seen since I left Galway five weeks before, and might be the last I would see for many more weeks, I sauntered up and down the main street, popping into a shop here and there to buy a few things.

[167] The Clifden railway line closed some years later, but part of it is today a walking route.
[168] A British clothing store chain.

At one shop I asked for stockings, the girl looked at me, then brought out a selection of very coarse ones at a shilling a pair. I said I thought I could go just a trifle dearer than that, and she brought some at one and six. Still they were coarse, and I said I might even consider dearer ones still. She looked doubtful as she produced a box at two shillings a pair. It happened there were none in my size, and in the end, to her great confusion, I bought a pair at half a crown. She tried to cover up what she felt to have been a dreadful *faux pas*.

'Sure, I thought you were just wanting a rough pair,' she assured me, 'for ladies often comes in and buys them cheap ones just for climbing the mountains, d'ye know?'

I went into another shop and could not get out under half an hour, in which time I had a rambling resume of the bird-like little woman's life story together with an invitation to accept the hospitality of a sofa in her sitting room for a few days and the loan of a bicycle with which to explore the neighbourhood.

'There's grand scenery round Clifden, and sure you couldn't go on without seeing it,' she said. She was so very insistent with her kindness that I found it hard to make plausible enough excuses. But in Clifden there were cars, there were hotels, there were tourists, and I had no wish to stay there. A bus came snorting up the road just then and saved me, for when I asked where it was going she told me it went to Leenane, so I said I thought I would go on towards there, and if the weather took up I might perhaps come back to Clifden later, as one needed good weather for cycling. Off I went then to get the bus that was now standing waiting outside one of the hotels further up, with, in the front seat, the two hikers from the train. Having thus caught one another out a second time, we all smiled.

I bussed for a mile or so of the way from Clifden, and then, as it looked like being a fine afternoon, I jumped off and walked slowly nearer and nearer to the mountains that, in a sudden flash of sunlight, seemed draped in green velvet.

I kept an eye out, as I went along, for a likely place to stay and, meeting an armlet of the sea again, I came to a village with a small, homely-looking hotel, where I thought I might stay for a few days while I wired my address and waited for letters.

The hotel proved just as homely as it looked. There was a friendly turf fire in the sitting room; there was a table on the landing upstairs with a little forest of white candlesticks from which, on going to bed, you helped yourself, and if you wanted hot water, there were a few cans under the table which in the morning were left outside as many bedroom doors as they would go round; those who were unlucky took their ewers and cheerfully went forth to the bathroom. It all made for a spirit of comradeship among the guests, for as well as enquiries as to how one had slept, there were such other queries as to whether you had been lucky with water that morning, and debates about who had been unpublic-spirited enough to have a bath and hold up the queue of those who waited, ewer in hand.

There was an air of sporting chance about everything, even to washing one's hands in the small basin in the bathroom, for the stopper was a size too big, and instead of fitting into the hole, it lay on top and wiggled about, letting the water run out all the time. I found washing my hair in it to be a most exciting business, for with one hand I had to try and hold the stopper, while with the other I swilled the water over my hair, and each time, just as I had got a good lather in the basin, the stopper shifted and away it all went. My bedroom window amused me too, for the gutter ran along outside, halfway down the window, so that, opening the top sash and leaning out, I looked down on the little trickle of water running along towards the next bedroom window. I sailed a little paper boat along it one day and watched it end its voyage by disappearing down the drainpipe at the end.

The village was equally homely, with its one or two small shops where buying a button would lead to an hour's chat. I thought it was time I did something about the ever-widening hole in my shoe, so one morning I set off to find the cobbler, who, I was told, lived in a cottage 'off down the road there'. It was rather vague, so meeting a man who was driving some cows into a field, I stopped and asked him if he could tell me where the cobbler lived. 'Sure 'tis meself's the cobbler,' he replied. I showed him the shoe and asked him if he could possibly put on a rough patch while I waited. 'Faith and I could if you'd just be waiting one minute now till I put the cows in.' He closed the gate of the field behind the last reluctant cow and I walked with him up the road to his cottage, a dreary, unkempt place, with no bustling woman in the kitchen to clear away the turf ashes of days, to rub the darkening dust from the small window, or to remove the remains of a scanty breakfast from the corner of the dusty table.

As he led me through the kitchen and into a tiny room at the back, he told me that 'herself' had been dead this ten year and that he had no one now to do anything for him. Round about his three-legged stool the floor was covered several inches deep with chips and cuttings of leather, and all around the room stood boots, old and new, finished and unfinished. Huge heavy country boots they were, whose soles bristled with big iron studs. I picked up one that felt as if it had been made for Hercules. 'Aye, I'm thinking they'd be a bit heavy for the likes of you,' he said; 'you'd want to have a few of their teeth drawn first.'

He had all the pride of a craftsman as he told me how he made every bit of them by hand. 'It was from me father I learnt it,' he went on, 'and he learning from his father before him, for it was all shoemakers was in our family.' It was, I think, a great grief to him that he had no son's steady hand waiting to take the awl from his when it grew old and shaky. Not that he was melancholy in his loneliness. It was there, but he hid it with a smile. I could imagine him sitting tapping and hammering away by the hour, and easing his sadness by letting it flow into the tune of some old Gaelic song. The village children, he said, liked to come in and watch him working, and it was telling stories to them he'd have to be.

I had asked him to put on a rough patch, but that apparently he could not do; everything that left his hand must receive the last touch. Fascinated I sat and watched him chisel the leather and smooth off the edges till, even and rounded, they satisfied him. When it was finished, he took me out to show me the view from the top of a sloping hillock at the back of his cottage.

'There's some as says 'tis up here the house should be, so that I'd have this grand view of the bay and the mountains, but sure 'twould be blew away on me entirely if I had it up here; 'tis bad enough where it is in the winter when the rough weather comes.'

The following afternoon I set out to walk round the inlet to where there is, at the end of a hilly promontory, a view of the open sea. It was a fresh day, a day of bright intense colour, with a strong sea wind that chased big lumpy white clouds across a clear blue sky, while their drifting shadows swept the sunlight from green sloping mountainsides and valleys, to be followed in their turn by a flood of flashing sunbeams. Connemara was herself at last. All her loveliness of quickly-changing colour, her sharp-pointed peaks of vivid green ranging back into distant purpling blue; her sudden gleams of sparkling waterfalls; her spreading sheets of calm, blue water; her fuchsia hedges glowing warm and red by the wayside. She had put on all her jewellery and was the charming, captivating Connemara who has ensnared the heart of many a worshipping artist.

Garry Hogg (1903–?)
Sneem, County Kerry in 1948

[Garry Hogg was a British journalist, broadcaster, university lecturer, and author. He had a total of thirty-six books – mainly about travel and nature – published during his writing career, which he only commenced at the age of forty-three. He particularly enjoyed exploring 'undiscovered' countryside, which led him to take long walking tours. He produced travelogues describing Norway and Brittany before coming to Ireland in 1948 to walk on the west coast.

His later works include *Portuguese Journey*, in which he describes a tour of that country on foot with his wife, Elizabeth Grey.

Hogg wastes little time with explanations about why he has chosen to walk, or how and by what route he got to the place he starts to walk; he starts his narratives as if simply beginning a new chapter, assuming you are there with him already, and this relaxed, no-sideshows format works very well. The excerpt below comes from his book, *Turf beneath my Feet*, describing a solo trek from Kerry to Donegal.

In it he relates how he walked a bit too far one day, along the coast of the Iveragh peninsula.]

The road turns west almost as soon as it is clear of Sneem, making for the end of the peninsula, for the strand (as all the beaches in Ireland seem to be called) near West Cove, and for a town which, from its name, I should have expected to find in the United States of America rather than on the extreme west coast of Ireland: Waterville.

There was, however, just as the road turned west, a narrow track heading apparently for the heart of the mountains themselves and most alluring to feet that had been too long now on hard, made roads.[1] Down it there came flying a most improbable figure on a bicycle. He wore a hard hat and a suit that would have looked more in place in the business quarters of a city than among the foothills. Balanced on his handlebars, and very precariously at that, was a bulging suitcase, with a length of bright material oozing out from a crack at one end. He raised one hand in salute, and I thought he was going to cry, 'Top of the morning to ye!' though he said no more than, ''Tis a grand mornin',' and was past me, wavering from rut to rut. He was the last person I saw for a long time that morning.

The track proved to be one of the most rewarding tracks that, in many hundreds of miles of track-walking, I have ever followed. I took it, not knowing whither it would lead me; but then that is an excellent reason for taking any track, literal or figurative, that lies to one's hand. After a mile or so of gentle climbing, it turned sharply south-west and, keeping to the same contour of the foothills nearly all the time, ran in a dead straight line parallel with the shore. It was wide enough to take wheeled traffic. There was in fact evidence that it was in regular use, not only by the flying

[1] Up until the mid nineteenth century this track was the main coach road along the coast; it fell into disuse when the new road was built, and was almost completely reclaimed by bog by the time it was brought into use again in 1988 as the Kerry Way walking route.

commercial traveller on the sturdy bicycle who was now out of sight behind me. There were wheel marks where the ground was soft, and horse droppings not more than a day or two old.

The most surprising thing about it, however, was its straightness. It was not merely more or less straight; it was, for furlongs at a time, as straight as any road could be. Peatbogs lay to right and to left of it, and there were men at a distance working in them. Theirs, I supposed, would be the carts that used the track; it was the sole means of access to one of the better areas of bogland in that district, and the turf cut there would be sold in Sneem and among the cottages on the hillsides beyond. It was a made road in the sense that such stone as had been extricated from the bog had been brought to it and used to give solidity to a sinking surface. Logically, therefore, the road had been made straight, to save time and labour and materials. But logic, one would say, is not a prime attribute of the Irish as a race.

Here and there I saw small homesteads standing a foot or two above the general level of the bog; a cottage, an outbuilding, a handkerchief-size field, green where the native turf was brown, dog tied to a staple in a wall; there would be the sound of a cow chewing, of a horse's hooves on stone. Near such smallholdings there would be a field ploughed into strips some four feet wide, separated one from the other by deep trenches. In those strips oats were growing. The earth was black between them.[2]

It seemed an odd method of growing corn, but I did not know then, as I knew later, that it was in fact the only way in which a crop could be grown where boulder and peatbog were rivals for every square foot of land. So thin was the good earth there that the only method was to dig it out of trenches and pile it in narrow strips between trench and trench, and there plant the oats. I saw it wherever good soil was at a premium, and that is over immense distances along the Atlantic coast from Cork to Donegal.

The track narrowed and climbed more steeply. Walking beneath a blazing sun and without a breath of wind for comfort was strenuous enough even at the leisurely pace I allowed myself. I stopped at length at one tiny farmstead and asked for a glass of water. There cannot have been many strangers who passed along that deserted trackway, and I knew as I stood there that I was under observation from behind the panes of the two small windows. The dog barked and leaped in its collar, but its chain held. I waited. Then there was a shuffling and an aged woman came to the door, one hand on the latch, her dark eyes peering out at me from beneath the peak of her black shawl.

---

[2] The ridges he describes are called 'lazybeds', a traditional cultivation method that was once widespread in Ireland, especially in areas of thin, poor soil.

'Could I have a glass of water, please – it's very warm walking, this weather.'

She did not answer at once. One hand clutched the folds of her shawl across her breast, the other still held the latch. She looked inquiringly at me, standing motionless. There was more shuffling behind the door, and I caught a glimpse of a second figure, well screened by the older woman, just darker than the darkness inside the cottage.

'Tis warm indade, sorr,' the old woman said at length. 'You would take a glass of milk maybe, would ye?'

I murmured something about water being quite sufficient, but she shook her head, turned, and spoke some words that I did not catch. There was some more shuffling, and then a glass of milk appeared, close behind the woman's elbow, held there by no visible agency. She reached round, took it in her own gnarled fingers and held it out to me.

'Twill hearten ye, sorr,' she said coaxingly. ''Tis the morning's milk, fresh and sweet.'

I drank. Milk is not a good drink when one is thirsty unless it comes from ice. This did not. It was warm, sweet, as the woman had said, sticky on the tongue and lips. I drank it, however, gratefully, and handed back the glass, empty.

'Would ye drink another?' she asked. 'You need not fear. There's plenty of it.'

I shook my head, and asked her what I might pay for the drink I had had.

'Ach, nothing at all, nothing at all,' she answered with emphasis. 'Sure, 'tis easier to be giving you milk than water. We've a long way to go beyond the fields for the water, but the cow herself is tied up forninst the house, and we have but to reach out to milk her, that's all.'

The track dipped and rose beyond the farm and deteriorated a good deal as it went. Long stretches of bog alternated with outcrops of rock, making it at times difficult to walk. As it ascended, clinging to the middle slopes of Esknaleughoge, the temptation to look away from one's feet and across the blue water to the dark slopes of the Slieve Miskish Mountains became greater and greater. Colour was filling them, pouring through the gaps as the sun rose higher behind them. It is hard to find the really adequate epithet for this colour that seems peculiar to Irish hills in certain conditions of light. The nearest that I can get to it is to say that they seemed to have the bloom that is seen on black grapes, velvety, deep, palpable.

As my track bore further southwards, the sun was in my eyes and the light reflected upwards from the Kenmare River was pure gold, finely hammered. If I stumbled once I must have stumbled a score of times in soft bog, the cold, dark, oily water rising up about my shoes and filtering in until my feet were chilled. There was more rock here and the track, which had long ceased to be straight and forthright, degenerated into a serpentining ribbon of mud and stone between two close, turf-covered walls of stone. The sides of rock closed in too, and for a time I missed the sense of spaciousness which was now lost to me.

Unexpectedly there was compensation. I came, after a short, steep, uneven rise, to a point at which the turf and rock approached to within a few yards of me. At one moment there was only blue sky between them and above the level of the track itself. Then I topped the rise, and saw spread out before me open sea that was the Atlantic Ocean. The gold was more thinly spread here, and there was blue-green beneath it, the hammered effect more pronounced. The Bull, the Cow and the Calf beyond Dursey Head, and the few rocks off Lamb's Head, were all that lay between me and the Americas. It was a point at which to cease walking and to drink one's fill.

I lay down on my back on a slope from which I could contemplate the seascape before me. I ate leisurely a handful of raisins and a slab of chocolate. Then, because the call of the sunlit water was strong, I scrambled to my feet and set off down the track westwards and at twice the speed at which I had been climbing it.

It was a curious track now, wider by far than it had been, and descending in a series of terraces marked by slabs of rock intersected by boggy ground and miniature waterfalls. Looked at closely it seemed to be no more than a length, and then another length, of natural ground; but taking in a long stretch of it westwards I could see that man had been at work there, shifting a rock or breaking a passage through a rock too big to shift, and filling in some of the bog with lumps of rock. There was a semblance of wall on either side, and the bogland beyond the wall to the right and left was rougher and even more forbidding than the track I was following.

I discovered later that this had once been the only road inland from the coast. It had been a smugglers' road, used by them to bring their dutiable goods through to those who had money or goods to barter, in the days before the lower slopes of the bog had been drained and the present road laid down from Sneem to Waterville. It can never, of course, have felt the pressure of wheels, but doubtless trains of pack animals had plodded up and down the track, led by silent men who chose the dark nights and day time mists for their journeys and abhorred the full light of day.

When it came near to sea level, however, the track vanished, swallowed up, doubtless, by the bog that so often has the final say. I rejoined for a time the made road and followed it to a curving, golden strand, where I shed my shoes and socks and paddled like a child in warm salt water. Only when I had paddled my fill did I remember that I had been walking all day, getting hourly further and further from my hay shed and sleeping bag. So I put on my shoes and socks, much shrunk now, it seemed, and took to the road again, walking with the sun low behind me and its light glowing ahead of me on the distant hills. Even when I realized that it had been a good fourteen miles by that winding track from Sneem I was not unduly perturbed; there was salt in the air, and there was a hard road beneath my feet, from which I should be able to gaze to left and to right without fear of stepping deep into bog.

At the end of three or four more miles, however, I came to realize that I had been foolish not to bring something more with me to eat than a handful of raisins and a slab of chocolate. I had, of course, banked on finding a place where at need I could get a meal, but because I had taken the mountain track I had not seen one. Nor, now I came to think of it, had I seen one since I rejoined the shore road.

My experience in England has been that one can rarely eat Hovis bread at any wayside cottage that advertises (with that entrancing sign): Teas with Hovis. But one can eat other bread, which may be hardly less good, and buns and cake and jam (and, in pre-war days, in the west, Devonshire 'splits'[3] and cream). This amenity has not penetrated to Ireland yet. At any rate I looked in vain for that or a similar sign all the way from Bantry to Bloody Foreland. Certainly it is not to be found between that golden strand where I had been so squandering of my time and the little town of Sneem.

I turned a corner in the road and, for a short space, walked in the shadow of high rocks close alongside me. The air was all at once surprisingly chill. I looked again at my map and there was absolutely no doubt that Sneem was still seven or eight miles away. I had a mile and more to walk on the other side of the town too, before I reached my hayshed. I had seen no sign of any public conveyance along this road, either as I looked down on it from the hill slopes early in the day or as I walked along it after leaving the track.

The road narrowed as it ascended, and rocks closed in on each side. At one corner I found two small, ragged children, a girl of eight and a boy perhaps a year older, spying on me. As I approached they closed in and, in a wheedling-whining chant, begged for pennies. They accompanied me for a hundred yards, wheedling turn and turn about, though I ignored them. Then, on a smooth, grassy patch beside the road, and sheltered by a steep wall of rock, I came upon the father and mother sitting over a small fire made in a triangle of stones. Beside them was a two-wheeled trap with a mangy pony still in the shafts, nibbling the dusty grass. The

---

[3] A kind of yeast bun split open and served with jam or cream.

woman broke into a murmured incantation as I drew level, opening her dark shawl and revealing a brown baby suckling her. The man eyed me with a sour look, his head turning with me as I passed by. Though I bade them good evening, they did not answer.

A hundred yards beyond them two more ragged children were waiting, evidently outposts stationed there to make contact with passers-by coming in the opposite direction. They followed me as the others had done, till a sharp call from the man turned them in their tracks and they abandoned me. There was no tent to be seen. Night was approaching, and I could only suppose that somehow father and mother, four children and the baby, would have to take shelter in and beneath the trap.

A mile further on, when I had begun to think even less cheerfully of the stretch of road that still lay ahead of me, I heard the sound of a car coming up astern, looked round, and saw that it was slowing down. A door swung open before it had come to a halt, and a hearty voice hailed me:

'Get in with ye, now, man, and take the weight off your feet!'

I got in gratefully. There was some scratching of gears, a jerk, and the car got under way again. The driver, an elderly man with a fringe of silver hair beneath an ancient green hat, turned in his seat, one hand on the wheel, the other pointing to the middle-aged woman seated at his side.

'Sure I'm glad of your company this day,' he said. 'Ye might not think it, but herself's after working up a breach-of-promise case on me, an' I'm feared she will have the law on me yet. Maybe a gentleman like yourself can make her see the unreason of it. Now, I ask ye: would ye say I'm a man would be making any woman a promise of marriage?'

He turned back to the wheel just in time to straighten out the car, which, all the time he had been addressing me, had been drawing nearer and nearer to the boggy side of the road, so that I was far more concerned with the prospect of having to dig it out of a ditch than of having to extricate him from the trouble he predicted.

By then he had forgotten what he was saying, if, indeed, there was anything at all in what he said. Almost at once he was asking me where I had been and whither I was bound and what parts I came from and whether there was a finer country in all the world than Ireland herself. And in the next breath he would have been asking me my views on Partition, which at this time was again exercising men's minds and emotions and affording an outlet for their oratory. But his companion, who till then had kept silence, stopped him short.

'Ach, O'Neill,' she said, and there was a caress in her soft voice as she spoke, 'sure the gentleman's travelled the world, ye can see it in his eye. So what for would ye be telling him that there's no finer country than Ireland, now? 'Tis for him to tell us, Padraic O'Neill.'

Sneem approached and I had not yet had to commit myself, though I had sung the praises of County Kerry till I stepped out of the car along-side my hayshed, saying that if I was lucky enough to meet them again when I had ended my journey, I could no doubt give them an answer that would be to their entire satisfaction.

The brightness of the day had served not only me but the farmer in whose hayshed I had camped. I returned to find it full to the roof with hay lifted from the fields during the past ten hours. It called for an acrobat's skill to climb to that new level and spread out a sleeping bag beneath the eaves. There was, when I settled down, hardly room for the slimmest bat in addition to myself, and half a dozen times during the night I woke to find that the hay had given at the edge beneath me, and I was in imminent peril of slipping off and crashing to the ground twelve or fifteen feet below me. So I slept cautiously, hoping for the best, and woke early to another brilliant morning of promise.

John Wood
Wicklow and Kerry, c.1949

[Yorkshireman John Wood walked a 1,000-mile circuit of Ireland in 1950 and published his account in a book entitled *With Rucksack round Ireland*. Wood fought as a Grenadier in the First World War, and after working in the railways and for a trades union, he volunteered for service at the outbreak of war in 1939, but was turned down on medical grounds. Frustrated, he went on to prove the doctors wrong, working as a mountain guide in Wales and the Lake District, and his performance ten years later during his walking tour of Ireland provided further evidence of his fitness.

He arrived in a 'taxiless Dublin' in July 1949, and found food very expensive (although the quantity of meat served was 'enormous'), many of the poor children barefooted, and, despite of the lapse of more than a quarter of a century since Ireland had become independent, he was surprised to find no Gaelic whatever spoken on the capital's streets.

Wood took the Military Road south through the mountains to Laragh, where he attempted to climb Lugnaquillia; delayed by rain, decided to turn back. In his second attempt, a catalogue of disasters occurred that could have brought his tour of Ireland to an abrupt and premature end. In his telling of the tale in the first excerpt I have chosen from *With Rucksack around Ireland*, he gives an excellent example of how, as in other extreme situations, an accumulation of small negative events in the mountains can culminate in a serious accident. In his case, the combination of exhaustion, heavy rain, nightfall, a defective compass and one critical decision made in a state of tiredness to try for a short cut home, were nearly his undoing. In the second excerpt, he describes his ascent of Ireland's highest mountain, Carrauntuohil.]

MOUNTAIN MISADVENTURE

Lugnaquillia, Prince of Leinster, head of all Ireland outside of Kerry, seemed to resent my hard-won conquest of his 3,039 feet. My first attack upon him by way of the desolately grand Lough Nahanagan, was repulsed, for by the time I had sat out a rainstorm and then reached the saddle between Conavalia and Table Mountain the afternoon was well advanced, and I had to return via the Wicklow Gap to my base at Laragh. The day would have been better spent on an ascent of the dark dome of Tonelagee (2,686), which I had admired the previous evening from the north side, and which commands the isolated dales where the rebels of 1798 kept camp for months after the defeat of their main force at Wexford.

Next day I resumed the onset, but from Laragh there is no way to Lugnaquillia except by a long detour, or by first surmounting a high barrier. This time I tackled Mullacor, a fairly level ridge rising to 2,179 feet between Glendalough and Glenmalure, but with a nearly disastrous result. The route from Glendalough past Poulanass Fall, though set out in the Youth Hostel handbook, led into a plantation of young conifers that covered most of the mountainside, and presently the path became impassable. Soon I was soaked by forcing my way past the wet and prickly branches, and then they became so densely interlocked that I could go no further. Unwilling to retreat, I adopted the alternative – I crawled under the lowest boughs, which left a space of about a foot. How many hundreds of yards I had to creep to the edge of the forest I cannot guess, but I thought it was miles. My palms and knees grew sore from the brown carpet of pine needles, and the rucksack sustained rents. Now and then I came to a clear space where grass grew, but elsewhere the gloom was deep.

Luckily the rain had stopped when at one o'clock I got out at last on to the bare hillside, and I removed all my drenched garments except the shorts, but during the hour I took as lunch interval the sun failed to appear and I had to resume the wet clothes. From the ridge top, when reached, I looked down into Glenmalure – refuge over the centuries of many fugitives from English law – and made out a zigzag track on the opposite slope which promised the easiest approach to my goal. Then a heavy shower came pelting down upon me as I dropped steeply into the glen.

A long narrow cul-de-sac of a boreen runs alongside Avonbeg with uncommon straightness at the bottom of Glenmalure. I was fated to make closer acquaintance with this lane, but now I crossed it and went over the stream by as rickety and unsafe a bridge as I had seen for a long time. After more struggling in a small but dense wood I got into the open again, and after a while struck the zigzag track. This was well engineered and had been made wide enough for carts, having probably served a mineral working at one time. When it petered out I still had a stiff climb before me, the first part being on to Cloghernagh (2,623), and then the way was easy for a mile and a half to Lugnaquillia's summit.

South-eastward views had been splendid during the climb, with Croaganmoira[1] – where gold has been mined – raising its shapely mass in the middle distance, and the coast in the vicinity of Arklow visible beyond. Lugnaquillia's own plateau had been in sight too, but as I approached scurrying clouds concealed it, and when I attained the summit cairn nothing was to be seen beyond a radius of a few yards. Worse still, the time was 6.30 and I had no food except one sandwich saved from lunch. My decision then should have been to make my way along the ridge to Carrawaystick and descend thence to the Glenmalure road at Drumgoff bridge, where the map showed an hotel, but it is easy to be wise after the event. Instead I decided to try to get around the head of Glenmalure and enter Glendalough at its western extremity.

I sat to leeward of the granite cairn for a few minutes and ate my sandwich, then took a compass bearing as the rain started again in deadly earnest. It was necessary to keep the compass in my hand and keep consulting it, but whilst doing so water must have penetrated the instrument, for the needle began to stick. As a result I went down the north-west spur to Glen Imail, whereas I should have gone northward to the saddle that precedes the rise to Table Mountain.

The headsprings of the Slaney are possibly less frequented than any other glenhead in Leinster – indeed, the map records that these boggy wastes of Imail have been used as an artillery range, though no sign of it remains. Most arduous the crossing proved to be, with its marsh, gorse, bracken, heather, hidden stones and old ditches, but I could see the way I now had to go, which was a light track that led up by an afforestation scheme and over the ridge called (or miscalled) Table Mountain. Up this I toiled in a veritable deluge. My oilskin cape became useless below the waist, and every few minutes the legs of my shorts had to be wrung out. Hidden reserves of energy must have come into play, for my only sustenance was a small tube of malted milk tablets, and with their help I

---

[1] The gold mine mountain is actually Crohan Kinsella, now called Crohan Mountain, some 15 km south of Crohan Moira.

dragged myself up to the top of the pass, almost at the summit (2,302) of Table Mountain.

The time was now ten o'clock, and dusk was fading into night. I could, I know, find my way fairly easily down the track into Glenmalure, but that would involve a twelve-mile walk, and Avonbeg might be unfordable at the foot of the pass. The alternative, though shorter, was a desperate venture over pathless peathags eastward to the head of Glendalough, continuing then in the same direction to Laragh. This might have saved four miles had my luminous compass been working properly, but it got worse and finally seized up with the wet.

After stumbling and slipping along until it was quite dark without reaching the steep descent that I hoped would be Glendalough, I had to confess myself lost, and resolved to follow the becks downhill and trust to luck for the rest. The next couple of hours gave me my worst experience for many years, dangerous rock, deep bog, darkness, and my wetness and exhaustion, all combining for my discomfiture. Lurching forward onto my face, sliding onto my seat, saving myself from other falls by clutching bushes that proved to be gorse, I felt the temptation to sit on a rock and let weariness get the better of me. Ever it rained, but I could get no wetter. My eyes were well accustomed to the gloom, but visibility was no more than five yards.

Getting down at last towards the floor of whatever glen it might be, I found myself on rocks that suddenly became precipitous. Below roared the mightily swollen torrent, and even could I have found holds for descent I should have been swept away at the foot. With a despairing spurt of energy I climbed back to find farther on a less perilous way to the beck-side, where I had to wade almost knee deep in mire that stank evilly, but after that I came to the walls of a ruined cabin and knew myself safe. A path must once have led to it by the waterside, I was sure, and so it proved.

During this time my mind was working in a detached way. I tried in vain to recall the music of Mussorgsky's *Night on the Bare Mountain*, and felt that the composer would have made it more poignant if he had shared my experience. But the only tune I could hum was 'The Old Folks at Home', though as my mother was long dead it was not really very appropriate.

Down on the level I could splash along through the muck without much fear that the next step might bring me grief, but before long I was pulled up short by a broad grey band that crossed my path and ended in the river. Too smooth and regular it seemed to be a tributary stream, but I put out a foot to test the depth and found it to be – a road. My lingering hope that I might be in Glendalough expired, and I staggered along like an automaton, waiting to find confirmation that it was Glenmalure. This was provided after a mile by the crazy bridge, now dimly seen, that I had used eight hours before, and I knew that I might have saved two hours and grave dangers and discomforts had I kept to the rudimentary track down from Table Mountain – always provided that Avonbeg had been fordable when reached.

Dragging one foot after another, and still prey to many miseries, I covered another two miles and then saw a light in a cottage not far from a crossroads. Reaching it I knocked and inquired of the man who came to the door what was the distance to Laragh. Six and a half miles, was the reply, by the Military Road over the mountain – an impossible walk at dead of night in my then condition. But I did not have to ask for shelter, for I was invited in, and found another man, a woman, and a girl of about 15 still sitting up, though the time was 1.30 a.m. A bed was soon made up for me in the parlour, and when I removed my saturated clothing clouds of vapour rose from my body, for by doggedly keeping on the move I had kept myself warm. A shirt and pyjama trousers were lent to me, and then a pot of tea and bacon sandwiches were brought.

Afterwards I slept until nearly seven, and then rose, donned my wet things, and tackled the mountain road. Two hours later I was back in Laragh, to the great relief of Mrs Toomey, who was thinking of reporting my disappearance to the civic guards. Somebody must have been praying for me, she declared when I told my story. I thought it unlikely in the extreme, but did not contradict her.

CARRAUNTUOHIL

Next morning, Sunday, found me on the way to Carrauntuohil and amazed by the number of chapel-bound people I met. A countryside that, if located in Britain, would have been all but uninhabited, seemed to be fairly proliferating. Within a mile and a half I must have met a couple of hundred hurrying to mass, on foot, cycling, or on donkeycarts, and my tongue was kept busy giving good morning.

Four and a half miles from Beaufort the boreen ends, and here the map shows the altitude to be only 417 feet, so there remained 3,000 (all but three) to ascend in order to attain Ireland's summit. A rough track ahead kept near the River Gaddagh, and climbed only steadily. This tourist route, I began to think, was unworthy of my mettle, besides which I had a notion to try the rocky edge (what is called in Wales a crib i.e., comb) from Beenkeeragh to Carrauntuohil. Accordingly I started up the steep scramble to the ridge past some overhanging boulders called the Hag's Teeth that would interest ropemen.

Since I saw them from Mangerton two days earlier the Reeks had been hidden in clouds, and now the mist began to lower. Whilst eating my sandwiches on Knockbrinnea (2,782), I had one glimpse of the lowlands to northward, like a green sea that rolled away to the Shannon's mouth. The rest was dank greyness above and around for four or five hours more, and thereout began to drop upon me sharp arrows of rain in unceasing flights. No sort of waterproof wear is practical on mountains, for the bodily heat generated by exertion precludes top-to-toe covering in heavy oilskins, not to speak of the necessity for freedom of the limbs, and a cape of any sort gets under the feet to trip you when ascending, or else blows up over your head when you are relying upon handholds. You can just make up your mind to get soaked, for even if the rain stops before it has penetrated to the body above the waist you will be wet enough in that region on account of the extra sweat induced by having to muffle up. It is at such times that you are thankful to be wearing shorts; bare knees will quickly dry when they get a chance, but wet trousers cause discomfort for hours longer.

Like most mountaineers who do not go in much for the too nearly stationary sport of rope-climbing, I love the thrill of a sharp edge that has a terrific precipice on each side, and I was anxious to compare the one in front of me with those in England and Wales. There was the interest too of a fresh medium in the old red sandstone of this range. Nothing out of the ordinary was encountered until I had conquered Beenkeragh (3,314), my third Irish three-thousander, and then followed an exciting drop to a saddle and a rather tricky ascent to Carrauntuohil itself. My verdict was that it was superior to Striding and Swirral Edges on Helvellyn and to Sharp Edge on Blencathra, but not in the same class with Crib Goch on Snowdon as a raiser of trepidation.

Conditions became worse, but one always hopes that the clouds will rise, if only for a few seconds, and vouchsafe a downward prospect. Now and again it really happens, but this was not my lucky day, and so I was denied a sight of the terrific descent on the west side to Coomloughra Glen, where a tarn of hourglass shape reposes on the 1,500-foot contour line, as it seems from the map. To the east was a still deeper drop to Loughs Gouragh and Callee, which I had seen on the first stage of my climb from Hag's Glen.

Of the many spellings of the anglicized name of Ireland's premier mountain I have used that given by the Ordnance Survey. In Gaelic it is *Corrán Tuathail*, meaning 'left-handed reaping-hook,' and the allusion must surely be to the entire ridge of the Reeks, with the sickle's handle at the eastern end, but the name has come to be attached to the highest peak only. This is grass covered, and said to be of narrow horseshoe shape, but I could not see far enough to check the statement. Visibility from the not very imposing cairn was about ten yards, and just within the radius was another fellow creature without wit enough to stay down below to leeward – a sheep; still, perhaps the sweetest grass grows at the top. For my part,

I could boast that I was nearer to heaven that day than any other human being in Ireland or England. I have been on Scafell Pike[2] in similar weather as only one of quite a crowd, but anyway that is 204 feet lower.

Rain continued to pelt pitilessly, and any hope of doing the ridge of the Reeks had to be abandoned. Had I been able to see the start of the faint track that comes up from Hag's Glen I would have followed it down and then retraced my steps of the morning, but a compass bearing brought me quickly to a precipice, and I was nervous of trusting to the instrument in rain since my misadventure on Lugnaquillia. Instead I battled against the storm for a mile westward in order to bag my third three-thousander of the day and fifth of the tour (Caher, 3,200), and then dropped down the uncomfortably close contours south-eastward to Curraghmore Lough. Much to my relief the sheet of water that appeared when, after a hair-raising slip-and-slide descent, I got below the clouds, showed the same outline as the map gave to Curraghmore.

Six o'clock saw me down at Dromluska, highest farmhouse on that side, and the dog's bark brought a woman to the door with the welcome inquiry if I should like some tea. As that was just what I was about to request of her, I went in thankfully, and whilst the water was being boiled I removed my sodden hosiery and poured the water from my boots. A pair of old carpet slippers was provided for my comfort, and my leather windjammer turned inside out to dry the lining at the turf fire whilst I was tucking in to the meal, of which my only criticism was that bread containing dried fruit was hardly the right accompaniment to eggs.

My hostess meantime chatted of her life in London as maid to the widow of an American author, and of how she had come back home to manage the farm when her brother died. (Her sister-in-law was present, but so subdued that I heard never a word from her.) When I broached the matter of payment she informed me that she usually got two-and-three or half-a-crown, thus displaying a commercial spirit altogether absent from other peasant homes where I had enjoyed hospitality. Perhaps the London training accounted for it, and it seemed that passers-by were not so rare as I should have thought, for the cabin was on a pass that linked the glens of the Caragh and Cummeenduff Rivers.

A rough three miles along the latter glen, in sight of brave cascades swollen with the recent rainstorm, brought me to the hairpin bend on the south side of Dunloe pass, and I had just reached the head of the Gap when the heavens opened and saturated my rear quarters all over again. Clouds as black as coal smoke overtook me and filled Finn MacCool's cleft, but my annoyance at the further soaking was mitigated by the awful

[2] In the Lake District, the highest peak in England.

impressiveness of the storm in such a setting. Between great boulders that lined the mountain foot on either side every trickle was become a torrent, and the sound of rushing waters competed with the howl of the wind in the gathering darkness. Not until 10.30 did I get back to Beaufort, much to the relief of Miss O'Sullivan, but the high tea she had prepared for me several hours before went untouched, for I was 'past it'.

Annraoí Ó Liatháin (1917–81)
County Kerry and County Cork *c*.1963

[Annraoí Ó Liatháin was born in Portumna, County Galway. He entered the Civil Service at the age of nineteen, and worked in various government departments, including the Department of Fisheries, until his retirement in 1981. He wrote a number of books in Irish for teenagers, in addition to works of fiction and history and a book on salmon fishing; he was also involved in Irish-language broadcasts on Radio Eireann. He was President of Conradh na Gaeilge from 1950 to 1952.

Ó Liatháin spent most of his childhood in Lismore, County Waterford, through which the Munster Blackwater flows, and two years in secondary school at Youghal, at the river's mouth. The Blackwater was very important to him, and in 1963 he set out from the river's source in the hills of east Kerry to follow its 75-mile course to the sea on foot, and his account of his journey was published in Irish in 1964 under the title *Cois Móire*, loosely translated as 'Beside the Blackwater'. The excerpt below, translated by Risteárd Ua Cróinín, is from this publication, and describes the beginning of his journey along the banks of the river.]

Even though the sun was high in the sky that day at the end of April, the east wind was strong and it was very cold at the side of Cnocan Finn[1] in north-east Kerry. The cattle and sheep were out on the mountain. The people were out too, boys here and there cutting turf and spreading it on the bog. The animals didn't notice me but the people did. They all rose from their tasks and stared at me.

What was a stranger doing on the mountain, on a cold windy day at the end of spring? Hea? It wasn't for the good of his health. He was up to

---

[1] Knockanefane.

something. Who was he, at all? An Inspector from the Department surveying the mountain for forestry? An engineer from the ESB assessing the turf for a new power station? A German looking for sanctuary free from the hustle and bustle of his own country? A Yank looking for oil or an eccentric scholar seeking out the grave of Finn Mac Cumhail? A crowd of men could spend a long, pleasant while, this weather, discussing a stranger on the side of the mountain. I quickened my step, for fear anyone might talk to me. They would only be disappointed if I told them my reasons for being there.

Cnocan Finn is a miserable mountain, a bare sloping hill without a rock or a feature to guide a climber. He sees a crest between him and the sky; he speeds up thinking he's near the top but when he gets there, he sees higher ground ahead.

The vista to the south gives the most extensive and wonderful mountain view in Ireland; Slemish in the west, shrouded with a mantle of mist, the high arêtes of the *Cruacha Dubha*,[2] the broad shoulder of Torc, the sprawling giant Mangerton, the inviting breasts of Dana,[3] *Caher Bhearnach*, Muisire, *Sléibhte Bealach Abraidh*[4] *Cnoc Maoldomhnaig*,[5] and the blue-grey shadow of *Slieve gCrot*[6] away to the east. I must return to this place again, to see the view properly, because I didn't really enjoy it on this particular day, anxious as I was not to lose my way on the broad slopes of Cnocan Finn. But when I cleared the topmost summit, I saw below me a deep narrow hollow with a sweep of grey rushes at the base. Somewhere among those rushes was my goal, but I spent half an hour trudging through the scrub and bog before I found it – a little pool of dark water between three clumps of heather. You would have thought it stagnant, but for its clarity. Its trickling source sprouted from under the rushes.

I sat down on a tussock, quite disappointed. It had hardly been worth a three-day journey to look at this black, rush-covered puddle. I recalled the well in the bog near Millstreet, from which the water surges so vigorously that it almost produces an instant river. I remembered the holy well near Mitchelstown that produces so much water that the eels are attracted to it. This was a miserable little black hole, in comparison.

There was a terrible loneliness in the hollow. There were high walls of heather between it and the world. There was no sound but a sheep, a bit

[2] The Magillicuddys Reeks.
[3] The Paps.
[4] The Ballyhoura Hills.
[5] The Knockmealdown Mountains.
[6] The Galtee Mountains.

below me, bleating at her lamb who was lost in the rushes. Stagnant water, rushes grey and lifeless after the winter, and the lamenting bleat of a sheep.

But after sitting for a while, I felt a spark of life stirring strongly in the mountain around me, like a giant awakening. I noticed that the hollow had a shape like a basket. And who but a giant would chose this deep, rushy cradle to rest in before taking on the world?

I looked reverently at the pool of stagnant water between these clumps of heather, because here in this hollow, on the side of Cnocan Finn rises the river referred to as the Daurona by Ptolemy,[7] which we call the Munster Blackwater. The red, rust-coloured streamlet ran through withered rushes, floating sods of soft black mud, creating an odd puddle that wouldn't satisfy a snipe's thirst.

This is the course of the Great One for a short while. Then one can hear a low, quiet trickle and see a narrow rivulet winding through the rushes. She disappears underground and re-emerges in a clump of sally.[8] She eats the mountain flag and strengthens. She cuts a stony passage for herself through the peat of the glen and throws off her rushy mantle. Her banks are red from devouring slices of the earth during the winter storms. But she is still but a stream in a mountain hollow. A little airy thing, frolicking constantly on a stony bed, gibbering nonsensically.

Now she arrives for the first time under the human yoke – the old stone bridge on the old route from Scairteach an Ghlinne to Áth Trasna. And you would imagine that the river, believing that it is no small honour to have a bridge built over her, makes a brave attempt to conceal her pride.

She gathers up heaps of gravel and sand and prepares dark, deep pools for herself. These pools are full of fish, including trout and young salmon. At the end of autumn and the beginning of winter when the river is in strong flood, the adult salmon come up here from the sea, hollow out deep cavities in the gravel and lay their eggs. And when the young salmon appear out of the nests they will stay in the pools for two years and it is a good man who can tell them from trout. Then the nature stirs in them, they leave the pools and follow the current on their long journey to Youghal harbour and the sea.

The mountain hollow has now become a valley. There are narrow islets on the banks of the river and trees growing from her sides. The alder, pet tree of the Great One, is here, its purple-brown buds about to burst, even though it still carries the dark seed pods of last year.

---

[7] Egyptian geographer and astronomer (*fl* AD 139–161); Ireland appeared on his map of the then known world, with seven rivers and five towns marked.
[8] Willow.

While witness to all this, the river attempts to practise prudence, but in spite of the islands, trees and salmon, she can still be capricious. After all, she is only a child, but three miles of age. No sooner has she made some dark, dreary pools, than she takes a fiery leap over a rock and lands with a splash on a bed of round stones, continuing in this childish, playful manner, until she realises that the fish and trees are watching. She composes herself then and returns to her task of creating more pools.

There were seven white ducks lying together on a river beach. I could have made my way past without disturbing them but they didn't know that. They got up and took to the water. They swam with the current and I couldn't pass them out. I reached the first settlement on the banks of the Blackwater with the flotilla of white ducks ahead of me, like a guard of honour.

Ballydesmond is a neat little village. It is surrounded by bogland, but that doesn't bother the inhabitants. Even though there are empty houses, showing that this place was not immune to the mortal plague of emigration, they are still a proud community. A straight, wide street, bright, newly-painted houses – and no alehouse in Dublin could beat the local tavern for cleanliness, comfort, food or drink. And where in Dublin would you get a fiddle hanging among the bottles, looking like it is often played? And doubtless, you wouldn't find in Dublin conversation as merry as I found in Bob Walsh's pub in Ballydesmond, the day I dropped in.

This neighbourhood spoke only Gaelic a hundred years ago and even though English was pressing hard on them at the beginning of this century they still loved the Gaelic. They have since surrendered to English and so you might think they'd have forgotten it all. But they still express themselves in the Gaelic way. They have phrases like 'in the run of the year' on their tongues, and maybe an Englishman mightn't understand them, but can express their thoughts well with clarity and humour! When they took on the King's English, they ignored the king's rules of language. They adapted the English from its miserly, stiff, Saxon form and changed it to a lively, imaginative, clever tongue so that it runs from their lips with rhythm, sparkling with colourful words and phrases.

A song was sung in Bob Walsh's pub in which each verse ended with 'Sweet King Williamstown', and with the pronunciation used by the singer, you'd imagine that 'Kingwilliamstown' was an ancient Gaelic word. It is the dreadful official name which was put on the place until recently. Ballydesmond is now the official name but it was known as *An Túirín Caoch*[9] in ancient times.

Isn't it amazing how the English planters used their imagination when

---

[9] The Crooked Tower

devising civilized names instead of the ugly Gaelic placenames used previously in Ireland, barbaric placenames like '*Cúl na Sméar*' (Blackberry Corner), '*Achadh na Sileann*' (Willowfield), and '*Ladhair na Carraig*' (Rocky Point); names that no Christian could get his tongue around.

If an honest Englishman named Thickpenny acquired a couple of thousand acres of Irish land for his loyalty to the King of England and for establishing the King's law among the wild Irish, he would first establish a neat little village for his English colony and then a fine big house for himself. Then he would attack the placename problem. After spending a long time thinking deep thoughts on the question, an idea would come to him like the kick of an ox, and a deluge of new names would flow into his skull. He would call the village 'Newtown-Thickpenny' and his new house 'Thickpenny Hall'.

From this lease of super-inspiration came the name 'Kingwilliamstown'.

There was a serenity on the countryside as I was going south to Cnoc na Croighe.[10] On the side of the hill a man was ploughing with a team. Because the hill was steep he didn't lower the ploughshare when they were ascending so that the horses had only to draw the idle plough behind them. Nearby, another man was waiting with a horse and harrow. Men and women in other fields were sowing potatoes. It was as if everyone in the neighbourhood was taking advantage of the sudden appearance of pleasant weather at the end of the spring.

I was puzzled why I found the countryside so quiet and tranquil. There was enough activity around me, men shouting at their horses and each other, dogs barking, birds singing in every tree and bush, the high-pitched squealing of pigs from the hill behind me and a couple of cows lowing miserably. In the end it dawned on me. The sounds around me were the natural sounds of the countryside in which I grew up, before that horrible, foreign monster, the tractor, came to local farms deafening the land with its hideous mechanical racket.

I see a huge trout in one of the river pools. Although it is but a hazy shadow in the dark depths of the water, I know it is more than twenty inches long. He sees me and moves slowly to the bank. His brothers scatter around the pool. This place is an angler's paradise with the amount of trout in these pools, but the whole day I have not seen anyone fishing as everybody is occupied with sowing crops.

But tonight after supper the young boys will arrive to show their fishing skills as I'm sure this bulky trout has not escaped their notice. And if the people in this place are anything like those who live where the river meets

[10] Knocknagree.

the sea, the old men will be here on the bank next Sunday, tempting their prey with a fly or a worm – or a canvas bag!

Peter Somerville-Large
Gougane Barra to Ballingeary, County Cork in 1972

[Peter Somerville-Large was born in Dublin in 1928. After graduating from Trinity College, he spent a decade abroad before returning to Ireland and writing a series of best-selling works on travel and social history. He has also written four thrillers. There are few authors who have characterized rural Ireland in the second half of the twentieth century as well as him. His interests are broad, his knowlege of the land and its peoples and history considerable, and he does not make the mistake of taking himself or anything he comes across too seriously, all of which makes him, through his writings, an entertaining and informative travelling companion.

On 31 December 1602, Donal Cam O'Sullivan Beare, Gaelic chieftain of south-west Cork, set out with a thousand members of his clan in an attempt to reach the safety of the lands of the O'Neill, 250 miles to the north. The forces of the Crown had been closing in since the Battle of Kinsale and the only way to survive was to run the gauntlet of the unfriendly territories that lay between Cork and Tyrone and seek asylum in the north. After fifteen days' travel in the bitter cold of winter, fighting numerous skirmishes along the way, O'Sullivan Beare reached the safety of Breiffne, where the county of Leitrim is today, his original party reduced by the hardships endured to but thirty-five persons. It was an epic journey, and in the winter of 1972 Peter Somerville-Large followed O'Sullivan Beare's route north to gain an understanding of what the trek was like, and to see if any folk memories of the passing fugitive clan remained. His account of his journey was published under the title *From Bantry Bay to Leitrim*. On the first day of his journey he walked from Glengarriff to Gougane Barra across the Shehy Mountains, a distance of almost twenty miles. The extract I have selected gives an account of the second day of his trek, a footsore walk to the village of Ballingeary, a distance of about five miles.]

Glaciers bruised and scarred Gougane Barra; it is a place where one is very much aware of their colossal imprint. Everywhere the earth has been scraped away and rocks bubble to the surface. On a wet day it is a penance to be within the small lakeside hollow under gloomy crags and dripping trees, but at other times the horseshoe of tawny hills enclosing the shiny black water has a special enchantment.

Gougane Barra seems to be a mini-Glendalough. They both attracted anchorites seeking solitude and they share similar mountain scenery dominating a lake. The atmosphere of Glendalough, which is too near to Dublin, has been largely eroded by tourism, and Gougane is not what it used to be either. In the nineteenth century a tourist wrote that 'the Ethiopian valley that Johnson in all the richness of his language describes as the abode of Rasselas, was scarcely more inapproachable on every side . . .'. Today you can drive up there easily enough and stay at one of the two hotels which continue the ancient tradition of pilgrim accommodation by attracting busloads of people in season. Although they had seemed beautiful on New Year's Eve with all their welcoming candles, by daylight they turned out to be startling eyesores. But they do not manage to destroy the serenity that still pervades the valley. Robert Gibbings thought it 'the holiest place I know',[1] and its mood catches most people, so that looking at the small island in the lake, they believe it was inevitable that a saint should choose it for his hermitage.

On Gougane Sunday at the end of September people arrive to pray and make the old rounds. Finbarr, 'the fair-haired', founded the monastery in the sixth century, having come here to kill off the last Irish dragon. Like all early Irish saints, biographical details about him are unreliable, but he is said to have been born in AD 560 and to have left Gougane sometime around AD 600. A few miles south of the lake there is a rock where he is supposed to have stood and looked back for the last time on the scene of his labours. He is credited with many miraculous cures, and the holy well still happily keeps up his high reputation.

All trace of the monastery and oratory that he built has vanished; so has the old causeway which used to link the island to the northern side of the lake. The buildings which are on Holy Island now are imaginative reconstructions of what might once have stood there. The eight small cells surrounding the court with its dead tree studded with coins are fakes, though perhaps it would be too harsh to call them follies. (The cells of the early monks would have been wattle huts.) These ruins, dating back from the early eighteenth century, were noted by the Cork historian, Charles Smith, in 1750 as 'a chapel, with some cells, a sacristy, chamber and kitchen erected by the late recluse, Father Denis O'Mahoney, who lived a hermit in this dreary spot for twenty-eight years'. Father O'Mahoney,

[1] Robert Gibbings (1889–1958), engraver, book designer and author. The quote is from *Lovely is the Lee*, Dent, 1945.

having timed his stay ten centuries too late to earn canonization, is buried in an enclosed grave facing the island.

The present oratory, designed at the turn of the nineteenth century by Samuel Hayes, was copied from Cormac's chapel on the Rock of Cashel. The ruins of an older chapel lie nearby, and it was probably here that O'Sullivan Beare's band of followers paused in the late dusk of New Year's Eve, 1602. At that time the island and lake were enclosed by oaks, since the forest survived in these hills until the nineteenth century. The Forestry Department has made a brave stab at replacing a section of the old woods by its plantation at the head of the valley, where for once the carefully planted larches and firs, allowed to grow to their full height, look entirely at home among the rocks.

My own experiences at Gougane were dismal. After an uncomfortable night my legs refused to function the next morning. Standing upright produced pain and walking downstairs meant creeping down foot by foot like a crippled penitent come to take the waters of the holy well. I hobbled to the island and cemetery where the Tailor and Anstey are buried.[2] When Eric Cross wrote of them in 1942 and reproduced the Tailor's wit and his mildly racy anecdotes, it was during the most repressive period of Irish censorship. The book was banned as being 'in general tendency indecent', and the Tailor was subjected to a macabre local boycott and persecution. On one occasion three priests appeared at his cottage and made him get to his knees and burn his own copy of the book. But now in this quiet churchyard he has been remembered by his friends for whom he epitomized a gentle society famous for storytelling and just good plain-speaking. Seamus Murphy designed his tombstone and Frank O'Connor chose an epitaph for him from *Much Ado About Nothing*: 'A Star danced and under that was I born'.[3] To be so remembered in this quiet church-yard is perhaps adequate and eases the other sour memories of his persecution.

The hundred yards back to the hotel seemed longer than the thirty miles I had walked the day before. I should have made proper preparations for the journey and hardened my sloppy muscles. Despondently I looked for the telephone in the hotel lounge and rang my wife.

'It's my legs – I can't walk on them. You'll have to come and fetch me.'

But over a long breakfast I reasoned that athletes gripped by agonizing pains often recover within a short space of time. Perhaps the discomfort would ease and I would be spared the humiliation of giving up so soon. Watched by the waitress, who paused as she brought me a chrome-covered

---

[2] Tim Buckley and his wife, Anastasia; he became a tailor when a leg injury he suffered made labouring impossible.

[3] 11.i.327.

pot of tea, I took some more trial steps over the floral carpet. They seemed a little easier; I thought I might get over a short distance today, and went back to the telephone to tell my wife I had changed my mind.

Before leaving I ditched some of the more cumbersome equipment, which I think is still in the hotel. The pack was a lot lighter as I stepped out again into the cold morning. Heads of clouds stooped round the hills and the lake shone black. On Holy Island the light flickered over holly and birch and the mass of rhododendron which in spring would be covered with candy-coloured flowers. People often describe this part of Ireland as tropical because of its heavy rainfall and the unusual luxuriance of under-growth in sheltered places. It seems a careless comparison; there is seldom anything remotely tropical about the stuffy chill of Cork and Kerry gardens under their rainwashed skies and mountains.

Above the valley the sun caught at a corner of a cloud, and its rays hitting the lake were not unlike the golden ladder that was seen to rise from St Finbarr's church up to the gate of heaven for twelve days after his death. Perhaps he exerted himself to push me on my way; I began to forget the state of my legs as I followed the road into the wet lead-coloured hills where O'Sullivan spent his first night on the march. I crossed a bridge over the Lee, a bubbling mountain stream that had just spilled out of the lake. Eastward the river slowed down and took its time through the long water meadows outside Cork, reluctant to wind below the hills near Shandon covered with their bright new suburbs, and carry the mailboat out into the harbour. Here it was a furious little torrent rushing between leafless alders, wreaths of soft brown moss and the dead tufts of fern which would uncurl in the sun when the spring came. A couple of rabbits sprang for the safety of the hedge. Rabbits seem to be re-establishing themselves and I had seen others the evening before as I approached Keimaneigh. But it would be a long time before they approached the density of the rabbit population of my boyhood, when they came out at dusk and covered the fields like lice. Conolly, the rabbit-catcher, with his dogs, iron bar and bag of ferrets, would put his ear to a rabbit hole and estimate the number of the community within. After myxo he took his ferrets to Australia where there was still work for him.[4]

I asked a farmer leading a small flock of black-faced sheep how far it was to Eachros.

'About four miles by our estimation. But by yours it would be a little farther.' Seemingly the old rule still applied here: 'The further from Dublin, the longer the mile.' Jonah Barrington had a theory that the

---

[4] Myxomatosis, a disease of rabbits; it was introduced into France in the 1950s to control the rabbit population, and from there spread rapidly to other European countries, including Britain and Ireland.

Irishman never computed distance 'from where you then are, but from his cabin, so that if you asked twenty, in all probability you would have as many different answers, and not one of them correct'. When it was in use, the Irish statute mile was longer than the English by a proportion of fourteen to eleven. I went on, wondering whether the farmer meant to addle a tourist, and how far it actually was to Eachros.

At midday it began to drizzle, and at the same time the country changed, receding into bogs and fields of rushes, a lowering empty landscape dominated by whirling black clouds. I rested in a dripping copse of birch and holly, easing my feet for a time until the rain ceased. I walked on slowly to the place off the crossroads at Gortenkilla, where O'Sullivan Beare and his weary followers made their first stop and camped beside the church at Eachros, 'a very rude and ancient church', according to an early traveller. It stands on the land of people named Cronin. Their farmhouse is typical of the area, a substantial two-storey building with outhouses and the yard behind, the whole place comfortably protected from the weather by walls and thick hedges. When I told Mrs Cronin, a matriarchal lady, that I had walked from Glengarriff, she said that that was nothing by the standards of the old days. Her neighbour used to walk to Bantry and back in a day for a shilling's work. I said that he had better legs than mine, and watching me limp around the yard, she agreed. She thought modern people weak; and the next generation would be weaker still. The children had never been the same since the school buses were brought in and they stopped walking four miles to Ballingeary and back each day to school.

She knew all about O'Sullivan Beare who had camped on this land, which had been forested then – the Cronins frequently found buried oak when they dug for turf. She also knew about his horse which was drowned in a boghole up beyond Ballingeary. Eachros was down towards the stream; following her directions I walked over the fields to its ruins above the little Bunsheelin river, some broken walls surrounding an elm tree. The first of many holy places where O'Sullivan chose to camp, its origins are at least as old as the oratory of Gougane Barra, and it was most probably in ruins when the column made its first night's rest. It was ringed by a cillín, one of many ancient burial places where the dead with odd souls are buried, mainly unbaptized children. All round the ruin small stones pushed out of the dank grass, and it was tempting to speculate how many had been there to trip up weary campers 370 years ago. Mrs Cronin had said that her own baby sister was buried in Eachros, and later the last to be interred there was a travelling man.

Before saying goodbye I asked her about the prospects of accommodation locally. 'Ballingeary is only a village,' she said, 'and Millstreet a scattering of houses.' She added rather illogically, considering her former remarks, 'And why haven't you a car?'

I walked fifty yards down the lane to view a grave of Finn MacCool on the neighbouring farm, a great wedge-shaped megalithic tomb stuck over the yard wall. Then I set out for Ballingeary. Originally I had thoughts of camping at Eachros, following as closely as possible the movements of O'Sullivan Beare, but even at this early stage I had given up all efforts at keeping pace with him and sharing his discomforts. I fell in with a man riding a scooter, whom I stopped to enquire about places for the night.

'You don't look the type who has to walk. If I were you I'd invest my money in a bike.' He told me that Mrs Connor, a countrywoman who had the misfortune to live in the village, would most likely look after me.

He didn't know about O'Sullivan Beare, but he could tell me all about the tithe war. In the old days the people had to pay a tenth of everything they produced to the Protestant clergyman, and it was in this very townland of Gortnakilla that they decided to take the law into their own hands. A battle was fought at the Pass of Keimaneigh between the local people and the forces of Lord Bantry.

'Are you with me?' he asked, and launched into *Caith Chéim an Fhia*, which is a long poem about the incident by Máire Bruí Ní Laoghaire who had been born in the shadow of the glen of Gougane Barra, and had lived there all her life until her death in 1849. He recited, translating line by line from Irish into English, while I held the umbrella over our heads to keep the rain off. It was a good battle, he said, because no one was killed. Then after telling me that the people of Ballingeary were nice decent ordinary folk and never went to law, he started up his scooter and drove away ahead of me into the rain.

When I reached the long scribble of grey houses, I found that he had warned Mrs Connor of my impending arrival, and a few minutes after I had knocked on her door I was sitting down to a good meal. Robert Gibbings wrote that Ballingeary is the friendliest village in the world. 'Everyone knows everyone and all about everyone. For anything you want there is always someone who knows someone who can manage it for you.' It was a crooked little village built around a crooked main street. There was a dark chapel filled with windows of Irish saints and the noise of a loud ticking clock. It had a garage, a post office, two pubs, houses with deep overhanging eaves, and plastic flowers in the windows, shops, an Irish college, some abandoned cars and a half-built laundry which, I was told, would deal with dirty linen all over West Cork. It was bounded by two rivers. At one end the Bunsheelin travelled behind some houses which used it as an overspill for garbage; at the other, near the Youth Hostel, the Lee turned up again with a fine old arched bridge thrown across its banks. In the four miles since leaving Gougane Barra on its way to the lakes at Inchigeela, it had dropped 269 feet and turned into a rippling brown stream streaked with crowfoot.

At this time of year the village was withdrawn, waiting for warmth to bring it to life. Under the rain the line of grey rooftops overshadowed curtained windows hiding interiors pervaded with winter languor – what Mary Lavin described in a marvellous phrase as 'the curfew of lethargy'. But it was only a seasonal pause; Ballingeary was in hibernation, relaxing after the hectic activities of its summer season.

Ballingeary is situated in the heart of the tiny West Muskerry Gaeltacht, which covers an area bounded by the Pass of Keimaneigh, Coolea and Ballyvourney. From June to August a rush of people from all over the country descends on the village to learn Irish – what the Tailor called the 'Boiling Programme', the intensive cultivation of the language. The majority of those who come are children, whose ages range from ten to eighteen. They stay with local families and bring a splash of colour to the area. In the main street houses advertise LEABA–BREICFEAST. 'We speak Irish in summer and English in winter,' a woman told me cynically. But it was the best Irish in Ireland.

Before the Famine 90 per cent of the people of County Cork were Irish speaking, and twenty years later a traveller could write of this part of Muskerry: 'Irish is the general language of the population, not only here, but throughout the district which we are now traversing, while English is as yet hardly known.' By 1883 native speakers in West Cork had shrunk to 35 per cent. Today two tiny, carefully-fostered communities, the one grouped around Ballingeary, the other on Cape Clear, still speak Irish. What particular spirit of pride and community or accident of location kept the language alive in these two small places alone in all Cork is difficult to identify. There are other isolated mountain areas, other islands, like Dursey, for example, where English has driven out Irish inexorably. In Ballingeary Irish survived against enormous odds, especially during the forties and fifties when so many people emigrated. Today there are more jobs, and the situation is said to be improving slightly. One recent survey of a class in the National School found that out of nineteen children enrolled, eight spoke nothing but Irish, three nothing but English and the rest were bilingual.

For four hundred years English was encouraged in Ireland until it almost won out. In 1537 a law was passed: 'Be it enacted that every person or persons, the King's true subjects, inhabiting the land of Ireland . . . to the uttermost of their power, cunning and knowledge, shall use and speak commonly the English tongue and language . . . and shall bring up his children in such places where they shall or may have the occasion to learn the English tongue, language, order and condition.' Fynes Moryson, ever consistent in his prejudices, wrote that Irish 'is a peculiar language; not derived from any other radical tongue (that I ever could hear, for myself neither have nor ever sought to have any skill therein). But all I have said thereof might well be spared, as if no other tongue were in the world, I think it would never be missed, either for pleasure or necessity.' Many of the Anglo-Irish of that period were bilingual, speaking according to one observer, 'a mingle mangle, a gallmaufrie of both languages, neither good English nor good Irish'.

The strong antipathy felt by the English towards the Irish language meant that there was less pressure on Irish people to change their religion. The seventeenth-century clergyman, John Richardson, who sought in vain to utilize Irish as a means of converting the Papists, wrote that English people in Ireland 'have a dislike to the nation, and this draweth them insensibly into a dislike of the language, for which no other reason can be given than that it is Irish'.

O'Sullivan Beare was proud of his education which had taught him other languages. We know that when he was making his claim for the chieftaincy, he felt that he had a strong point when he stated that his uncle, Sir Owen O'Sullivan, only spoke Irish, while he himself 'had been brought up in learning and civility, and could speak English and the Latin tongue'. His spoken Latin would have been colloquial, while his written Latin was fluent; his letters to his Spanish contacts were in that useful lingua franca in which the men of Europe could communicate a lot more easily than they can today. (Later, during fourteen years of exile, he would have learned Spanish.) Latin was widely spoken in Ireland well up to the beginning of the nineteenth century, not only among the educated, but among more rustic speakers of 'bog Latin'. In 1588 Don Cuellar, the Spanish survivor of one of the shipwrecked vessels of the Armada, who had to make his way through Ireland as a fugitive, was able to make himself understood on a number of occasions through Latin alone.

Standards of culture among educated Irishmen in the sixteenth century were high. Not everyone, however, strove to better himself by learning English, and others probably felt like Shane O'Neill: "One demanded why Oneile . . . would not frame himself to speak English. 'What,' quoth the other in a rage, 'thinkest thou that it standeth with Oneile his honour to writhe his mouth in clattering English?' His kinsman, Conn O'Neill, is said to have cursed 'any of his pedigree who should learn English, build houses or sow corn'.

From early times Irish was used almost as a test of nationality. When Hugh O'Donnell attacked Connacht in 1595, he slaughtered all the English settlers between fifteen and sixty who could not speak Irish.

At Mrs Connor's a candle shone in the window, for this was New Year's Day, and the same custom applied here as at Gougane Barra. Under pictures of saints, three popes and a framed Memory of Irish Freedom I ate a massive fry with slabs of thick country bacon, sausages and eggs. In the kitchen Mrs Connor and her family, sitting around the range, enticed me into the circle of heat with cups of tea. Was I an Englishman? How far had I travelled? It was a bad time to be on the road. They chanted their fine West Cork English with its cadences and idiosyncrasies that derived from another language – Sullivan to rhyme with soothe, any direction prefixed by a compass bearing, and so on. Later, I said goodnight and went upstairs to scatter my clothes and climb into the double bed. I lay for a time listening to the patter of rain on the gabled window announcing the close of a long slow winter's day.

Paul Theroux
Londonderry and Antrim in 1983

[Paul Theroux is a novelist and a travel writer of international renown, particularly for his narratives of railway journeys such as *The Great Railway Bazaar* and *The Patagonian Express*. His book *The Kingdom by the Sea* describes a circumnavigation of the coast of the United Kingdom seeking the true condition of Britain in the early 1980s, for as he says: 'Britain is her coast'. Northern Ireland is included in this journey; at the time the Troubles were at their height there, but, for a writer who pulls no punches and is anything but romantic about what he describes, Theroux is kind to the Irish. It was, however, like 'being shut up with a quarreling family and listening to cries of "You started it!" and "He hit me!"', and he wanted to tiptoe to the front door and leave quietly.

The conversations Theroux has with people tend to be one-way; that is, all the revelations and information flow his way and he contributes little; he interacts with those he meets no more than is absolutely necessary. As a result, he can concentrate on listening carefully, and therefore he captures conversations perfectly, even down to the finest nuances of accent. In this extract from *The Kingdom by the Sea*, Theroux describes his walk from the town of Portrush to the Giant's Causeway.]

It was drizzling at Coleraine, where I boarded a two-coach train to Portrush, a small seaside resort, emptier than any I had so far seen in Britain. But emptiness had given the place its dignity back; Portrush was rainswept and poor, and part of it was on a narrow peninsula with waves breaking on three sides.

The rain intimidated me for an hour or so. I had lunch with a man named Tubby Graham – there were only the two of us in the restaurant. Tubby was seventy and from Bangor. He liked motoring around, he said. 'But I stay out of those ghetto places. Bushmills for example – that's a completely Protestant town, and Derry's a Catholic one'. He recommended Magilligan Point Did I want a lift?

I said I had other plans, and when he was gone I sneaked down to the beach and started walking toward Bushmills to see what a Protestant ghetto looked like. It was still raining, but I thought if I kept walking, it might stop; and so it did, by the time I reached Dunluce Castle, three miles away. I walked along the sandy beach – not a soul in sight. And the cliffs were like battlements, made of white chalk with flint embedded in it. The only sounds were the gulls and the wind.

Farther on I climbed the cliff and walked through the wet grass to Bushmills. The more prosperous a place was in Ulster, the sterner and more forbidding it looked. Bushmills, rich on whiskey, was made of flat rocks and black slates and was cemented to the edges of straight roads. And now I saw what Tubby meant: the Orange Hall was large enough to hold every man in town.

I began to develop a habit of asking directions, for the pleasure of listening to them.

'Just a munnut,' a man in Bushmills said. His name was Emmett; he was about sixty-odd and wore an old coat. He had a pound of bacon in his hand, and pressing the bacon to the side of his head in a reflective way, he went on.

'Der's a wee wudden brudge under the car park. And der's a bug one farder on – a brudge for trums. Aw, der used to be trums up and down! Aw, but they is sore on money and unded it. Ussun, ye kyan poss along da strond if the tide is dine. But walk on da odder side whar der's graws.' He moved the bacon to his cheek. 'But it might be weyat!'

'What might be wet?'

'Da graws,' Mr Emmett said.

'Long grass?'

'In its notral styat.'

This baffled me for a while – *notral styat* – and then I thought: of course, in its natural state!

Kicking through bracken, I pushed on and decided to head for the Giant's Causeway.

> Boswell: Is not the Giant's Causeway worth seeing?
> Johnson: Worth seeing? Yes; but not worth going to see.

I stayed on the coastal cliffs and then took a short cut behind a coastal cottage, where I was startled by a big square-faced dog. The hairy thing growled at me and I leaped to get away, but I tripped and fell forward into a bed of nettles. My hands stung for six hours.

The Giant's Causeway was a spectacular set of headlands made of petrified boilings and natural columns and upright pipe-shaped rocks. Every crack and boulder and contour had a fanciful name. This massive coastal oddity had been caused by the cooling of lava when this part of Ireland had oozed during a period of vulcanism. I walked along it, to and from Dunseverick Castle – 'once the home of a man who saw the Crucifixion' (supposed to be Conal Cearnach, a roving Irish wrestler who happened to be in a wrestling match in Jerusalem the day Christ was crucified).

The basalt cliffs were covered with black slugs and jackdaws, and at seven in the evening the sun broke through the clouds as powerfully as a sunrise, striping the sea in pink. It was very quiet. The wind had dropped. No insects, no cars, no planes – only a flock of sheep baaing in a meadow on a nearby hilltop. The coves and bays were crowded with diving gulls and fulmars, but the cliffs were so deep, they contained the birds' squawks. The sun gleamed on the still sea, and in the west above Inishowen Head I could spy the blue heights of Crocknasmug. Yes, the Giant's Causeway was worth going to see.

It had been a tourist attraction for hundreds of years. Every traveler to Britain had come here to size it up. There had been tram lines out to it, as Mr Emmett had told me in Bushmills. But the Troubles had put an end to this, and now the coast had regained a rough primeval look – just one stall selling postcards, where there had been throngs of noisy shops.

This landscape had shaped the Irish mind and influenced Irish beliefs. It was easy to see these headlands and believe in giants. And now with people too afraid to travel much, the landscape had become monumental once again in its emptiness.

In pagan Ireland cromlechs[1] had been regarded as giant's graves, and people looked closely at the land, never finding it neutral but always a worry or a reassurance. Hereabouts, there had been caves that had been the homes of troglodytes. And it seemed to me that there was something in the present desolation that had made the landscape important again. So the Irish had been returned to themselves in this interval, and their fears restored to them, for how could they stand amid all this towering beauty and not feel puny?

Enough of these natural wonders, I thought, and at the hotel that night I buttonholed Mr McClune from Ballywalter. "Oh, I like Ballywalter! Oh,

---

[1] Stone monuments of the neolithic or bronze ages, usually consisting of a series of great slabs supporting a capstone.

yes, Ballywalter's pleasant, it is! We only get the odd bomb in Ballywalter!"

But he was worried about his sister.

'My suster is going down to Cavan this weekend. I don't unvy her. She's a Protestant girl, you see.'

'Where is Cavan exactly?'

'In the free state', Mr McClune said.

I smiled; it was like calling Thailand 'Siam', or Iran 'Persia'.

'A pig farm,' he explained. 'I mean to say, that's where my suster's staying. Now at this piggery there's a foreman. He is a member of the IRA.'

'I see why you're worried,' I said.

'But that could be a good thing, couldn't it?' he said. 'It could keep her safe.'

He meant that no one from the IRA would murder his sister, because a man from the IRA was employed by his sister's friends.

'We'll see what hoppens,' he said.

We were having coffee at the Causeway Hotel, sitting in front of the fire. We were the only two guests. An Ulster hotel could be very restful. I was never asked personal questions. People talked, in general, on harmless subjects, unless I took the plunge. Mr McClune, who was seventy-three and very wealthy – he had a Jaguar out front – said he had been to Australia and Canada and California.

'But I've never set futt on the continent of Europe,' he said. 'And I've got no desire to.'

I said I was going to Londonderry.

'I haven't been to Derry for thirty-three years.'

The next morning I walked back to Portrush. I passed a signboard indicating the way to Blagh. It was eight fifteen and there were no cars on the road, and it was very quiet except for the birds – crows and finches. I kept walking, toward the train. It was green as far as I could see, and I could see twenty miles up the lovely coast.

Eric Newby
Croagh Patrick, County Mayo in 1986

[Eric Newby, born in London in 1919, is nothing if not a well-rounded man. At the age of eighteen he was a crew member on one of the last wind-jammers to round the Horn, he served in the Special Boat Section of the Black Watch during the Second World War, and spent three years as a prisoner of war. After the war he became a fashion executive and a publisher, and for the past thirty years has been a best-selling travel writer. He has an insatiable curiosity and an eye for the incongruous, which characteristics were overworked when he came on a cycling tour of Ireland in 1986 with his wife, Wanda. When she had to return briefly to England to make the annual strawberry jam, he occupied himself by climbing Croagh Patrick, Ireland's holy mountain where St Patrick is said to have fasted during the period of Lent in AD 441. The extract I include is from his book, *Round Ireland in Low Gear*.]

At Murrisk, on the coast road from Westport to Louisburg, I left my bike behind Campbell's pub, above which, at present invisible in mist, the quartzite cone of Ireland's most holy mountain, otherwise known as 'The Reek', rises from sea level in Clew Bay to 2,150 feet in a horizontal mile and three-quarters. Here, I bought a supply of fruit and nut chocolate, filled one of the bottles off the bike with water and bought a pamphlet from old Mrs Campbell, entitled *Croagh Patrick, The Mount Sinai of Ireland*, by F. P. Carey, an irresistible title if ever there was one, which cost 20p Irish. Published by the *Irish Messenger*, it contained powerful endorsements: A *Nihil Obstat* (No Objection) from *Gulielmus Dargan, SJ Censor Theol. Deput.*, and an *Imprimi Potest* (You Can Print It) from *Joannes Carolus, Archiep. Dublinem, Hiberniae Primas*, which put the book on pretty sound ground, theologically speaking.

The last time I had climbed Croagh Patrick had been in 1966, the year we had gone to the Aran Islands. Then, two of us had done it in an hour; but to do this meant reaching the saddle at the foot of the summit cone in thirty minutes. For it is at the far western end of this saddle, at the foot of the cone, that the pilgrim's troubles really begin.

I was by now in fairly good condition after all this biking and I decided to try for the top in an hour again, something Wanda would have forbidden, had she been present.

I left at eleven in brilliant sunshine under a cloudless sky. Only the summit had a wig of white vapour firmly clamped on it, against which the gleaming white statue of St Patrick, where the climb begins, loomed dramatically. From here to the saddle the track through the heather was channelled and eroded by rain and the feet of innumerable pilgrims, and full of stones. To the right was the deep, dark combe known as *Log na nDeamhan*[1] which runs up to the precipitous north-east face of the mountain, into which a horde of demons who were bothering the saint

[1] 'The place of the demon'.

were cast by divine intervention. Soon after I set off I overtook a very fragile, elderly man who looked as if he was taking his first steps after a long illness, accompanied by what appeared to be his wife and daughter. Supporting himself with two sticks, he was climbing the mountain barefoot with infinite slowness; he had obviously spurned the help of his companions.

On this section, the last part of which is pretty steep, I passed six more people, including a woman with two children of about six and eight. All of us, with the exception of the barefooted man, whom the Almighty appeared to spare this further discomfort, were assailed by a sort of yellowish-green horsefly which flourished here in large numbers.

I got to the eastern end of the saddle five minutes late, at 11.35. This is the place where *Tóchar Phádraig*, Patrick's Causeway, the original route to the summit, joins the modern route from Murrisk. It was this causeway that the Saint used when he climbed the mountain on Quinquagesima Sunday 441, the Sunday preceding Ash Wednesday, to begin his forty days of fasting. He started from the church of Aghagower, which he himself founded, some five miles to the east of the mountain. In fact the Causeway is much longer; it has been traced at least as far as the Abbey of Ballintober, north of Lough Mask some fourteen miles from the mountain, which, together with Aghagower formed the last link in a chain of religious houses which catered for pilgrims from distant parts of Ireland in the same way as eastern caravanserais.

From the saddle the mountain fell away northwards, the direction from which I had climbed it, to the innermost part of Clew Bay which is filled with innumerable grassy islets. To the south it fell away to a lonely lough beyond which what looked like a rough sea of hills and mountains – an area called The Murrisk – extended as far as the eye could see, down towards the border of counties Mayo and Galway. Westwards now the track stretched away up the length of the saddle for just over a mile, an easy walk to the foot of the summit cone, before climbing steeply toward the top around its south face. The mist had now dispersed completely. This part of the route had a number of small, roofless shelters along it, occupied on the nights and days of pilgrimage by sellers of refreshments, and I remembered on my first visit the track glittering in the sunshine with the glass of innumerable broken bottles, rather as the open spaces in Russian cities used to shine, but more dully, with the metal caps of equally innumerable vodka bottles. Now, there was very little glass to be seen at all. Then, after passing a couple of sets of official loos, I reached the first of the penitential stations: *Leacht Mhionnáin*, the Memorial of St Benignus, a heap of stones on the track near the head of *Log na nDeamhan*, into which the demons were consigned. Benignus, otherwise Benen, Patrick's very youthful companion on his missionary travels, acted as his driver and servant. Later he became his psalm singer in charge of music for religious services, was ordained and eventually became second Bishop of Armagh. Of him, the most impetuous of Patrick's native-born bishops, it was said, 'Restrain him not, that youth shall yet be heir to my kingdom.' There is a legend that Benen remained at this spot, being too tired to continue to the summit, and that when Patrick came down from it he found that Benen had been killed by the retreating demons; it was Patrick who caused the monument to be raised in his memory. Here, the pilgrims making their *turas*, or journey, recite seven 'Paternosters', seven 'Ave Marias' and make seven circuits of the station, and the ground had been worn smooth by their constant passage. At one time these rounds, and the rounds at all the other stations on the mountain, were performed on the knees, often bare knees.

The next part up from the monument to the summit on what is called *Casán Phádraig*, Patrick's Path, over steep, loose scree which here pours down the slopes in torrents, is really tough for almost anyone. It is certainly difficult to imagine how anyone who is in any way infirm – and some of the pilgrims who make the climb are literally on their last legs – can reach the top, even with assistance. On this final section the terrible flies were still out in force and there were a few sheep chewing away at the sparse vegetation. Here, I caught up with a young Dutch couple who had left a few minutes earlier than I had. Inspired by this competition the girl went away with a very strong finish to beat me to the top. It was 12.10 when I reached it; I was ten minutes slower than I had been twenty years before. I was unlikely to be doing it in 2006, even with the aid of sticks. As a prize I gave her one of my fruit and nut bars.

The summit is not in fact the point of a cone. The cone is truncated; the summit a flat, stony area covering about half an acre. On it stands an oratory, built in 1905 to replace an earlier building with the help of subscriptions from all over the world, and constructed with great diffi-culty in such a remote place. The first mass, on 30 July that year, was attended by a thousand pilgrims (the figure is now around sixty thou-sand), and it was the Archbishop of Tuam, Dr Healy, who served it, who was chiefly responsible for saving the pilgrimage from extinction. Unfortunately, it is not a very attractive building.

Here on the summit, kneeling pilgrims, having overcome the agonies of the ascent in darkness and often pouring rain, saying the rosary on the way, say seven more 'Paters', seven 'Aves' and the Creed at *Leaba Phádraig*, PAtrick's Bed, a bit like the mouth of a well to the north-east of the modern oratory, and make seven walking circuits of it. Then at the altar of *Teampall Phádraig*, Patrick's Church, the vestigial remains of an earlier oratory, fifteen 'Paters', fifteen 'Aves' and the Creed are said, also kneeling, and the pilgrims make fifteen circuits of the entire summit, praying all the while.

After this, back to *Leaba Phádraig* for seven more 'Paters', seven 'Aves' and the Creed, and seven rounds before repairing to *An Garraí Mór*, the Great Garden or Enclosure, some way down the side of the mountain in which there are three mounds of stones. There, they recite a final seven 'Paters', seven 'Aves' and the Creed, and walk seven times round each of the three mounds and seven times round the perimeter of the Enclosure. This brings to an end this remarkable pilgrimage and penance, although some conclude by making further rounds at a holy well at Kilgeever, on a hill at the foot of the mountain to the west.

On a day such as this, from the top of Croagh Patrick you could see almost for ever: north-west across Clew Bay to Achill Island and out across the wastes of County Mayo to Slieve League, the high cliffs on the north side of Donegal Bay; westwards to Clare Island and south-west to the Twelve Bens in Connemara. Looking out across the screes seawards it was not difficult to believe that it was supposed to be possible from a certain point to see the streets of New York.

St Patrick spent forty days and forty nights on the mountain, fasting and keeping the discipline of Moses and Elias and Christ. The first account of his sojourn was in the *Breviarium* of Tírechán, who lived in the second half of the seventh century. The account was subsequently enlarged upon in the *Vita Tripartita*, the Tripartite Life, written at the end of the ninth century. During his sojourn the Saint was visited by demons in the guise of hideous black birds who subjected him to awful temptations and who were so numerous that they blacked out the sky and rendered the sea invisible as they swooped around him, attempting to savage him with their beaks and beat him with their wings. Meanwhile, the saint-to-be chanted psalms, prayed to the Lord for assistance, and rang a bell given to him by St Brigid, all without success, until finally his prayers were answered and he threw the bell after the demons, breaking a piece off it as they fled down *Log na nDeamhan*, to sink into the sea beyond Achill Island. There they remained for seven years, seven months and seven days and nights, after which they surfaced once more on the north-west coast to make life a misery for its inhabitants, until they were finally driven out by St Colmcille. Patrick was then visited by an angel who arrived with a flock of white birds, representing in material form the souls he was to save in the future. Local folklore, not the Tripartite Life, goes on to say that after sending the demons helter-skelter down the combe he had to face an even more formidable enemy in the shape of the Devil's mother, the *Corra*. He succeeded in driving her down into the lonely lough below the saddle on the south side, now known as *Lough na Corra*, from which she subsequently escaped to perish later in Lough Derg.

There is a much less arduous route to the summit from the saddle near the station of St Benignus, as I discovered when I came to make the descent. It runs along the edge of the precipice above the demons' combe and is mostly over heather. It was at this moment being used by a band of, like me, *nicht so jung* Germans who were plodding doggedly upwards. A further mockery of human effort was made by the arrival overhead of a helicopter with a sack suspended below it loaded with a ton of sand and cement and planks for the repair of the Oratory. During my descent, which if anything is more tiresome than going up, it made several journeys at a cost to the Church of £3,000. By the time I got to the eastern end of the saddle the barefooted man with the two sticks had just reached it. The two women with him looked completely exhausted by the emotion of watching him. I always wonder if he made the summit.

Later that afternoon, sitting in brilliant sunshine outside P. Dunning's pub in the Octagon, surrounded by boys and girls in T-shirts, drinking Harp under the gay pub umbrellas provided by You Know Who, what I had seen and felt on the mountain seemed like yet another dream.

Colm Tóibín
County Derry in 1986

[Born in County Wexford in 1955, Colm Tóibín had a distinguished career as a writer, journalist and magazine editor before becoming a successful, award-winning novelist.

In 1986, at the height of the Troubles in Northern Ireland, Tóibín set out on a unique journey – to follow the border between the Irish Republic and Northern Ireland that meanders along county boundaries from Lough Foyle to Carlingford Lough. His experiences were published in 1987 under the title *Walking along the Border*, an account of a journey that was at times dangerous, at times hilarious, and for the most part surreal, highlighting as much the artificiality of the border as the essential differences between the two communities that live along it. In the extract I have selected, Tóibín recounts his experiences as he set out from the city of Derry at the beginning of his odyssey.]

A BED FOR THE NIGHT

I walked out of Derry towards the border on a beautiful, cloudless afternoon, past the broken-down public houses, past the abandoned shirt factory, past the new housing estates and the sailing boats on the Foyle. It was Saturday. I was wearing a rucksack. When I crossed the border I would turn right and take the road to Lifford.

In half an hour I would be in the Republic of Ireland, where the price of petrol would be much higher, where the price of drink would be a constant source of discussion and where just about everything else – new cars, hi-fi, televisions, videos – cost more than in the North .

The river widened. There was a smell of cut grass. Men were playing golf on the other side of the river; down below the road there were boys fishing.

The soldier at the border stepped out from his hut as I came towards him.

'Walking, sir,' he said to me.

'I am,' I said.

'To Lifford,' I said.

'You turn there, sir,' he said, pointing to the road.

'How far is it?' I asked.

'I don't know sir, ten miles, twenty miles.'

I walked on towards the customs posts. The first one, which belonged to Her Majesty, was closed up. No one would dream of smuggling from the South into the North. The Irish customs official sat in the second hut, waving each car by. They were all locals, he said, he knew them; there was no point in stopping them, it only annoyed them. They were probably just driving over to get cheap petrol. *Fáilte go Dún na nGall* the sign said, 'Welcome to Donegal'. It was getting warmer; I could see the Foyle again in the distance. What I found odd was the opulence of the houses, the size of the fields, the sense of good, rich land. I had taken this road on the Republic's side of the Foyle because I thought it would be quieter. I also thought the land would be poor. I was expecting dry stone walls and wet pasture land with small cottages.

As I moved beyond the village of Carrigans (where three men talked in a pub about the price of drink, one having gone through £32 on New Year's Day) down to St Johnston, I began to notice the outhouses behind the farmhouses, how beautiful the stonework was, how well painted the woodwork was. I passed by farm after farm, noticing the well-trimmed hedges, the big houses, the huge fields used for silage or tillage, the large herds of cows in other fields; above all the outhouses.

I had a drink in the next village, St Johnston, and, since every small group in the pub made sure that no one else could hear what they were talking about, I finished up quickly and took a walk around the town. On the right-hand side stood the Orange Hall, painted in bright colours. The Orange Hall explained the well-kept farmhouses and big farms. This, though in the South, was Protestant territory.

'Is the hall used much?' I asked a passer-by.

'It's used a bit for bowling,' he said.

The sound of a band could be heard in the distance and as I moved down the street I caught sight of an accordion and pipe band, with several cars in front, and I could hear a version of 'When the Saints go Marching In' being played. The band was led by a boy carrying the Irish flag; people had come out from the pubs and the houses and stood watching as the parade passed by. It was a school band and mixed tunes such as 'Amazing Grace' with well-known Republican anthems like 'Roddy McCorley':

O Ireland, Mother Ireland, you love them still the best
The fearless brave who fighting fell upon your hapless breast.

I decided to visit Toland's pub and have a pint; it was getting near six o'clock and I was tired of walking. If Lifford was ten miles away, then I could be there by ten o'clock. I would be tired, dog tired, but I could rest a few days, and if there was a festival on, as the women behind the bar in Toland's confirmed that there was, I could join in the festivities.

The women behind the bar began to interrogate me: Where was I from? Where did I live? How had I made my way to St Johnston? The clientele ranged around the horseshoe-shaped bar listened carefully, and when I said I had walked they drew in their breath. From Derry? Walked? And was I not tired? I was, I said.

The two young men on my right at the bar disappeared to get a guitar and were away for some time. In their absence a smallish man with red hair in the corner, who had been watching me very attentively, was prevailed upon to sing. He took a huge gulp of his drink, cleared his throat and began an extremely heartfelt and high-pitched version of 'Nobody's Child' with his eyes closed.

There was a thorn in his side, however, in the guise of an old man, who was drunk, and couldn't stop himself interrupting with comments which I couldn't make out. The woman behind the bar told him to stop and we listened as best we could to the song. As soon as the red-headed man had finished, the old man started up. This time I had no difficulty under-standing him. His song was about an Orangeman who went to Cavan where he met the devil. It was directed at the previous singer, who, from his protest at the song, I took to be an Orangeman, or at least a Protestant. The women behind the bar tried to stop the old man, but he had to finish the song, in which the Orangeman ended up in a black hole.

Outside, the summer afternoon was fading fast over the Foyle. It was time to go. There would be plenty of traffic, they said, I'd have no trouble getting a lift.

I went out and stood on the road. I had made certain arrangements with myself about walking. I had made rules. All progress along the border must be on foot, I had agreed. If I wanted to go and see something that was off my route I could do so by taxi or I could hitch a lift, but every move towards my ultimate destination, Newry, must be on foot, except if there was danger, and then I would do anything – hire a helicopter if necesssary – to get out fast.

This meant that I could march into Lifford tonight, or I could stay somewhere along the way. The women behind the bar, however, didn't believe that there was a boarding house between St Johnston and Lifford. I passed a church and graveyard facing the Foyle and went to look at the gravestones and the Protestant names: Roulston, McCracken, Barr, Moody, Hanna, Buchanan. 'This congregation founded in 1726' a notice said. The church was like a New England church. It had been built in 1849 and re-built in 1984, having been struck by lightning.

The road began to deteriorate. Twilight. The pink sun was going down against the hills. Dotted along the road were new bungalows with Spanish arches and multi-coloured brickwork as well as picture windows and tiled roofs. But the area, despite the odd patch of bogland, was still full of huge old houses, flat, fertile fields, large holdings. On gate after gate the signs read: 'Beware of Alsatian Dog'. Even some of the smaller cottages had the sign up.

Cars began to speed along the road towards Lifford, and for half an hour cars came from the opposite direction as well; they had been at the dog racing in Lifford. I had to be careful walking on the narrow road. The evening was settling in, and there was a white mist on the hills above the Foyle. Black beetles were crawling out from low ditches. I tried not to walk on them. Coloured lights flickered from the mast on the opposite hill.

It was half past twelve when I arrived in Lifford and the pubs were still open; opening hours had been extended due to the festival. The hotel, however, was closed up. It had closed a few months previously and there was talk that it would never open again: business was bad. There were a few bed and breakfast houses in the town and I was directed to these but they were all full. There was only one other place, someone said, but they thought it was full too. But I should go and try, they said. I went and tried. I was tired and I would have slept in a hole in the wall. My feet were like two concrete blocks full of frayed muscles. I rang the bell of the house but there was no reply. I stood there for a while until a Garda car with several women in the back arrived and stopped outside the house; one of the women got out and said she was the proprietor. I explained my plight to her and she explained to me that the gardai were giving herself and her friends a lift to a dance a few miles away. The gardai were looking out at me. I could stay the night, if I wanted, she wouldn't see me stuck, but I would have to sleep on a sofa. I said that was fine. She was in her late thirties, and seemed very friendly and genuinely concerned that I should have somewhere to stay.

Why didn't I come to the dance with herself and her friend? I told her about my feet. She said I should drop my bag and come to the dance as her child was asleep in the house and her aunt and her aunt's son were coming to babysit until she came back from the dance. I said that was all right with me. I would just go to bed. But that was the problem, she then told me, there was only one room where they could sit and that was where the sofa was.

The gardai had become impatient, and began to blow the horn of the car. I told her I would be happy if I had somewhere to sit down and at that very moment the aunt and the aunt's son arrived. The woman said she'd see me later and went to rejoin her friends in the Garda car. I was now at the mercy of her aunt and her aunt's son. I looked at them. I wanted to sleep in the room they wanted to sit in. The son turned on the television, the aunt went to make tea. When she came back I suggested to her as politely as I could that she and her son could go home and I would babysit.

'And have the child wake up and see you?' she peered at me.

'Well, if you told me what to do,' I said feebly.

'You'll just have to wait now until the dance is over,' she said firmly. 'The child would get an awful fright', she said, looking over at me again. She poured the tea and her son switched the television from channel to channel. It was past one in the morning and there was only tennis on the box. 'We'll not bother with that,' he said and turned it off. We were now left to our own devices. We discussed the festival, the closing of the hotel, my birthplace, my business, until the aunt asked: 'Do you do the amusements?' I didn't know what she meant.

'The amusements,' she repeated, and her son examined me carefully to see what I would say. 'You know, the amusements, one-armed bandits, slot machines,' the woman said. 'No,' I answered, 'I don't really know anything about them.' They both expressed disappointment. They worked in an amusement centre. I had noticed several as I searched Lifford for a place to stay. It was very popular, they both agreed. It would be open the following day and I could go if I wanted to.

The clock on the wall ticked slowly. It was now only a quarter to two and the dance wouldn't be over until two and it would surely be half an hour after that before the owner of the house would get home. I asked about Strabane, just over the bridge in the North, but they said they didn't go there much. Fifteen minutes was then filled with an account by the aunt of a robbery at the amusement centre. We agreed that times were bad, but it was still only five past two.

They talked between themselves for a while, the two of them, while I sat on the sofa immersed in self-pity. I was going to rest for several days,

I decided, and in future I was going to walk in small doses. Over the next hour we made several efforts to talk to each other, some of which succeeded to a limited degree. The proprietor finally returned and relieved the aunt and her son at a quarter to four. She found me blankets and opened out the sofa to make a bed.

I fell into a deep sleep, to be woken in the morning by a question: what would I like for my breakfast? I sat up and looked around. It was nine, she said, some of the other lodgers were having breakfast. Did I want mine now? I said I would wait for a while.

It was afternoon when I woke again and the sun was hot. It was time to wash myself, pay the bill and move on.

There was still a festival on in Lifford. A group of boys had brought a huge transistor radio to a piece of grass near the customs post at the bridge. They sat with their shirts off drinking cans of beer, trying to attract the attention of a group of girls who were sitting on the window ledge of a nearby shop and indulging in horseplay. In the main square a man sat on the stage and played traditional Irish tunes on an accordion; people stood and listened.

Around the corner there was a field where there were to be races and games, but most of the children were attracted by a huge empty factory building, with the doors wide open, damp and dark inside with offices near the factory floor. Children were screaming their heads off to hear their voices echo.

The pubs in the town were full, with fellows standing outside, pints in their hands. One pub had sunshades, tables and chairs in a garden with a man playing well-known tunes on an organ: 'Yesterday', 'The Way We Were'. Further up a crowd sat in a run-down bar and listened to a live band play pop songs. I had a few drinks and decided that there wasn't much future in this festival, and left to walk across the border into Strabane.

The army were stopping some of the cars at the checkpoint but they paid no attention to me as I wandered by. There was nothing happening in Strabane. A few kids hung around an amusement arcade; the pubs would remain shut all day as this was the North. The Fir Trees Hotel was at the other end of town.

The woman at reception said they could accommodate me for one night only. The hotel bar was open; it was doing good business.

For the entertainment of guests, the hotel had provided a free copy of a magazine called *The Ulster Tatler*, full of fashion photography, with a column on social life in Belfast by a woman who called herself 'The Malone Ranger' and went to parties on the Malone Road. There wasn't a word about the Anglo–Irish agreement, signed the previous November by the British and Irish governments, which had increased tension in the

North and sparked off a campaign by Protestants with the slogan 'Ulster Says No'. The North according to *The Ulster Tatler* was full of wild parties, nice big houses, good-looking women wearing expensive clothes, and great restaurants. Over the next few months, I was to discover that things were, in fact, rather different from the world depicted in *The Ulster Tatler.*

Cameron McNeish
County Kerry in 1988

[Cameron McNeish is a former Scottish track and field athlete who became an accomplished mountaineer. He was involved in founding the outdoor magazine, *Footloose*, in 1982, and went on to take over *The Great Outdoors* in 1991. He has presented a number of very successful radio and television programmes about mountain climbing, including two series of the popular *Wilderness Walks*. Author of over fifteen books on walking and climbing, he has twice climbed all the 284 Scottish peaks of over 3,000 feet, and has climbed in almost every part of the world where there are hills. He enjoys Irish traditional music and frequently visits Ireland to combine his love of music with his passion for climbing. The following extract from *The Great Outdoors Book of the Walking Year* of 1988 describes a trip to Ireland in that year.]

I'd decided that I probably wouldn't have time to do anything in Connemara for I had a fair bit of work to get through in County Clare, of all the Gaeltacht areas the finest for collecting traditional music. But I couldn't have a week in Ireland and not visit Kerry. County Kerry, where I would stay with the Doonans, grand Gaelic-speaking people who had a fund of good songs and stories of the *Fianna*. My journey was planned. Tonight Kilkenny, tomorrow Killorglin, County Kerry, and the next day Carrauntuohill, the highest mountain in Ireland.

There must be a word for the area of land where softness and harshness come together. The Gaelic probably has it, for that ancient language is so much more expressive than our own, and in Ireland, particularly in Kerry, there is more interplay between these two states than anywhere else I have seen. Look down on the counterpane of fields from the rocky slopes of

MacGillycuddy's Reeks. There is no landward 'machair'[1] here, only the thin dividing line of an old drystone dyke separating the rich green from the rugged browns and ochres of the lower slopes. Kerry landowners of the past have wrestled with a wild landscape to scourge every inch of uncompromising soil from the possession of the great hills that dominate them. The effect is one of great charm, for the hillwalker gets the impression of being in a living landscape rather than a desert, where the reek of turf smoke can be sensed high above the patchwork below and occasionally even the drone of voices may be heard, lifted by thermals to the topmost crags of the hills themselves.

One has to be blessed to experience these sensations, blessed by uncharacteristic calm and dry weather which is not common in this land where life is so often dominated by the great troughs of depression which are spawned out in the anonymity of the vast Atlantic swells. To a person raised and nurtured on the unpeopled highlands of Scotland, where the only sign of human habitation in the glens is more often than not in the bony skeletons of ruined shielings, such an interchange between wild and tamed is both novel and quite delightful.

Lying, trying to attract what there was of a weak spring sunshine, beside a hawthorn bush which was alive with the sound of chattering tiny wrens, it is easy to tumble back into the time when this land was dominated by those who are now folk heroes. Down below by Glencar lies the spot where the bold Oisín, bardic son of the renowned Fionn MacCumhail, or Fingal as he is recognized in Scotland, returned to the land of the living after reputedly spending three hundred years in *Tír na nÓg*, the Land of the Ever Young. It was here that he searched for his *Fianna* brothers, celebrated in mountain and glen names in all the Celtic lands.

Even further back the land was peopled by the mysterious Tuatha Dé Danann, a strange and cultured folk who may have been wanderers from Sicily, Sardinia, Italy and Spain, the ancient Tartessia, or were they figments of a Celtic imagination? Could it be that the great mountain that rose behind me, Carauntuohill, or *Corrán Tuathuill*, the highest in all Ireland, was named after these Tuatha Dé Danann people? The thought appealed to me. The hill of the faery folk, for it was the De Danann who were the archetypal faery people. Their ways were mysterious to the Celts who occupied Erin on their arrival. Their culture, it seems, was significantly more advanced than the Celts' and they surrounded themselves

---

[1] A word used in Scotland to mean a strip of sandy, grassy land just above the shore, used for grazing or arable land.

with an aura of magic. The magic people, the Faery Folk, Tuatha Dé Danann.

There certainly was an aura of magic around their mountain this hazy springlike day. I was prompted from my daydreaming into activity. The days were still short and there was work to be done. The softness of the scene was about to become harsher, as harsh as anything in the British hills.

A horseshoe of high rugged hills rose sheer from a figure-of-eight lough held deep in their bosom. From the shores of that lough the rocky walls rose to a jagged skyline, steep walls, seared and riven by scree runnels and prominent ribs of sandstone. The shape of the cliffs, together with their great height, created an atmosphere not unlike that of an immense cathedral. The contrast between the mountain savagery and the pastoral softness of the earlier scene left me awed, breathless and excited, and impatient to get to grips with the tight ridges which enclose this Coomloughra horseshoe of Carrauntuohill.

I grew hot as I made my ungainly way up loose scree towards the ridge crest which leads to Caher, the fort, at 3,250 feet. By the time I reached the first of the three summits the watery sunshine took a tangible form, a thin drizzle hung in the air like a veil. I was glad to crawl into the tiny stone structure which perches there. The latter-day pilgrim who built this remote oratory was certainly not concerned with physical comfort. I couldn't help but recall the words of a tenth-century Irish poem,[2] describing the basic hut of a hermit priest:

The size of my hut, small yet not small, a place of familiar paths; the shebird in its dress of blackbird colour sings a melodious strain from its gable.

The stags of Druim Rolach leap out of its stream of trim meadows; from them red Roighne can be seen, noble Mucraimhe and Maenmhagh. A little hidden lowly hut, which owns the paths which you may reach; you will not go with me to see it, but I shall tell of it. . . .

After this first summit of Caher the going becomes steeper. Tracings of a track run down to a high col, then steeply up to the real summit, before winding a tormented zigzag towards the south-west ridge of Carrauntoohill. The immediate approaches to this ridge offer easy walking on good springy turf, giving an eagle's eye view of the rest of

[2] 'The Hermit Marbán'.

these unlikely named MacGillycuddy's Reeks. The great coums, or corries, split the hills into a series of high, ridge-linked peaks, looking higher than their 3,000 feet would suggest against the flat plains of mid Kerry and Cork. To the north a great finger of land thrusts its way out across the dark waters of Dingle Bay, reaching out, stretching into the Atlantic. Close to the end of that finger, like an afterthought, rises the bulk of Brandon, Brandon of the blessed. To my Celt-sodden mind it is certainly the most atmospheric of mountains in whose brooding corrie bowels dwell the legend of the banshee, the little people, and the finest of all the Fingalian tales, a bubbling pot of lore and legend, a place where one may dream unashamedly and where the simple strum of a harp could bring tears streaming down one's face like the waters of its Paternoster Lakes. A remarkable mountain, to be sure.

The flat-topped summit of Carrauntuohill, some 3,414 feet above the Atlantic, is, like Brandon, a strangely humbling place. A huge cross stands here, a boxed metal construction of a thing which even in its rusting and dilapidated condition does not fail to register a holy presence. Even on this grey day of Irish softness this great Christian emblem cast its aura of peace and grace across the entire scene, its very presence in such a place re-emphasizing the wonder of God's creation and the base beauty of it which we so often take for granted. I was glad of the cross.

Like an ecstatic evangelist I left the summit of Carrauntuohill behind me leaping from rock to rock until the narrow Aran-like ridge to Beenkeragh stopped me dead in my tracks. I had been here before. Several years ago, on my first visit to Kerry, I had wandered onto this ridge and onto a steep scramble which led to rocky walls and great drops. I made sure I didn't make the error again. I believe this is the spot where most of Ireland's mountain accidents take place, with about twenty people dying in the past thirty years. Care is required.

The arête runs northwards for about three-quarters of a mile to a col which lies on the 3,000-foot contour, a col which offers superb crag-framed views into Beenkeragh's hidden loch and corrie, and across the wilds of the Hag's Glen to the other hills of the Reeks. All the guidebooks suggest that there are sheep tracks which, if found, skirt the worst (or the best – it depends how you look at such things) of the ridge. I couldn't find them. Not that I searched for them particularly hard, for there is nothing finer than a good scramble on coarse rock. As I scrambled the rocky jumble of slab and block, the watery sun appeared again, lighting up the corrie below with an ochrous glow. Despite the wetness of the rock, and the coldness of it on my bare hands, I enjoyed the rocky thrill of the scramble, tiptoeing along the crest, searching out the simplest line over the rocky jumble. I could easily have been on the rocky ridges of *A'Chir* or *Beinn Tarsuinn* in Aran, or on the best of the *Aonach Eagach* or even the Cuillin itself, such was the thrill of the ridge. Who wants to follow sheep tracks when there are scrambles like this on offer? A rough boulder field separates the end of the ridge from Beenkeragh's summit, the Peak of the Sheep at 3,314 feet, an anticlimax after the exertions of the ridge. The remaining walk to Skregmore, the final top of the horseshoe, looked fairly dull, a bit like having to watch the B movie after enjoying the main one.

Needless to say, like many minor summits, it offered the best view of the day, a grand panorama of the group as a whole. The entire ridgeline appears serrated and rugged with plunging precipices dropping into the great scooped cauldron that holds the loughs, and above all, a sky that was now smiling, the only hint of benevolence left in the whole scene. But within half an hour I was back in the soft country and I lingered to enjoy the last of the winter daylight. The lowing of cattle sounded close and I could smell the turf smoke in the air once more. I began to look forward to Mrs Doolin's soda scones.

The village of Dingle is one of contrasts, old Ireland living uncomfortably with the new. Donkeys and jaunting cars are common, and in season the commercial interests of tourism tend to jar. I was thankful it was February. 'Who wants to go to Dingle in February?' I had overheard someone ask in the pub in Killorglin the night before. Well, I had two reasons: to climb Brandon, one of the finest mountains in the British Isles, and to experience the delights of a seafood meal in Doyle's, a restaurant world-famous for its fruits of the sea.

But I was to be disappointed. Doyle's was shut and I had to make do with a bar meal in the hotel. It wasn't the greatest of food but that didn't matter too much for I believe that Guinness is both food and drink to a hungry man and I had enough to feed a regiment later on in Flaherty's Bar, a grand place for music. Flaherty's is a bit of an institution in Dingle, and some years before I had been enjoying the music there when a little slip of a man wheedled his way up beside me and whispered, 'How are ye, Matt, me bhoy? Will ye give us a tune?'

'Pardon', said I, a bit put out.

'Come on, Matt, give us a tune. If ye don't have yer flute with ya, one o' the lads'll lend you theirs.'

'I think you're mistaking me for someone else,' I said.

'Holy Jeysus,' said the diminutive one, 'Are ye not Matt Molloy?'

'Holy Jeysus I'm not,' said I, delighted that someone would confuse me with a man who is possibly one of the finest flautists in all Ireland. Like me, Matt Molloy is balding and has a beard, and I suppose that through Guinness-soaked eyes one could be excused for noting a resemblance. The wee man was most apologetic, and insisted on showing me to the entire bar. 'Whad ye look at this, fellas, is he not Matt Molloy's double?' For the first time in my life my balding head and beard earned me an entire evening of free Guinness. I now carry a flute in my top pocket . . . just in case history should repeat itself . . .

I was late in starting in the morning. I had a bit of a head and had some difficulty sorting out some of the recordings I had made the night before. It's amazing how material that sounds great at one o'clock in the morning in a busy pub sounds awful in the cold grey light of dawn. Motoring over the Conair Pass to Cloghane, north of Dingle, I was dismayed to see Brandon cloaked in swirling mists and cloud. I had hoped for a view from the summit, a view which I'd been told the night before takes in the skyscrapers of New York!

Low cloud dominated the scene and I set off from the tiny village of Faha for what must be one of the most signposted mountain walks in the country. Signs proclaiming *Aire! Cnoc Géar* (Take care! Dangerous Hill) appear every couple of hundred yards. There is an annual pilgrimage walk to the summit of Brandon and the signposts are primarily for the benefit of pilgrims. Indeed at the start of the walk, just outside Faha, there is a grotto to the Blessed Virgin and I was delighted to see around it the first daffodils of the year. Spring at last. As confirmation of the fact, later in the day, I heard my first oystercatcher and curlew of the year. Good old Gulf Stream. Good old Ireland. Even in February she will bless you with her softness.

The path ran on into the murk of the mists. It was mild enough, but a real dampener. In several visits to Brandon I have only had it clear the once and I knew, as I surmounted the initial ridge and followed the path upwards, that I would soon be in one of the finest coums in Ireland. I longed to see it. Onwards I went, up steep slabs of rock, running with water. It's like climbing up a giant's staircase in this coum and on each giant-sized step there is a small tarn, still and black. These are the Paternoster Lakes; seen from above they resemble a rosary chain! There was little in the way of wildlife today. I've seen peregrines here, and buzzards, and fir club moss, starry saxifrage, wild thyme and St Patrick's Cabbage, the well-loved London pride. But it was too early in the season for botany.

As I climbed up the last steep scree-filled section towards the summit ridge, my miracle happened. A breeze, no doubt born somewhere beyond in the solitude of the wild Atlantic, caught the curtain of cloud and rent it apart, billowing it upwards, wrestling with it until it evaporated into streams far above me. The landscape that was revealed below made me gasp. Cliffs, broken and riven by great seams and clefts, rose on all sides, the result of glaciation more than 12,000 years ago. The loughs, each spilling over into another, dropped away like a string of black pearls as far as I could see into the peat-covered valley below. If there is such a thing as a banshee, this must surely be its home. The whole place was glistening black and I loved it.

The summit ridge after this was something of an anticlimax; I longed to be back in the bowels of that deep natural gash. But duty bid and I duly made my pilgrimage to the ruins of St Brendan's oratory, right on the summit of this 3,127-foot mountain.

What a man St Brendan must have been. Instead of choosing a cave, or a forest, or even a lonely isle for his prayer cell, St Brendan chose the summit of this mountain, right on the very edge of the Atlantic. Perhaps it was the ensuing deprivations of fasting in such a wild spot that trained him for his later explorations. It is said that he made evangelical forays to France, England, Scotland and the Faroes. Indeed his *Navigatio*, a Latin account of journeys of Homeric proportions, has enthralled generations, and it was this journal that inspired an Englishman, Tim Severin, to undertake a voyage in Brendan's wake. This modern undertaking used a craft of Brendan's day, a leather-skinned curragh, to sail to Iceland and then America – a fabulous journey which proved that Brendan's original voyage, in the seventh century, was indeed possible.

It's now generally accepted that when Christopher Columbus landed in America, Vikings and Irish monks had preceded him.

I wandered back down the ridge and into the depths of the coum, my mind full of great deeds. I was surprised to meet another walker. 'It's a grand day now,' I shouted.

'Indeed it is, praise God,' was the reply, 'Yer man Brendan was a hardy one to be sure.'

I agreed. Tom McDonagh was a schoolteacher from County Fermanagh, and he was on strike. He'd brought some schoolchildren down to Kerry for a few days but they in turn had gone on strike when they saw the weather that morning. We fell into easy conversation and found out that we had mutual friends in Dublin and in Glasgow. We sat there talking and savouring our surroundings for a good hour, sharing our lunch and our mutual gossip. It was good to be there. The next day I had to drive north to County Clare in search of ancient music, which I didn't find. But it didn't matter. I had re-acquainted myself with the hills of Ireland, I had met friends, old and new, and I had even found springtime in a month that can be as wintry as any. Ireland had been good to me, yet again.

Three days after our meeting Tom McDonagh was killed in a car accident. I read about his death in a Galway newspaper and I felt fortunate to have shared those moments with him on Brandon, his last mountain. However we come and go within this world, our existence is frail against

the aeons of the hills. I am left with a February memory of a place and a
time, edged with sadness for a friend I will not meet again on Brandon:
Brendan's – and Tom's – hill.

John Montague
The Hill of Silence

[While themes based on walking in the countryside were major foundation
stones of English Romantic poetry, there is a scarcity of poetry about
walking in the Irish context. Among contemporary Irish poets John Montague
is one of the few to deal directly with walking. He was born in New York in
1929, and came to live in Ireland with his aunts in County Tyrone at the age
of four. He was educated at University College Dublin, and at Yale, and went
on to live in Paris for a while before taking up lecturing posts at Berkeley
and then University College Cork. Among many themes, his poetry
comments upon birth, growth and decay and contemporary Irish life, particularly in Ulster, from a sophisticated, cosmopolitan viewpoint. I have chosen
his poem 'The Hill of Silence' for its succinct encapsulation of the essence of
walking in the countryside, the importance of tiny details of the landscape,
the sense of history, the sense of silence, the healing power of nature.]

The Hill of Silence

I
From the platform
of raised stones

lines appear to lead us
along the hillside

bog Tufts softening
beneath each step

bracken and briar
restraining our march

clawing us back, slowing
us to perception's pace.

II

A small animal halts,
starts, leaps away

and a lark begins
its dizzy, singing climb

towards the upper skies
and now another stone appears

ancient, looming, mossed
long ago placed,

lifted to be a signpost
along the old path.

III

Let us climb further.
As one thought leads

to another, so one lich-
ened snout of stone

still leads one on,
beckons to a final one.

IV

Under its raised slab
Thin trickles of water

Gather to a shallow pool
In which the head stone

Mirrors, and rears
To regard its shadow self,

And a diligent spider weaves
A trembling, silver web

A skein of terrible delicacy
Swaying to the wind's touch

A fragile, silken scarf
A veined translucent leaf.

V

This is the slope of loneliness
This is the hill of silence
This is the wind's fortress
Our world's polestar
A stony patience.

VI

We have reached a shelf
That surveys the valley

On these plains below
A battle flowed and ebbed

And the gored, spent warrior
Was ferried up here

Where water and herbs
Might staunch his wounds.

VII

Let us also lay ourselves
Down in the silence

Let us also be healed
Wounds closed, senses cleansed

As over our bowed heads
The mad larks multiply

Needles stabbing the sky
In an ecstasy of stitching fury

Against the blue void
While from clump and tuft

Cranny and cleft, soft-footed
Curious, the animals gather around.

David Boyd
The Shannon Estuary in 1993

[David Boyd took early retirement from the Northern Ireland Civil Service in 1992, and set out the following March to walk the coast of the island of Ireland. Among his reasons for embarking on such a venture at the age of 62 were the challenging aspects of the trek, a thirst to learn more about Ireland, the chance to raise money for an African relief programme he was interested in, and simply to enjoy what he refers to as 'one of the greatest long distance walks in the world.'

His account of the journey, soon to be published, is a unique description of the edge of Ireland at the end of the second millennium; some southern Irish readers may be surprised that a northern Presbyterian can have such interest in and warm feelings towards an Irish nation to which he is proud to belong.

He completed the 3,720-mile odyssey in November 1993, having walked through 19 counties and having discovered a 'great, unifying and kindred identity', whether in Wexford or Kerry, Mayo or Antrim. He succeeded in collecting £26,000 for his African charity.

In the excerpt I have selected from his forthcoming book, he describes walking around the Shannon Estuary, and an Ireland that is far removed from that described in the earlier excerpts in this anthology.]

The Shannon – 250 miles of it – is by far Ireland's longest river. Rising in its 'Pot' below the long slopes of Cuilcach, it flows through eight counties before its waters become mixed with the salt of the Atlantic north of Limerick. The name translates from the Irish as 'the Old One', almost 'Old Man River', implying an ancient river god personified by the flowing water. I knew little of it except for fleeting glimpses across parapets of bridges at Carrick, Athlone and Limerick. I was to make up for my neglect as I walked its estuarine banks for 270 miles, through Foynes and Askeaton up to Limerick and then down again to Loop Head past Shannon Airport, Clarecastle, Kilrush and Carrigaholt. I became almost landlocked, away from the great cliffs which I had been walking for two months since Waterford, but I felt neither restrained nor impatient. It was all another intriguing part of the Irish coast which, even if it did not move me northwards, still led me onwards. I smiled off the suggestion that taking the ferry from Tarbert to Lakyle would not really be cheating and would save me a week. Apart from anything else, I felt that I owed it to the 'Old Man' to keep him company in his last hours.

And so I headed eastwards to Glin with the intention of staying in the Castle, home of Desmond Fitzgerald, the Knight of Glin, but Ladybird Johnson, widow of LBJ, former president of the United States, was staying, and the house was full up with her security entourage; no fewer than nine security staff members which, given that her husband has been dead for twenty years seemed to me somewhat excessive. But I followed Ladybird's signature into the visitors' book and was shown around the unpretentious dignified Georgian house with its treasures displayed artistically as befits its owner, a former curator of the Victoria and Albert Museum in London.

I held to the road as far as Foynes where I wandered into the railway station to seek permission to walk four miles of the track across the estuary of the Ahacromane river. The line has a Percy French[1] atmosphere about it and I remain unsure whether the trains run weekly or monthly or only to the requirements of the huge aluminium works on nearby Aughinish Island. Indeed the only obstacle I came across was a heavily barricaded level crossing, closed in favour of road traffic. It did save me a significant detour, for the shore line lay deep in tidal mud and the single track was fringed with thyme and stonecrop and in the wetter areas, ragged robbin and orchids. I sat on the fortuitous bridge and listened to curlews and oystercatchers and watched a grey heron tread delicately along the water's edge, outlined against the white trailing plume from the tall chimney of the aluminium plant. I speculated idly on choice – if we had to choose between the two – and came to the conclusion that economies and so-called progress would win the day and that the heron would follow the impending demise of that other evocative bird, the corn-crake.

The weather was fitful all the way to Limerick, with short snappy showers coming in from the west and catching me with the same precision as the transatlantic jets setting down on the runways of Shannon airport four miles across the river. There were other traffic noises too, for there is a regular hovercraft service downstream from Limerick. I came across a 16–seater parked on the shore, empty but with its door locked in much the same manner as I leave my car. I looked in vain for the pilot and could only surmise that he was having lunch with his mother in a large rambling house a quarter of a mile across the fields. Near Ringmoylan Quay I met with four fishermen hauling in their nets, pessimistic of a catch, for in the last eight trawls they had caught only one salmon. And so it turned out: a few crabs, starfish, seaweed, but of the 'King of Fishes' not one. They

[1] William Percy French (1854–1920), Irish humourist, songwriter, poet and painter.

were part-timers, also working at Tarbert power station. They were noncommittal when I asked if the Tarbert and Money Point power stations were a factor in salmon decline. A more likely cause they said was the overall reduction in world stocks and changing patterns of distribution.

Some of the walking was not easy as the levees were overgrown and the thistle season was at its height. Never had I encountered so many, and while, initially, I was much taken with bed after bed of waving purple, my bare legs underwent continuous pricking until finally I had to stop to put on overtrousers. There was wide expansive grassland particularly where the Maigue river meandered down from Ferrybridge, crisscrossed by drainage channels too wide to jump. I had to keep a close lookout too for bulls, for each herd of heifers was zealously – and jealously – lorded over by half a ton of prime beef. I recalled the wording of fairly recent Northern Ireland legislation in which I had been involved, relating to public footpaths and the rights of both farmers and walkers. Roughly speaking, as I recollect, it was in order to have a bull in the vicinity of a path provided it was of the beef variety, was running with heifers, or was less than six months old. The confused public therefore had to have some agricultural expertise before running the gauntlet. I used a part mnemonic, 'Beef Rule, OK', but still kept an escape route to hand. In fact I was only seriously threatened once when one Hereford giant did his best to demolish a fence to get at me.

I came ashore, as it were, past the cement works and walked the last mile and a half into Limerick along the road to the docks where again I sought permission for entry. The gatekeeper, clearly not used to such a law-abiding request, waved me through with an encompassing sweep of both arms. But he had not lived in Belfast where the fascinating port area, which I used to roam through twenty-five years ago, is barred to all without security passes. The quays were empty except for the 'MV Solo', one of the cutting edges used by Greenpeace in focusing – with some success – on some of the world's environmental 'nasties'. I had last seen the ship off the Cumbrian coast during a high profile protest involving the pop group U2 against the proposal to reprocess spent nuclear fuel at Sellafield.

After an overnight in Limerick, I met the Mayor in the new council offices commanding a spectacular view of the river. It seemed to me that the building married in well with those of the old city which I first discovered in my rugby playing days. I handled reverently the ball with which Munster had defeated the All Blacks in a historic encounter in 1978. We talked of rugby, local politics and walking, for the Mayor was a keen member of the local Rambling Club. She regretted that Council commitments prevented her from doing a stint with me, but provided me with an enthusiastic fellow-walker over the rather dull twenty miles to Shannon Airport. Apart from the first four miles out of Limerick, we tramped the road and at Bunratty Castle sat on a wall eating our lunch in the drizzle and discussing the lure that Ireland had for the throng of tourists milling around the Castle and the Folk Park.

The three days of good weather gave way to five of sustained rain and low cloud. I spent more than an hour walking round the perimeter of Shannon Airport although the smart, if irresponsible, thing to do would have been to nip across the southern end of the main runway, saving three miles. I kidded myself that it would be interesting to see something of the successful industrial estate even though its gridiron pattern of roads had me confused. The Fergus estuary is formidable and I had several long days to Killadysert, six miles across from Shannon. The bridging point was Clarecastle where I stayed the two nights. The mist and rain prevented me from seeing across the Shannon which, at this time, is little more than a mile wide. Just short of Lakyle, I suffered humiliation which had me standing in the middle of a lane waving my stick furiously at a receding car. The surface was an almost continuous sheet of water from which rose up islands of cow dung recently clapped down by a large herd of Friesians which I passed later. Into this scene came a car driven at speed. I sensed what might happen but there was nowhere to go and all I could do was turn away and hope that the driver would slow down. If anything, he accelerated and I was covered from head to foot with instant slurry. I had just taken delivery of a new anorak and overtrousers whose technical properties I had been invited to test. The manufacturers could hardly have asked for more. So I rolled ineffectively in the damp grass and thought longingly of the car wash back at my local garage. But I soon saw the funny side and kept walking; past the car ferry jetty and along the shore of Clonderalaw Bay to Kilmurry McMahon with its church and pub and not much else. It was now 7 p.m. and I had been walking for nine hours with a further two miles to go. The area was short on accommodation and I had some 'dead walking' to do before reaching Woodland Farm where, fortunately, there was a room.

The next day came my reward. The sun shone and, eating my first blackberries of the season, I sat and watched two young foxes playing in the bracken. Only the sulphurous smoke from the towering chimneys of the power station at Money Point dented my good humour. I had been told that the government had failed to insist on the full provision of scrubbers and the yellow vapour testified to the omission. I wondered if this was why the 'Solo' was in the vicinity. I raised my cup to all those people – mostly young – who campaign for 'clean industry', to conserve the environment for future generations.

I had time in Kilrush, for it was a short day's walk. I went to see Percy

French's old railway station, visited the Scattery Island Visitor Centre and mingled with the crowds of holidaymakers at the new marina. I inspected the statue to the Maid of Éireann in the town centre and looked in vain for the damage said to have been inflicted on it by British troops in 1921. The marina has greatly enhanced the town's waterfront, which is not always the case with marinas. Sometimes boats and their elaborate moorings are allowed to take over but next morning I made good use of it, nipping across the dock gates, saving myself another walk through the town.

I caught up with Percy French again near Moyasta and followed the track of the old West Clare Railway, now sadly overgrown. Percy French was an Inspector of Drains, as well as a railway engineer and is remembered well for his songs about the West Clare. The stretch of line on which I walked not only captures French's romantic appeal, but has real potential for use as a long-distance footpath. I went rooting about in thick brambles, and at the site of the old junction near Moyasta, which took the line into Kilkee, came across some minor railway treasure-trove – old catch points, sleepers and the like.

At Kilcredaun Point four men from Irish Lights were painting the rather soulless property around the now automatic lighthouse. They were glad enough to put down their brushes and have the usual discussion about the past versus the present and the future. I walked across the drowned forest at Rinevella Bay hopping from peat islet to islet, a welcome change from shingle and pebbles. The sea had broken through within living memory, inundating the trees and leaving only an offshore reef as evidence. While technically still within Shannon Mouth, I felt that I had now left the river behind me and, as if in celebration, the skies cleared. I looked over to Kerry Head and beyond to the fast appearing shape of Mount Brandon. I stopped overnight with friends in Kilbaha and visited the Church of the Little Ark. To circumvent the law in 1852 a small hut where mass could be celebrated was built on the shore between high and low water marks. It is now in one of the transepts of the church. I talked to local people about the Rural Resettlement Scheme initiated in County Clare to combat population decline in rural areas. The scheme is still in its infancy and success is by no means assured, but if rural Ireland is to survive into the next century as a vibrant homogenous society, and not just an attractive theatre for tourists, then it must retain people committed to a rural lifestyle – who have realistic prospects of permanent employment.

I left Kilbaha armed with the information that the local farmer now had his bull running with the cows and had increased the voltage of his electric fences. This latter fact was new to me, for I thought that by this time I knew all there was to know about electric fences. As it turned out I had nothing to worry about, as I walked through sea asters along the lonely empty cliffs to Loop Head. The Head itself was impressive, not just because of its geographical location, but its 200 feet of vertical rock which had a corresponding off-shore stack of equal height, on which had been built a stone cairn; a feat requiring considerable rock climbing skills. There were a few sightseers for there is a road to the lighthouse, but they contented themselves with a short stroll from the car park to the cliff edge where I sat munching my lunch. Some spoke, but all seemed impatient to be back into their cars and away to the next camera point.

It was a different matter half an hour later near the Ross Arch, when a lone figure came walking purposefully towards me. It was another member of the Limerick Rambling Club and his stride was light and balanced and he was uncumbered with gear. Pat Donoghue is a doctor in Galway and on his day off had come looking for me to walk a mile or two, or 'maybe more'. He accompanied me almost to my next stop at Goleen Bay and gave me useful advice on what lay ahead. Pat knew his Galway better than most for he was just finishing his thesis on the Thatched Buildings of the County. He was of the opinion that I would find Connemara the most troublesome of coasts with its myriads of tiny islands, peninsulas and seaweed-infested shore. And so indeed it turned out, for I often had difficulty in determining what was island and promontory and where the seaweed started and where it ended. But that was two weeks and more away, and in between lay the Burren and most of Galway Bay.

Mike Harding
County Mayo in *c*.1995

[Mike Harding was born in Manchester in 1944. He is the author of a number of very successful books on walking travel, notably *Walking in the Dales* and *Footloose in the Himalayas*, and is a Fellow of the Royal Geographical Society and a life Vice-President of the British Ramblers' Association. He has also written poetry, particularly for children, plays and short stories, and has achieved acclaim for his photography, his acting, his work as a stand-up comic, and as a musical entertainer; he is very much an all-rounder.

His Irish Catholic family background engendered a love for Ireland and its conversation, music and landscape, which comes through in his book *Footloose in the West of Ireland*, from which the following extracts are taken. The extracts I include deal with the ascents of two of Mayo's bare summits,

Devil's Mother, which name Harding explains is an innacurate translation from the Irish, and Mweelrea, where he gave himself a scare and had a strange meeting with a raven.]

THE DEVIL'S MOTHER

The Devil's Mother (*Magairlí an Deamhain*) lies at the eastern end of Killary Harbour, an outlier of the Partrey Mountains. From the Leenaun–Louisburgh road, it doesn't look much of anything, a great hump of a hill with steeply sloping flanks. In truth, it's a stiff climb but a rewarding one because the views from the summit are superb and you are almost certain to have it all to yourself because, like many of the hills of Mayo (Croagh Patrick excepted), the Devil's Mother gets few visitors. The day I climbed it had a glum and grey beginning. Killary Harbour was funnelling all the foul weather from the Atlantic along the fjord, and once the weather hit the Devil's Mother, it just rolled up it and squatted there. The mountains all around were no better, Ben Gorm and Mweelrea had vanished in the thick mist and drizzle that was driving in out of the west. However, when a sliver of blue showed just after breakfast, I decided to hang around Leenaun to see if it would clear long enough for me to get on the hills at all that day. I sat on the car park wall by the Leenaun Cultural Centre, looking down the lough and listening to the morning news from Radio Éireann on my car radio. The IRA had called a ceasefire and, as the news was coming through from Dublin, Belfast and London, the sky began to break and the first sun of the day came streaming down the fjord, almost as though the weather was in sympathy with the awakening of hope.

I parked in a fisherman's lay-by two miles out of Leenaun on the Louisburgh road and filled the rucksack with waterproofs, food and cameras. I was going to follow a straightforward route up the flanks of the mountain onto the ridge which would take me directly to the summit. From there I planned to travel southeast then north following a long spur back down to the road. The climb to the ridge was long, hard and dirty; it was slippy underfoot and the flanks of the hill turned into a severe boggy slope with lots of nothing at the bottom. Had I slipped badly and rolled, I would have gone a long way. The clouds drove in again and the wind got up to gale force by the time I made the shoulder below the first of the mountain's summits. You could have sat on the wind. I carried on climbing the near vertical bog to the first unnamed summit which, when I checked the map, is only 1,815 feet high. At first I wondered why I had found it so tough, but then realised that I had started off at sea level, so I didn't feel too bad about puffing and gasping up the last hundred or so feet.

From the summit I followed a wonderful, though fairly boggy ridge to the Devil's Mother proper. I stood there holding myself stiffly against the wild winds; black clouds raced overhead with sudden slashes of sun; below me was a sullen and dark land, Lough Nafooey to the east in rolling shadows, and Killary in the west all murky and forbidding. Then, just as suddenly, the sun broke through and the land was transformed again. Aross the valley, the corrie of Ben Gorm and, beyond that, the confused mass of Mweelrea were burnished by the wild light. I got in the lee of a small crag to have lunch and then began the descent. I described it in my journal for that day as 'a hard but not impossible descent. In mist, it would be easy to take the wrong spur and end up back in Leenaun, which would mean a three-mile road walk back to the car.' Going down was a bit of a knee-shaker but I dropped down fairly quickly. The weather closed in yet again and as gusty showers swept down the fjord I found a fairly easy way off the last of the ridge, though, as ever, there was a bog, a ditch and a barbed wire fence iust before the road. When I got back to Leenaun, I sat in the Cultural Centre having a cup of tea with Michael O' Neil, the local historian, writer and fluent Irish speaker who built the centre.

'*Táimid ag siúl ar an sléibhe*', (I've been walking on the mountain), I trotted out in my beginner's Irish.

'*Cad Sléibhe*? (Which mountain?)

'*Magairlí an Deamhain*,' I replied. 'The Devil's Mother.'

Michael took a sip of tea, looked at me over his glasses and checked to see if any nun or Japanese lady tourist might be in earshot:

'You see, that isn't the real name of the mountain at all. When the sappers[1] came round here making the maps of the country, they asked the local people what the names were of the various hills and rivers and loughs. "That's the Devil's Mother," said the old man they asked, because he was too embarrassed to say the proper word. Not that the old Irish were embarrassed among themselves, only when there were strangers amongst them. You see, the real translation is the Devil's Bollocks – but that would not look very nice on a map now, would it?'

I told him I thought it was a shame that the robustness and the bawdi-ness of much of Irish literature and art, such as is found in Merriman's poem '*The Midnight Court*', had all become part of a secret sub-culture. Then I remembered something John B. Keane had said to me once when we were talking about the works of one of Ireland's great folk poets, a man whose work has hardly ever appeared in the anthologies of Irish poetry: Sigerson Clifford. Clifford was a schoolteacher from Kerry and his work, though it owes much to the folk ballad, is fine poetry, some of it glorious.

---

[1] Presumably the old man meant 'surveyors'.

Although he was loved in his native Kerry, he was ignored by the critics and scholars of the Dublin literary scene. 'Those middle-class intellectuals in Dublin,' said J.B., 'have done more to destroy Irish culture than the British ever did.'

That night in my hotel bedroom I took out my Irish–English *foclóir*. I was almost sure the colloquialism wouldn't be found there so I looked up 'testicle'. There it was, as true as Michael had said 'testicle – *magairle*', and the plural would be *magairlí*, and Magairlí an Deamhain is nothing to do with the Devil's Mother at all. I had spent the day climbing the Devil's Bollocks and felt a great deal better both for knowing it and having done it.

MWEELREA

Mweelrea (*maol ribhach* – bald grey hill) is the highest mountain in Connaught, a hard unforgiving massif standing between the dark and ghost-riddled waters of Doo Lough and the great fjord of Killary Harbour. The horseshoe walk that takes in Mweelrea and Ben Lugmore and Ben Bury has some fierce cliffs and crags that make it, in my opinion, one of the toughest hills in Ireland. In poor weather it could be a killer. I wondered at the names of Ben Lugmore and Ben Bury. Ben Bury, known also as Oughty Caraggy could perhaps be *Binn Bur* (Peak of the Boar) but Ben Lugmore is harder to translate. Being a romantic old fool I would like it to mean Great Mountain of Lugh – the god of light who gave his name to Lughnasa, London and Lyons, but Paddy Dillon[2] reckons it is really *Binn Log Mhor* -The Peak of the Big Hollow, which I think may be correct but much more boring.

Climbing the Mweelrea horseshoe one autumn, I had one of the hardest days out in the hills I have ever had. I had been staying in Clifden and was making my way northwards to Louisburgh and Westport, hoping for some climbing on the way. Mweelrea had eluded me all summer, seven days out of ten it had been hidden under a cap of thick cloud when the rest of the country was under clear blue skies. That morning, coming north towards Leenaun, it was obvious that, although the valleys were clear and in full sun, there was still a great deal of cloud hanging around the mountains. Strange, inverted cloud was rolling over the Maumturks like a waterfall, pouring down the flanks of the hills into the Inagh Valley. The sun, burning through the mist, gave a sharp, almost unreal edge to the morning. I looked over at Mweelrea. For the first time all summer it

[2] Paddy Dillon is an Englishman who specialises in writing about walking travel in Britain and Ireland.

was almost clear of cloud, just a fine, white, thin veil hanging over the last few hundred feet. It looked as though I might be in with a chance.

At Leenaun I filled the rucksack with cartons of drinks. Mweelrea was going to take five hours at least and I wanted to make sure that I had plenty of liquid. I drove to Delphi just south of Doo Lough, parked the car and looked up at the horsehoe. Mweelrea was clear, although there was a constant thin cloud swirling around on the ridge between Ben Lugmore and Ben Bury. But it looked as though it was set to clear out completely and had all the signs of turning into a lovely day, so I set off walking towards Doo Lough and the footbridge that crosses the stream at its southern end. On the east side of the lough the Sheeffry Hills were wearing a hood of cloud, but everywhere else seemed clear.

I crossed the footbridge and began climbing. It was a tough slog up the shoulder of Ben Lugmore with the occasional hands-on pull over slabs that were steep but not too exposed. I stopped every so often to look back at the glen falling away below me; a school bus purred along the valley road beneath my eyrie like a tiny white maggot. Above me I could see that the cloud I had seen rolling over the ridge had dropped slightly lower but it still looked passable. The summits had been just above the clouds when I left, so I assumed that the mist would still just be clinging to the ridge. I climbed on, soaked with sweat, through air that was alternately still and chill, an indication of why the cloud inversion was taking place. Still air rising up the south side of the ridge was meeting cold air on the knife edge itself. I climbed through the cloud into warm sunshine and sat below the summit to take a break, laying my shirt out to dry on a boulder, sitting there bare-chested in the warm sun.

I scrambled on through craggy outcrops, following a set of bootprints I had noticed lower down on the mountain, and a couple of stiff pulls brought me onto the summit of Ben Lugmore just as the mist closed in again. The summit was a fairly featureless waste of rock outcrops and peaty pools but the stranger's footprints led on in the right direction so I followed them through the mist. As the mist suddenly cleared for a moment I saw that I was on a very impressive knife edge, leading between Ben Lugmore and Ben Bury. The arête is safe enough if you keep slightly below it to the south, but to the north there are some horrific cliffs.

I took a bearing and went on, the going underfoot much better now. Then the mist thickened and visibility dropped down to a handful of yards. I had a good map and a compass so I checked my position carefully. One thing I had to avoid was going too far north and making a descent on to the north-east ridge where rope work is needed. The mist ebbed and flowed and at times I walked above a milky sea with the black fang of Ben Bury rising through it like an island. I made the summit just as the mist closed in again and then a very strange and unsettling thing happened.

A raven suddenly flew at me through the cloud, skimming my head. I flinched as its wings beat above me then turned to watch it settle on a rock close by, where it screeched out a harsh rattle-like cry. It may well have been my imagination but I could have sworn that the bird was directing its calls at me, whether warning or mockery I don't know, but in the rolling mist on that sharp peak with all the crags about me, I felt more than a little inclined to believe the bird knew something. In the Buddhist Himalaya, ravens are birds of good luck and are often kept as pampered pets, fed on titbits and wear little brass bells round their necks – but I wasn't in Nepal or Zanskar, I was in Mayo in the west of Ireland and in Celtic mythology the raven is always a bird of ill omen. Every raven in Ireland is said to have three drops of the Devil's blood in it, and there I was, mist-bound on a savage summit with lots of nothing on either side of me, being heckled by a black thing with three drops of Old Nick inside it. My membership of the Catholic Church has lapsed but I now tried to remember the Perfect Act of Contrition as I saw my obituary passing before me: 'Kind to most animals and a good climber for his size. Perished while trying to strangle a raven on an Irish mountain in thick mist.' Then, with one last strange gargling call, the black messenger flapped away into the cloud.

I knew that I couldn't sit there all day waiting for the mist to clear so I took a careful bearing and scrambled down from the peak towards the saddle between Ben Bury and Mweelrea. As I set off the cloud piled in again, turning from a light mist into dense fog, and the world about me became a grey ghost. There was nothing but nothing all around me, and some of that nothing had big holes in it. I walked on the bearing for a few hundred yards and found myself on the edge of a very nasty-looking crag with more nothing beneath. I sat down. The new 1:50,000 Irish maps are good but they don't show crags, just lots of contour lines close together and, since a good deal of the horseshoe is like that, I hadn't a clue where the hell I was; even with map and compass, it was impossible to decode the landscape around me in this mirk. I was alone, the weather was foul, I was on a mountain I didn't know and nightfall was at the most three hours away. Then I remembered the two most important words in any mountaineer's lexicon – 'Don't Panic'. I looked at the map again. Then I panicked. I was in dense clinging fog on a high mountain summit with no visible way off and the land falling away from me on three sides. I could hear running water to my right which could, I reckoned, have been the Bananakee River that runs down from the saddle to Killary. Following that down would take me miles out of my way to Uggool or the road end at Dadreen where, if I was very lucky, I might be able to get a thirty-pound taxi ride back to Delphi.

I knew I needed to head more to the east but sensed nothing but empty space in that direction. The friendly bootprints had vanished in a jumble of scree and boulders. Whoever it was had either sprouted wings or had had better weather than me and had found his way off. All I could see before me was a steep shale slope leading to nothing. I cast around looking for clues and came to a crag edge that was a serious scramble leading to who knows what. I checked the map again, setting it against the compass. It told me I was in a fix. I had been making a mental note of escape routes and knew that, if I had to, I could climb back up a little and make my way off by a steep flank that looked as though it might be hard work but at least seemed free of crags and cliffs. I decided to sit it out for half an hour. The day was wearing on and, even if I got lucky, I would be getting back to the car as the sun was falling. But I reckoned I could spare thirty minutes.

It felt like a terribly long wait, but after quarter of an hour the cloud lifted and I could just see my way down on to the saddle between Ben Bury and Mweelrea. I scrambled down and belted along the col, losing more height than I liked, and then climbed through thickening mist along the ridge to the summit of the Bald Grey Hill. Here again I could have gone wrong, for there are three peaks to choose from, but the compass and map guided me through porridge to the highest mountain in Connaught. Below me (2,688 feet below) was Killary Harbour. It could have been ten feet below for all I knew. I took another bearing and found my way off down the ridge towards the valley, eventually dropping below the cloud into early evening sunshine.

It was five o'clock and I still wasn't off the mountain. It was here I made another bad decision. One of the guidebooks shows a route that drops down to a saddle and climbs another unnamed hill before leading down to the road. I decided to walk out by the glen to avoid another climb. It would have been easier climbing the hill. The walk out was a nightmare, boggy and slutchy. Every few hundred yards there were gullies and ditches full to the brim with the run-off from forestry plantations. I wasted time trying to go round these drains and in the end gave in and either leaped them or sploshed through. It took a long, long time and I was very, very, very miserable. I didn't get back to the car until almost seven o'clock, and there was peaty water and slutch up to my *magairlí*. I had had what you might call an interesting day out, one that underlined the fact that you should never ever take Irish hills lightly – they are serious places. The mood I was in was not lightened by the drive northwards. Doo Lough was dark and oppressive but I stopped at the side of the road above the lough as I always do, to stand in silence by the memorial there, for the story is one that demands silence. It is a testimonial to a terrible tragedy.

At the height of the Famine, six hundred starving people came into the town of Louisburgh looking for food or admission to the workhouse. They were turned away and told to see the two paid Poor Law guardians who would be holding a board meeting at Delphi Lodge the next day. The following morning four hundred of them set off, some in rags, some half naked, all of them barefoot, through a bitter cold spring day to cross ten miles of the wildest and bleakest country in the west of Ireland. At Glenkeen they were forced to ford a river swollen by recent rains, and between there and Doo Lough they followed a high goat track, fording more streams and rivers along the way. When they reached Delphi Lodge, the guardians, Colonel Hograve and Mr Lecky, were at lunch and would not be disturbed, so the soaked and starving people were left to wait amongst the pine trees. When the two gentlemen finally came out they refused the people relief and told them to make their way back to Louisburgh. There were no roads through that grim pass between the Sheeffry Hills and the Mweelrea Mountains, just narrow high goat tracks above the lough. Night was closing in and a savage wind brought a hailstorm in from the north-west and, as they passed above a cliff known as the Stoppabue, sudden gusts of wind drove many of them off the cliff and down into the lough. The rest carried on northwards through worsening weather. Those who did not die along the way died at the second crossing of the Glenkeen River. Not one of the four hundred survived. I turned away from the memorial and drove northwards, the autumn night gathering around me as I left the great glen behind and crossed the rolling boglands to Louisburgh under a sky as dark and dour as the waters of Doo Lough.

Select Bibliography

Barrow, John	*A Tour of Ireland*	1837
Barry, William	*Walking Tour around Ireland in 1865 by an Englishman*	1867
Bartlett, Phil	*The Undiscovered Country*	1993
Bence-Jones, Mark	*A Guide to Irish Country Houses*	1990
de Bougrenet, J. L.	*A Frenchman's Walk through Ireland 1796–97*	1798
Foster, John Wilson	*Nature in Ireland*	1997
Gamble, John	*A view of society and manners in the north of Ireland in the summer and autumn of 1812*	1813
Gibbons, John	*Tramping through Ireland*	1930
Gittings, Robert (ed.)	*Letters of John Keats*	1970
Gwynn & Hadcock	*Medieval Religious Houses, Ireland*	1988
Gwynn, Stephen	*Highways and Byways of Donegal and Antrim*	1899
Hogg, Garry	*Turf beneath my Feet*	1950
Jarvis, Robin	*Romantic Writing and Pedestrian Travel*	1997
Lewis, Samuel	*A Topographical Dictionary of Ireland*	1837
Lloyd Praeger, R.	*Some Irish Naturalists*	1949
Milligan Fox, Charlotte	*Annals of the Irish Harpers*	1911
Montague, John	*Collected Poems*	1995
Nicholson, Mrs Asenath	*Ireland's Welcome to the Stranger*	1847
Ó Laoghaire, Peadar	*Mo Scéal Féin*	1915
Ó Liatháin, Annraoí	*Cois Moire*	1964
Ó'Dalaigh, Brian	*The Stranger's Gaze – Travels in County Clare 1534–1950*	1998
Rice, John Herman	*Moonbeams*	1917
Rice, John Herman	*The Devil's Punchbowl*	1926
Rossetti, W. M. (ed.)	*Wordsworth's Poetical Works*	1880
Sleater, Matthew	*Topography & Itinerary of the Counties of Ireland*	1806
Somerville-Large, P.	*From Bantry Bay to Leitrim*	1975
Taylor & Skinner	*Maps of the Roads of Ireland*	1778
Theroux, Paul	*The Kingdom by the Sea*	1984
Trotter, J. B.	*Walks through Ireland in 1812, 1814 and 1817 in a Series of Letters*	1819
Wallace, Anne D.	*Walking, Literature and English Culture*	1995
Welch, Robert, (ed.)	*The Oxford Companion to Irish Literature*	1996
Withey, Lynne	*Grand Tours and Cook's Tours*	1997
Wordsworth, William	*Guide to the Lakes*	1810

Index

Index